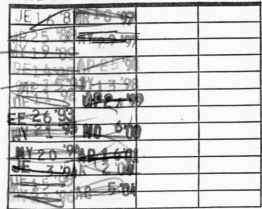

Modern Critical Views

These and other titles in preparation

Modern Critical Views

WILLIAM WORDSWORTH

Modern Critical Views

WILLIAM WORDSWORTH

Edited with an introduction by

Harold Bloom

Sterling Professor of the Humanities
Yale University

1985
CHELSEA HOUSE PUBLISHERS
New York

THE COVER:

Wordsworth is shown against the background of his poetry's Scene of Instruction, the hills and wild secluded places of his boyhood home.—H.B.

PROJECT EDITORS: Emily Bestler, James Uebbing
ASSOCIATE EDITOR: Maria Behan
EDITORIAL COORDINATOR: Karyn Gullen Browne
EDITORIAL STAFF: Linda Grossman, Peter Childers
DESIGN: Susan Lusk

Cover illustration by Michael Garland

Printed and bound in the United States of America

Library of Congress Cataloging in Publication Data

William Wordsworth.
    (Modern critical views)
    Bibliography: p.
    Includes index.
    1. Wordsworth, William, 1770–1850—Criticism and interpretation—Addresses, essays, lectures. I. Bloom, Harold. II. Series.
PR5888.W45 1985   821'.7   85–3800
ISBN 0–87754–613–4

Chelsea House Publishers
Harold Steinberg, Chairman and Publisher
Susan Lusk, Vice President
A Division of Chelsea House Educational Communications, Inc.
133 Christopher Street, New York, NY 10014

Contents

Editor's Note

   This volume gathers together a representative selection of the best criticism devoted to Wordsworth from 1950 to the present day, arranged in the chronological order of publication. The editor's "Introduction" centers upon two of Wordsworth's prime emphases, the marriage of the mind of man to a redeemed Nature, and the infinite dignity of the natural man. Frederick A. Pottle's classic exposition of Wordsworth's endeavor to keep his eye steadily upon the natural object begins the chronological sequence, which continues with the late Paul de Man's equally definitive essay on the intentional structure of Wordsworth's images of nature. This opposition between Pottle and de Man is only partly mediated by Geoffrey Hartman's vision of how Wordsworth composed his "romance of nature" through an original mode of negation.

   John Hollander's subtle analysis of the trope of sound in Wordsworth can be regarded as the most advanced instance of A. C. Bradley's vision of Wordsworth as poet of the Sublime. The essay by M. H. Abrams juxtaposes Bradley's tradition to that of Matthew Arnold in Wordsworthian criticism. Subsequent readings of Wordsworth's Sublime by Thomas Weiskel and by the editor can be regarded as further additions to the middle way between Bradley and Arnold sketched out by Abrams.

   The essay on the "Immortality Ode" by Frances Ferguson is a distinguished instance of the deconstructive criticism fostered by de Man and by Jacques Derrida. Thomas McFarland's profound analysis of Wordsworth's increasingly rigid political and social stance contributes toward understanding the sorrow of the later Wordsworth, whose poetry falls away so astonishingly from the work of the great decade 1797–1807. Finally, Kenneth Johnston's account of the unfinished *Recluse* fragment presents us with a vivid impression of Wordsworth at the heights of his power in 1800, a power beyond that of any other poet in the language since the death of John Milton.

Introduction

The *Prelude* was to be only the antechapel to the Gothic church of *The Recluse*, but the poet Wordsworth knew better than the man, and *The Prelude* is a complete and climactic work. The key to *The Prelude* as an internalized epic written in creative competition to Milton is to be found in those lines (754–860) of the *Recluse* fragment that Wordsworth prefaced to *The Excursion* (1814). Wordsworth's invocation, like Blake's to the Daughters of Beulah in his epic *Milton*, is a deliberate address to powers higher than those that inspired *Paradise Lost*:

> Urania, I shall need
> Thy guidance, or a greater Muse, if such
> Descend to earth or dwell in highest heaven!
> For I must tread on shadowy ground, must sink
> Deep—and, aloft ascending, breathe in worlds
> To which the heaven of heavens is but a veil.

The shadowy ground, the depths beneath, and the heights aloft are all in the mind of man, and Milton's heaven is only a veil, separating an allegorical unreality from the human paradise of the happiest and best regions of a poet's mind. Awe of the personal Godhead fades before the poet's reverence for his own imaginative powers:

> All strength—all terror, single or in bands,
> That ever was put forth in personal form—

> Jehovah—with his thunder, and the choir
> Of shouting Angels, and the empyreal thrones—
> I pass them unalarmed.

Blake, more ultimately unorthodox than Wordsworth as he was, had yet too strong a sense of the Bible's power to accept this dismissal of Jehovah. After reading this passage, he remarked sardonically:

> Solomon, when he Married Pharaoh's daughter & became a Convert to the Heathen Mythology, Talked exactly in this way of Jehovah as a Very inferior object of Man's Contemplations; he also passed him by unalarm'd & was permitted. Jehovah dropped a tear & follow'd him by his Spirit into the Abstract Void; it is called the Divine Mercy.

To marry Pharaoh's daughter is to marry Nature, the Goddess of the Heathen Mythology, and indeed Wordsworth will go on to speak of a marriage between the Mind of Man and the goodly universe of Nature. Wordsworth is permitted his effrontery, as Solomon the Wise was before him, and, like Solomon, Wordsworth wanders into the Ulro or Abstract Void of general reasoning from Nature, pursued by the ambiguous pity of the Divine Mercy. But this (though powerful) is a dark view to take of Wordsworth's reciprocal dealings with Nature. Courageously but calmly Wordsworth puts himself forward as a renovated spirit, a new Adam upon whom fear and awe fall as he looks into his own Mind, the Mind of Man. As befits a new Adam, a new world with a greater beauty waits upon his steps. The most defiant humanism in Wordsworth salutes the immediate possibility of this earthly paradise naturalizing itself in the here and now:

> Paradise, and groves
> Elysian, Fortunate Fields—like those of old
> Sought in the Atlantic Main—why should they be
> A history only of departed things,
> Or a mere fiction of what never was?
> For the discerning intellect of Man,
> When wedded to this goodly universe
> In love and holy passion, shall find these
> A simple produce of the common day.

No words are more honorific for Wordsworth than "simple" and "common." The marriage metaphor here has the same Hebraic sources as Blake had for his Beulah, or "married land." The true Eden is the child of the common day, when that day dawns upon the great consummation of the reciprocal passion of Man and Nature. What Wordsworth desires to write is "the spousal verse" in celebration of this fulfillment:

and, by words
Which speak of nothing more than what we are,
Would I arouse the sensual from their sleep
Of Death, and win the vacant and the vain
To noble raptures.

This parallels Blake's singing in *Jerusalem*:

Of the sleep of Ulro! and of the passage through
Eternal Death! and of the awaking to Eternal Life.

But Wordsworth would arouse us by speaking of nothing more than
what we already are; a more naturalistic humanism than Blake could
endure. Wordsworth celebrates the *given*—what we already possess, and for
him it is as for Wallace Stevens

As if the air, the mid-day air, was swarming
With the metaphysical changes that occur,
Merely in living as and where we live.

For Wordsworth, as for Stevens, the earth is enough; for Blake it
was less than that all without which man cannot be satisfied. We need to
distinguish this argument between the two greatest of the Romantics from
the simplistic dissension with which too many readers have confounded it,
that between the doctrines of innate goodness and original sin. Wordsworth is not Rousseau, and Blake is not St. Paul; they have more in
common with one another than they have with either the natural reli-
gionist or the orthodox Christian.

Wordsworth's Imagination is like Wallace Stevens's *Angel Surrounded
by Paysans*: not an angel of heaven, but the necessary angel of earth, as,
in its sight, we see the earth again, but cleared; and in its hearing we hear
the still sad music of humanity, its tragic drone, rise liquidly, not harsh or
grating, but like watery words awash, to chasten and subdue us. But the
Imagination of Wordsworth and of Stevens is "a figure half seen, or seen
for a moment." It rises with the sudden mountain mists, and as suddenly
departs. Blake, a literalist of the Imagination, wished for its more habitual
sway. To marry Mind and Nature is to enter Beulah; there Wordsworth
and Blake are at one. Blake insisted that a man more fully redeemed by
Imagination would not need Nature, would regard the external world as
hindrance. The split between Wordsworth and Blake is not theological at
all, though Blake expresses it in his deliberately displaced Protestant
vocabulary by using the metaphor of the Fall where Wordsworth rejects it.
For Wordsworth the individual Mind and the external World are exqui-
sitely fitted, each to the other, even as man and wife, and with blended

might they accomplish a creation the meaning of which is fully dependent upon the sexual analogy; they give to us a new heaven and a new earth blended into an apocalyptic unity that is simply the matter of common perception and common sexuality raised to the freedom of its natural power. Wordsworthian Man is Freudian Man, but Blake's Human Form Divine is not. "You shall not bring me down to believe such a fitting & fitted" is his reaction to Wordsworth's exquisite adjustings of the Universe and Mind. To accept Nature as man's equal is for Blake the ineradicable error. Blake's doctrine is that either the Imagination totally destroys Nature and puts a thoroughly Human form in its place, or else Nature destroys the Imagination. Wordsworth says of his task that he is forced to hear "Humanity in fields and groves / Pipe solitary anguish" and Blake reacts with ferocity:

> Does not this Fit, & is not Fitting most Exquisitely too, but to what?
> —not to Mind, but to the Vile Body only & to its Laws of Good & Evil
> & its Enmities against Mind.

This is not the comment of an embittered Gnostic. Blake constructs his poetry as a commentary upon Scripture; Wordsworth writes his poetry as a commentary upon Nature. Wordsworth, while not so Bible-haunted as Blake, is himself a poet in the Hebraic prophetic line. The visible body of Nature is more than an outer testimony of the Spirit of God to him; it is our only way to God. For Blake it is the barrier between us and the God within ourselves. Ordinary perception is then a mode of salvation for Wordsworth, provided that we are awake fully to what we see. The common earth is to be hallowed by the human heart's and mind's holy union with it, and by that union the heart and mind in concert are to receive their bride's gift of phenomenal beauty, a glory in the grass, a splendor in the flower. Until at last the Great Consummation will be achieved, and renovated Man will stand in Eden once again. The human glory of Wordsworth, which he bequeathed to Keats, is in this naturalistic celebration of the possibilities inherent in our condition, here and now. That Wordsworth himself, in the second half of his long life, could not sustain this vision is a criticism of neither the vision nor the man, but merely his loss—and ours.

The Old Cumberland Beggar (1797) is Wordsworth's finest vision of the irreducible natural man, the human stripped to the nakedness of primordial condition and exposed as still powerful in dignity, still infinite in value. The Beggar reminds us of the beggars, solitaries, wanderers throughout Wordsworth's poetry, particularly in The Prelude and Resolution and Independence. He differs from them in that he is not the agency of a revelation; he is not responsible for a sudden release of Wordsworth's imagination. He is not even of visionary utility; he is something finer, beyond use, a vision of reality in himself. I am not suggesting that *The Old Cumberland Beggar* is the best of Wordsworth's poems outside *The Prelude;* it is not in the sublime mode, as are *Tintern Abbey*, the Great Ode, *Resolution and Independence*. But it is the most Wordsworthian of poems, and profoundly moving.

Nothing could be simpler than the poem's opening: "I saw an aged Beggar in my walk." The Old Man (the capitalization is the poet's) has put down his staff, and takes his scraps and fragments out of a flour bag, one by one. He scans them, fixedly and seriously. The plain beginning yields to a music of love, the beauty of the real:

> In the sun,
> Upon the second step of that small pile,
> Surrounded by those wild unpeopled hills,
> He sat, and ate his food in solitude:
> And ever, scattered from his palsied hand,
> That, still attempting to prevent the waste,
> Was baffled still, the crumbs in little showers
> Fell on the ground; and the small mountain birds,
> Not venturing yet to peck their destined meal,
> Approached within the length of half his staff.

It is difficult to describe *how* this is beautiful, but we can make a start by observing that it is beautiful both because it is so matter of fact, and because the fact is itself a transfiguration. The Old Man is in his own state, and he is radically innocent. The "wild unpeopled hills" complement his own solitude; he is a phenomenon of their kind. And he is no more sentimentalized than they are. His lot is not even miserable; he is too absorbed into Nature for that, as absorbed as he can be and still retain human identity.

He is even past further aging. The poet has known him since his childhood, and even then "he was so old, he seems not older now." The Old Man is so helpless in appearance that everyone—sauntering horseman or toll-gate keeper or post boy—makes way for him, taking special care to keep him from harm. For he cannot be diverted, but moves on like a natural process. "He travels on, a solitary Man," Wordsworth says, and then repeats it, making a refrain for that incessant movement whose only meaning is that it remains human though at the edge of our condition:

> He travels on, a solitary Man;
> His age has no companion. On the ground
> His eyes are turned, and, as he moves along,

They move along the ground; and, evermore,
Instead of common and habitual sight
Of fields with rural works, of hill and dale,
And the blue sky, one little span of earth
Is all his prospect.

He is bent double, like the Leech Gatherer, and his vision of one little span of earth recalls the wandering old man of Chaucer's *Pardoner's Tale*. But Chaucer's solitary longed for death, and on the ground he called his mother's gate he knocked often with his staff, crying, "Dear mother, let me in." Wordsworth's Old Man sees only the ground, but he is tenaciously alive, and is beyond desire, even that of death. He sees, and yet hardly sees. He moves constantly, but is so still in look and motion that he can hardly be seen to move. He is all process, hardly character, and yet almost stasis.

It is so extreme a picture that we can be tempted to ask, "Is this life? Where is its use?" The temptation dehumanizes us, Wordsworth would have it, and the two questions are radically dissimilar, but his answer to the first is vehemently affirmative and to the second an absolute moral passion. There is

a spirit and pulse of good,
A life and soul, to every mode of being
Inseparably linked.

The Old Man performs many functions. The most important is that of a binding agent for the memories of good impulses in all around him. Wherever he goes,

The mild necessity of use compels
To acts of love.

These acts of love, added one to another, at last insensibly dispose their performers to virtue and true goodness. We need to be careful in our reaction to this. Wordsworth is not preaching the vicious and mad doctrine that beggary is good because it makes charity possible. That would properly invoke Blake's blistering reply in *The Human Abstract*:

Pity would be no more
If we did not make somebody Poor;
And Mercy no more could be
If all were as happy as we.

Wordsworth has no reaction to the Old Man which we can categorize. He does not think of him in social or economic terms, but only as a human life, which necessarily has affected other lives, and always for the better. In particular, the Old Man has given occasions for kindness to the very poorest, who give to him from their scant store, and are the kinder for it. Again, you must read this in its own context. Wordsworth's best poetry has nothing directly to do with social justice, as Blake's or Shelley's frequently does. The old beggar is a free man, at home in the heart of the solitudes he wanders, and he does not intend the humanizing good he passively causes. Nor is his social aspect at the poem's vital center; only his freedom is:

> —Then let him pass, a blessing on his head!
> And, long as he can wander, let him breathe
> The freshness of the valleys; let his blood
> Struggle with frosty air and winter snows;
> And let the chartered wind that sweeps the heath
> Beat his grey locks against his withered face.

Pity for him is inappropriate; he is pathetic only if shut up. He is a "figure of capable imagination," in Stevens's phrase, a Man perfectly complete in Nature, reciprocating its gifts by being himself, a being at one with it:

> Let him be free of mountain solitudes;
> And have around him, whether heard or not,
> The pleasant melody of woodland birds.

Mountain solitudes and sudden winds are what suit him, whether he reacts to them or not. The failure of his senses does not cut him off from Nature; it does not matter whether he can hear the birds, but it is fitting that he have them around him. He has become utterly passive toward Nature. Let it be free, then, to come in upon him:

> if his eyes have now
> Been doomed so long to settle upon earth
> That not without some effort they behold
> The countenance of the horizontal sun,
> Rising or setting, let the light at least
> Find a free entrance to their languid orbs.

The Old Man is approaching that identity with Nature that the infant at first knows, when an organic continuity seems to exist between Nature and consciousness. Being so naturalized, he must die in the eye of Nature, that he may be absorbed again:

> And let him, *where* and *when* he will, sit down
> Beneath the trees, or on a grassy bank
> Of highway side, and with the little birds

Share his chance-gathered meal; and, finally,
As in the eye of Nature he has lived,
So in the eye of Nature let him die!

The poem abounds in a temper of spirit that Wordsworth shares with Tolstoy, a reverence for the simplicities of *caritas,* the Christian love that is so allied to and yet is not pity. But Tolstoy might have shown the Old Cumberland Beggar as a sufferer; in Wordsworth he bears the mark of "animal tranquillity and decay," the title given by Wordsworth to a fragment closely connected to the longer poem. In the fragment the Old Man travels on and moves not with pain, but with thought:

He is insensibly subdued
To settled quiet . . .
He is by nature led
To peace so perfect that the young behold
With envy, what the Old Man hardly feels.

We know today, better than his contemporaries could, what led Wordsworth to the subject of human decay, to depictions of idiocy, desertion, beggars, homeless wanderers. He sought images of alienated life, as we might judge them, which he could see and present as images of natural communion. The natural man, free of consciousness in any of our senses, yet demonstrates a mode of consciousness which both intends Nature for its object and at length blends into that object. The hiding places of man's power are in his past, in childhood. Only memory can take him there, but even memory fades, and at length fades away. The poet of naturalism, separated by organic growth from his own past, looks around him and sees the moving emblems of a childlike consciousness in the mad, the outcast, and the dreadfully old. From them he takes his most desperate consolation, intimations of a mortality that almost ceases to afflict.

FREDERICK A. POTTLE

The Eye and the Object
in the Poetry of Wordsworth

This year, the centennial of Words-
worth's death, has seen the publication of a good many essays with
some such title as "Wordsworth Today." The purpose of such essays
has been to read Wordsworth as though he were a contemporary
poet, to decide what portion of his works is really available to present-
day sensibility. My purpose is rather descriptive than judicial: I shall try to
isolate qualities of Wordsworth's poetry that look as though they were
going to be apparent to all historical varieties of sensibility, though the
values assigned to them by different sensibilities may differ. And I think I
can best get to what I want to say by the method of texts: by inviting you
to consider two prose statements made by Wordsworth himself about
poetry in general and about his own poetry in particular. They are both
from the famous Preface: "Poetry takes its origin from emotion recollected
in tranquillity" and "I have at all times endeavoured to look steadily at my
subject." It is my notion that the latter of these texts usually gets, if not a
false, at least an impoverished, interpretation; and that the two, taken
together and rightly understood, go a long way toward placing Wordsworth
in literary history.

At first sight it looks as though they were what Bacon calls "cross
clauses": that is, they appear to be hopelessly contradictory. The natural
image that rises in one's mind as one reads the statement "I have at all
times endeavoured to look steadily at my subject" is that of an artist
painting from a model or an actual landscape; and since Wordsworth's

From *The Yale Review*, vol. 40, (Autumn 1950). Copyright © 1950 by Yale University.

poetry contains a good deal of landscape, the obvious meaning of his words would appear to be that he composed poetry while looking earnestly and steadily at the natural objects that he introduces into his poems. But if poetry takes its rise from "emotion recollected in tranquillity," it is hard to see how this can happen. In fact, the only way in which we can leave any place for the actual model, in poetry that starts from recollection, is to suppose that after poetry *has* taken its rise, the poet goes back to natural objects and pores over them as he composes. And we know that Wordsworth did not do that. His normal practice, like that of other poets, was to paint without the model. He very seldom made a present joy the matter of his song, but rather turned habitually for the matter of poems to joys that sprang from hiding-places ten years deep.

More than that, a good many of his poems, including several of his finest, either have no basis in personal experience at all, or show autobiography so manipulated that the "subject" corresponds to nothing Wordsworth ever saw with the bodily eye. His extensive critical writings deride the matter-of-fact and speak over and over again of the power of the imagination to modify and create. Yet there is a widespread belief that Wordsworth was Nature's Boswell, in the old erroneous sense which defined Boswell as a man who followed Johnson about with a notebook, taking down his utterances on the spot. Actually, like Boswell, Wordsworth relied on memory, and says so quite explicitly. But then he says other things in which he appears to be vindicating the rightness of his poetry, not on the ground that it is well-imagined, but on the ground that the things described in the poem really did happen in that fashion and in no other. I do not mean merely the notes which he dictated in old age to Miss Fenwick. There is his impassioned defense of *The Leech Gatherer* against the mild and sisterly strictures of Sara Hutchinson, a defense made before the poem was published: "A young Poet in the midst of the happiness of Nature is described as overwhelmed by the thought of the miserable reverses which have befallen the happiest of all men, viz Poets—I think of this till I am so deeply impressed by it, that I consider the manner in which I was rescued from my dejection and despair almost as an interposition of Providence. . . . 'A lonely place, a Pond' 'by which an old man *was*, far from all house or home'—not stood, not sat, but '*was*'—the figure presented in the most naked simplicity possible. . . . I cannot conceive a figure more impressive than that of an old Man like this, the survivor of a Wife and ten children, travelling alone among the mountains and all lonely places, carrying with him his own fortitude, and the necessities which an unjust state of society has entailed upon him. . . . Good God! Such a figure, in such a place, a pious self-respecting, miserably infirm . . . Old Man telling such a tale!"

Who would believe from reading this that in real life Wordsworth met the old man, not on the lonely moor, but in the highway; that the old man in real life was not demonstrating resolution and independence by gathering leeches under great difficulties, but was begging? In short, that the narrative is from first to last an imaginative construction—the account of an imagined meeting between Wordsworth and the beggar as Wordsworth imagined him to have been before he was finally reduced to beggary?

What, then, are we to make of Wordsworth's boast that he endeavored at all times to look steadily at his subject? I shall try to answer the question by tracing the steps that he followed in writing one of his most famous poems, *I wandered lonely as a cloud*, commonly (though with no authority from Wordsworth) called *Daffodils*. The starting point is the entry in Dorothy Wordsworth's *Journal* for April 15, 1802. That entry is fairly long, but it is all good reading; and I have my reasons for not eliminating any of it:

"It was a threatening, misty morning, but mild. We set off after dinner from Eusemere. Mrs. Clarkson went a short way with us, but turned back. The wind was furious, and we thought we must have returned. We first rested in the large boat-house, then under a furze bush opposite Mr. Clarkson's. Saw the plough going in the field. The wind seized our breath. The Lake was rough. There was a boat by itself floating in the middle of the bay below Water Millock. We rested again in the Water Millock Lane. The hawthorns are black and green, the birches here and there greenish, but there is yet more of purple to be seen on the twigs. We got over into a field to avoid some cows—people working. A few primroses by the roadside—woodsorrel flower, the anemone, scentless violets, strawberries, and that starry, yellow flower which Mrs. C. calls pile wort. When we were in the woods beyond Gowbarrow Park we saw a few daffodils close to the water-side. We fancied that the lake had floated the seeds ashore, and that the little colony had so sprung up. But as we went along there were more and yet more; and at last, under the boughs of the trees, we saw that there was a long belt of them along the shore, about the breadth of a country turnpike road. I never saw daffodils so beautiful. They grew among the mossy stones about and about them; some rested their heads upon these stones as on a pillow for weariness; and the rest tossed and reeled and danced, and seemed as if they verily laughed with the wind, that blew upon them over the lake; they looked so gay, ever glancing, ever changing. This wind blew directly over the lake to them.

There was here and there a little knot, and a few stragglers a few yards higher up; but they were so few as not to disturb the simplicity, unity, and life of that one busy highway. We rested again and again. The bays were stormy, and we heard the waves at different distances, and in the middle of the water, like the sea. Rain came on—we were wet when we reached Luff's, but we called in. Luckily all was chearless and gloomy, so we faced the storm—we *must* have been wet if we had waited—put on dry clothes at Dobson's. I was very kindly treated by a young woman, the landlady looked sour, but it is her way. She gave us a goodish supper, excellent ham and potatoes. We paid 7/- when we came away. William was sitting by a bright fire when I came downstairs. He soon made his way to the library, piled up in a corner of the window. He brought out a volume of Enfield's *Speaker,* another miscellany, and an odd volume of Congreve's plays. We had a glass of warm rum and water. We enjoyed ourselves, and wished for Mary. It rained and blew, when we went to bed. N.B. Deer in Gowbarrow Park like skeletons."

I said this was the starting point, for it is as near the raw matter of the poem as we can get. The true raw matter consisted of certain perceptions, visual, auditory, tactile, which Wordsworth and his sister had on that windy April morning—and those we have no way of recovering. In Dorothy's entry this raw matter has already been grasped and shaped by a powerful imagination, and it has been verbalized. The entry is not a poem, because it contains a good deal of true but inconsequential statement (the rum and water, the volume of Congreve), but much of it is prefabricated material for a poem. And the fact is (though this is doctrine little heard of among men) that Wordsworth made grateful use of prefabricated material whenever he could get it of the right sort. As Professor Lane Cooper showed us long ago, he went regularly to books of travel for material of the right sort, but his best source was his sister's journal.

The function of the imagination, as Wordsworth and Coleridge insisted, is, at the first level, to make sense out of the undifferentiated manifold of sensation by organizing it into individual objects or things; at the second, and specifically poetic, level, to reshape this world of common perception in the direction of a unity that shall be even more satisfactory and meaningful. Dorothy has made extensive use of the secondary or poetic imagination. Notice the devices by which she has unified and made sense of the experience of the daffodils. First, and most important, she has endowed them with human qualities. They are a social group engaged in busy concerted activity. The notion of the social group, the crowd (she does not actually use the word) is reinforced by her further figure of stragglers. Secondly, besides being active, the crowd of daffodils is happy: they look gay, they toss and reel and dance (their very activity is sport) and seem verily to laugh. And thirdly, some of the crowd have danced so hard that they are tired: they rest their heads upon the stones as on pillows.

Wordsworth recollected the scene in tranquillity and wrote his poem a full two years afterwards. He fixes on Dorothy's fine central perception of "the simplicity, unity, and life of that one busy highway," and condenses it into the one word "crowd," which, as we have seen, she did not use. He takes over, too, her impression that the daffodils were "dancing," that they were "gay," that they were even "laughing." Ever since 1807, when Wordsworth published this poem, daffodils have danced and laughed, but there is nothing inevitable about it. The Greek myth of Narcissus is not exactly hilarious; and even Herrick, when he looked at a daffodil, saw something far from jocund:

> When a Daffadill I see,
> Hanging down his head t'wards me;
> Guesse I may, what I must be:
> First, I shall decline my head;
> Secondly, I shall be dead;
> Lastly, safely buryed.

The literal, positivistic, "scientific" fact was that Wordsworth and his sister saw a large bed of wild daffodils beside a lake, agitated by a strong, cold spring wind. The rest is all the work of the imagination.

The mark of the poetic imagination is to simplify: to make the manifold of sensation more meaningful by reducing it to a number of objects that can actually be contemplated. Wordsworth continues Dorothy's process of simplification: he eliminates the bitterness of the wind, which is so prominent in her account; reduces the wind, in fact, to a breeze. It may appear here that he has simplified more than was necessary or wise. Shakespeare, in the most famous lines ever written about daffodils, kept the wind:

> daffodils
> That come before the swallow dares, and take
> The winds of March with beauty.

Admittedly, it is a higher mode. Wordsworth, on some occasions, would have kept the wind, too; but to have kept it here would have made a more complex—if you will, a more tragic—poem than he felt like writing. He felt this poem as something very simple and very pure; when he came to publish it, he put it in a group called "Moods of My Own Mind." But he is impartial: as he throws out matter on the one hand because it is too serious, he throws out matter on the other because it is too playful. The prettiest thing in Dorothy's realization—her image of the daffodils pillowing their heads on the stones—drops out. He dispenses too with Dorothy's stragglers. He fastens on her central image of the dancing, laughing crowd, and lets everything else go.

But now the idea of the crowd calls for a modification, and a modification of a fundamental sort. The social glee of the crowd can be made more significant if it is set over against solitary joy; and so in the poem he makes himself solitary, which in literal fact he was not. He now has what for him is a promising situation. The solitariness of the poet and the sociability of the daffodils are set up as poles between which the poem discharges itself. I have said that the situation is for him a promising one. Everyone knows of Wordsworth's love of solitude, his conviction that the highest experiences came to him when he was alone. What we need constantly to remind ourselves of is that his theory assigned an only slightly lower value to the love of men in societies. (The subtitle of Book VIII of *The Prelude* is "Love of Nature Leading to Love of Man.") The trouble was that, though he had the best of intentions, he could never handle close-packed, present, human crowds in the mode of imagination. If he were to grasp the life of a great city imaginatively, it had to be at night or early in the morning, while the streets were deserted; or at least in bad weather, when few people were abroad. The Seventh Book of *The Prelude* ("Residence in London") is one of the most delightful things Wordsworth ever wrote, but as he himself tell us, it is almost all in the mode of fancy—almost all poetry that groups with *The Kitten and the Falling Leaves*. But in the figure of a bed of daffodils endowed with human characteristics, he can handle with feelings of approval and exhilaration the concept of a crowd, of ten thousand individuals packed close together. He begins and ends solitary: at the beginning, we may assume, filled with joy, but a joy somewhat solemn, somewhat cold and remote, as the symbol of the cloud indicates. He is surprised by the sensation of mere unmixed human gaiety and lightheartedness, yields to it, and finds it good; so good that ever after he can derive refreshment from the memory of the experience.

I ought perhaps to be no more specific, but my purposes demand a somewhat closer analysis of Wordsworth's formal devices. The extension in space which he secures by linking the daffodils to other objects in nature— stars and waves—is characteristic of his poems of the imagination, but I shall defer discussion of this. The second stanza is ostensibly introduced merely to reinforce the idea of number ("continuous" echoing "crowd" and "host"), but of course there are other meaningful parallels. "Stars" looks back to "golden," and "twinkle" echoes "fluttering." So, too, the third stanza professes only to reinforce the idea of dancing, but actually reinforces also the idea of number (waves are always numberless); and "sparkling" looks back to "twinkle," and back of that to "fluttering." The progress toward explicit identification of the symbol is gradual. First we have "fluttering" (literal: the flowers are self-moved); then "tossing their heads in sprightly dance." (The flowers are self-moved and are having a wonderful time. "Dance" is the key word: you will have noticed that it occurs in either the last or the first line of each of the four stanzas.) Finally—but not until the third stanza is reached—we get the quite explicit series "glee," "gay," "jocund," "pleasure." Wordsworth is always (or almost always) explicit in this fashion: he tells you just how you are expected to take his figures. Of course it is the figures that convey the emotion. No one can make us joyful merely by using the word "joy" or any of its synonyms. But there is impressive agreement among readers of all periods that by giving us a simple figure, reinforcing it by certain devices of varied iteration, and explicitly interpreting it, Wordsworth does evoke the emotion of joy.

We can now see what Wordsworth meant by looking steadily at his subject. So far as his subject is expressed in imagery drawn from nature (and that means in all his best poetry), there is implied a lifelong habit of close, detailed, and accurate observation of the objects composing the external universe. By "accurate" I mean something the same thing as "naturalistic," but not entirely so. Wordsworth scorned the merely analytic vision of the naturalist ("One that would peep and botanize Upon his mother's grave") because in his opinion that kind of apprehension empties the object of life and meaning by detaching it from its ground. "His theme is nature *in solido*, that is to say, he dwells on that mysterious presence of surrounding things, which imposes itself on any separate element that we set up as an individual for its own sake. He always grasps the whole of nature as involved in the tonality of the particular instance." But, except for those portions of the scientist's vision which require (let us say) dissection and magnification, there is little in the scientist's vision that Wordsworth misses. A *merely* matter-of-fact, an *exclusively* positivistic view of nature fills him with anger, but his own apprehension includes the matter-of-fact view without denying any of it. Dr. Leavis has perhaps put this more intelligibly when he remarks, as the chief virtue of Wordsworth's poetry, a "firm hold upon the world of common perception," though I myself should like to phrase it, "in the mode of perception which has been common in Western civilization since some time in the late eighteenth century." In a literal, physiological sense, Wordsworth did look steadily at the natural objects that appear in his poetry.

But the subject he is talking about in the sentence in the Preface is not an object in external nature; and the eye that looks steadily is not the physical eye. The subject is a mental image, and the eye is that inward eye which is the bliss of solitude. The mental image accompanies or is the source of the emotion recollected in tranquillity; it recurs in memory, not once but many times; and on each occasion he looks at it steadily to see what it *means*. Wordsworth in his best poetry does not start with an abstraction or a generalization, a divine commonplace which he wishes to illustrate. He starts with the mental image of a concrete natural object. He feels this object to be very urgent, but at first he does not know why. As he looks steadily at it, he simplifies it, and as he simplifies it, he sees what it means. He usually continues to simplify and interpret until the object becomes the correlative of a single emotion. It is a great mistake to consider Wordsworth a descriptive poet. When he is writing in the mode of the imagination, he never gives catalogues, in fact never provides a profusion of imagery. He employs few images. His images are firm and precise ("literal"), but, as one of my undergraduate students acutely said, they are very spare. Of the daffodils we are given nothing but their habit of growing in clumps, their color, and their characteristic movement when stirred by the wind. Wordsworth's method (I am trying to be just as hard-headed and precise as I know how) is not the method of beautification (Tennyson), nor the method of distortion (Carlyle); it is the method of transfiguration. The primrose by the river's brim remains a simple primrose but it is also something more: it is a symbol (to use Hartley's quaint terminology) of sympathy, theopathy, or the moral sense.

We can also see now the main cause of Wordsworth's dissatisfaction with the poetry of Pope: "It is remarkable that, excepting the nocturnal Reverie of Lady Winchilsea, and a passage or two in the Windsor Forest of Pope, the poetry of the period intervening between the publication of the Paradise Lost and the Seasons does not contain a single new image of external nature; and scarcely presents a familiar one from which it can be inferred that the eye of the Poet had been steadily fixed upon his object, much less that his feelings had urged him to work upon it in the spirit of genuine imagination. To what a low state knowledge of the most obvious and important phenomena had sunk, is evident from the style in which Dryden has executed a description of Night in one of his Tragedies, and Pope his translation of the celebrated moonlight scene in the Iliad. A blind man, in the habit of attending accurately to descriptions casually dropped from the lips of those around him, might easily depict these appearances with more truth." For Pope's usual method is the exact contrary of that which I have been describing. Pope starts with an abstraction or a generalization concerning human nature and then looks for a correlative in the world of nature apart from man. His habit of observation of external nature is not detailed and precise; indeed, he thinks it unimportant whether the "facts" of nature which he alleges in his illustrations are really facts or superstitions. The natural history of Pliny and the old bestiaries are as much grist to his mill as the latest papers of the Royal Society. He appears also to me to have at times no clear, detailed, and consistent mental picture of his own figures. To illustrate: in the couplet near the beginning of the *Essay on Man*,

> The latent tracts, the giddy heights explore
> Of all who blindly creep or sightless soar,

he means, I suppose, moles and birds of some sort. If so, in order to enforce his doctrine that "the proper study of mankind is man," he appears to be making use of the ancient and medieval notion that all birds except the eagle blind themselves by looking at the sun. Surely, by Pope's time it was generally known that the high-flying birds are not "sightless"; that on the contrary they have telescopic vision.

> When in the same poem he says that man
> Touches some wheel, or verges to some goal,

I cannot convince myself that he could draw a diagram of the machine he has in mind. Or consider a famous passage from the Second Dialogue of the *Epilogue to the Satires* (he is referring to satire itself):

> O sacred Weapon! left for truth's defense,
> Sole Dread of Folly, Vice, and Insolence!
> To all but Heav'n-directed hands deny'd,
> The Muse may give thee, but the Gods must guide.
> Rev'rent I touch thee! but with honest zeal;
> To rowze the Watchmen of the Publick Weal,
> To Virtue's Work provoke the tardy Hall,
> And goad the Prelate slumb'ring in his Stall.
> Ye tinsel Insects! whom a Court maintains,
> That counts your Beauties only by your Stains,
> Spin all your Cobwebs o'er the Eye of Day!
> The Muse's wing shall brush you all away.

"Tinsel" to me means "shining or glittering like cheap metal foil," and my natural image of a "tinsel insect" would be some kind of beetle ("this Bug with gilded wings"). But the word can mean no more than "pretentiously showy" and so may not have been intended to identify the kind of insect Pope has in mind. "Stains," however, can hardly mean anything else than moths or butterflies ("Innumerable of stains and splendid dyes, / As are the tiger-moths deep-damask'd wings"). But the trouble with that is that Pope's insects spin cobwebs, which no butterfly or moth can do. I think we shall do Pope no injustice if we conclude that his insects have the combined characteristics of beetles, moths, and spiders, and hence do not belong to any order known to naturalists.

Looking steadily at a subject, then, for Wordsworth means grasping objects firmly and accurately in the mode of common perception and then looking at them imaginatively. And we have not said all that needs to be said about the second half of the process. I have made a great deal of *I wandered lonely*, and must add now that Wordsworth had doubts about putting that poem in the central group of his short pieces called "Poems of the Imagination." In the collected edition of 1815, where the grouping first appeared, he added the following note to *I wandered lonely*: "The subject of these Stanzas is rather an elementary feeling and simple impression (approaching to the nature of an ocular spectrum) upon the imaginative faculty, than an *exertion* of it."

It is hard for us nowadays to understand why Blake, Wordsworth, Coleridge, and Shelley made such a fuss about the imagination, and why Wordsworth and Coleridge labored so to distinguish the imagination from the fancy. Make no mistake about it: it was for them a matter of vital importance, nothing less than a vindication of their right to exist as poets. In the reigning psychology of Locke extended by Hartley, imagination and fancy—pretty much interchangeable terms—were handled as modes of memory. That in itself was proper enough, but there was a strong tendency to make a total and exclusive philosophy out of this mechanistic naturalism. Wordsworth and Coleridge were convinced that imagination and fancy were creative; and they wished to make imagination not merely creative but a power for apprehending truth. It is a pity that neither of them was ever very clear on the subject. Perhaps the problem is too profound to allow of perfectly clear statement, but it is possible to be a lot clearer than either of them ever was. In particular, I should advise the reader to note carefully what Wordsworth says about fancy in the Preface of 1815, but not to bother with what is said there about the imagination, for he will only find it confusing. Here is the passage about fancy:

"The law under which the processes of Fancy are carried on is as capricious as the accidents of things, and the effects are surprising, playful, ludicrous, amusing, tender, or pathetic, as the objects happen to be appositely produced or fortunately combined. Fancy depends upon the rapidity and profusion with which she scatters her thoughts and images; trusting that their number, and the felicity with which they are linked together, will make amends for the want of individual value: or she prides herself upon the curious subtilty and the successful elaboration with which she can detect their lurking affinities. If she can win you over to her purpose, and impart to you her feelings, she cares not how unstable or transitory may be her influence, knowing that it will not be out of her power to resume it upon an apt occasion. But the Imagination is conscious of an indestructible dominion;—the Soul may fall away from it, not being able to sustain its grandeur; but, if once felt and acknowledged, by no act of any other faculty of the mind can it be relaxed, impaired, or diminished.—Fancy is given to quicken and to beguile the temporal part of our nature, Imagination to incite and to support the eternal."

Fancy deals with images that are fixed, detailed, and sharply defined; its effects are "surpising, playful, ludicrous, amusing, tender, or pathetic." Furthermore (and most important), these effects are transitory because the deep relationships of things will not permit a serious, steady contemplation of them in that mode. Dorothy's charming image of the tired daffodils resting their heads on the stones was for Wordsworth an image of fancy; her image of the daffodils as a busy crowd expressing social glee, an image of the imagination. He did not disparage poetry of the fancy, but he considered it inferior to poetry of the imagination. He thought that an unfortunately large portion of metaphysical poetry was fanciful rather than imaginative, because of the definiteness and fixity of its images; and he would probably have passed the same judgment on modern poetry. Imagination, in his opinion, gets at relationships that are true at the deepest level of experience. He was, in short, a religious poet; and nothing for him was deeply imaginative unless it attained (I fall back on Hartley's terminology again) to theopathy and the moral sense. And since Wordsworth was a mystic, subject to occasional mystic rapture, he felt that the deepest truth was not attained until the light of sense went out. He always connected deeply imaginative effects with the sense of infinity. So long as you can see sharply, clearly, with the kind and degree of detail that accompanies common perception, he might say, you should suspect that you are either engaged in merely practical activity or are resting in the mode of fancy. You will know that you are dealing with imagination when the edges of things begin to waver and fade out. In two brief texts he sums up the whole business far more satisfactorily than in the entire Preface devoted to the subject. The first is in the Sixth Book of *The Prelude* (he is speaking specifically of the imagination):

> in such strength
> Of usurpation, when the light of sense
> Goes out, but with a flash that has revealed
> The invisible world, doth greatness make abode,
> There harbours; whether we be young or old,
> Our destiny, our being's heart and home,
> Is with infinitude, and only there;
> With hope it is, hope that can never die,
> Effort, and expectation, and desire,
> And something evermore about to be.

The sound occurs in a letter to Walter Savage Landor, January 21, 1824. Landor has said that he is disgusted with all books that treat of religion. Wordsworth replies that it is perhaps a bad sign in himself, but he has little relish for any other kind. "Even in poetry it is the imaginative only *viz.*, that which is conversant [with], or turns upon infinity, that powerfully affects me—perhaps I ought to explain: I mean to say that, unless in those passages where things are lost in each other, and limits vanish, and aspirations are raised, I read with something too much like indifference."

It is not difficult by Wordsworth's own standards to establish the right of *I wandered lonely* to be considered an imaginative poem. The impression that the daffodils are joyous is not for him what Ruskin called pathetic fallacy. Under steady, prolonged, and serious contemplation daffodils can remain for him a symbol of joy because it is his faith (literally—no figure of speech) that every flower enjoys the air it breathes. Again, *I wandered lonely* is imaginative because the impression of joy deepens into *social* joy: since the daffodils stand for men in society, the poem attains to sympathy on Hartley's ladder. But Wordsworth was not willing to rank the poem as an example of the higher exercise of the imagination, because it lacks the fade-out. In it things only just begin to be lost in each other, and limits to vanish, and aspirations to be raised. He was quite aware of the fact that *I wandered lonely* is a very simple poem.

The Solitary Reaper has the degree of complexity necessary for full illustration of Wordsworth's theory. The Highland Lass is *single*, is *solitary*, is *alone*, and her song is *melancholy*. I said that the situation of *I wandered lonely* was promising, but here is what is for Wordsworth the optimum situation: solitude, in the single human figure against the landscape with more than a hint of visionary dreariness in it; society, its affections and passions presented not directly but felt in the distanced, muted, managed form of song. Actual men in crowds are to him an unmanageable sight, a crowd of daffodils can stand for humanity if no more is called for than a gush of social joy; but this symbol of the singing reaper will express the whole solemn mystery of human existence. The limits begin to vanish in the first stanza with the figure of the sound overflowing the rim of the vale.

The mystery of human existence: that is the first meaning of the bird metaphors of the second stanza. The song can stand for mystery because it is itself mysterious. Like the song of the nightingale and the song of the cuckoo, it is in a foreign tongue. It is one of those Gaelic occupational chants that go on and on like the drone of a bagpipe ("the Maiden sang / As if her song could have no ending"); the poet feels it to be melancholy from its tone and rhythm, though he cannot understand the words. But he is also at work in other ways to make limits vanish: he pushes his boundaries out in space from Arabia to St. Kilda. And the third stanza, besides reinforcing "melancholy" by the more explicit "old, unhappy, far-off things, And battles long ago," extends the boundaries in time: from "long ago" to "to-day," a plane of extension cutting across the plane of space. Again, we have the extension in human experience: from the unnatural sorrows of battles to the natural pain of everyday life. It is by devices such as these that Wordsworth transfigures the matter of common perception.

It would be perverse to attempt to identify the basic ideas of Wordsworth and Blake on the imagination. Blake by his "double vision" no doubt meant much the same thing as Wordsworth with his two ways of looking steadily at objects. Wordsworth might well have joined Blake's prayer to be kept from single vision and Newton's sleep. But Wordsworth believed that poetry must hold firm to the vision of the outward eye, and Blake, I think, wanted to relinquish the control of common perception altogether. "I assert for My Self that I do not behold the outward Creation & that to me it is hindrance & not Action; it is as the dirt upon my feet, No part of Me. . . . I question not my Corporeal or Vegetative Eye any more than I would Question a Window concerning a Sight. I look thro' it & not with it." Still, detached from Blake's private interpretations, his lines state very well what Wordsworth proposed:

> To see a World in a Grain of Sand
> And a Heaven in a Wild Flower,
> Hold Infinity in the palm of your hand
> And Eternity in an hour.

PAUL DE MAN

Intentional Structure
of the Romantic Image

In the history of Western literature, the importance of the image as a dimension of poetic language does not remain constant. One could conceive of an organization of this history in terms of the relative prominence and the changing structure of metaphor. French poetry of the sixteenth century is obviously richer and more varied in images than that of the seventeenth, and medieval poetry of the fifteenth century has a different kind of imagery than that of the thirteenth. The most recent change remote enough to be part of history takes place toward the end of the eighteenth century and coincides with the advent of romanticism. In a statement of which equivalences can be found in all European literatures, Wordsworth reproaches Pope for having abandoned the imaginative use of figural diction in favor of a merely decorative allegorization. Meanwhile the term *imagination* steadily grows in importance and complexity in the critical as well as in the poetic texts of the period. This evolution in poetic terminology—of which parallel instances could easily be found in France and in Germany—corresponds to a profound change in the texture of poetic diction. The change often takes the form of a return to a greater concreteness, a proliferation of natural objects that restores to the language the material substantiality which had been partially lost. At the same time, in accordance with a dialectic that is more paradoxical than may appear at first sight, the structure of the language becomes increasingly metaphorical and the image—be it under the name of symbol or even of myth—comes to be considered as the most prominent dimension of the style. This tendency is still prevalent today, among poets as well as among critics. We find it quite natural that theoretical studies such as, for example, those of Gaston Bachelard in France, of Northrop Frye in America, or of William Empson in England should take the metaphor as their starting point for an investigation of literature in general—an approach that would have been inconceivable for Boileau, for Pope, and even still for Diderot.

An abundant imagery coinciding with an equally abundant quantity of natural objects, the theme of imagination linked closely to the theme of nature, such is the fundamental ambiguity that characterizes the poetics of romanticism. The tension between the two polarities never ceases to be problematic. We shall try to illustrate the structure of this latent tension as it appears in some selected poetic passages.

In a famous poem, Hölderlin speaks of a time at which "the gods" will again be an actual presence to man:

> . . . nun aber nennt er sein Liebstes,
> Nun, nun müssen dafür Worte, wie Blumen, entstehn.
> ("Brot und Wein," stanza 5)

Taken by itself, this passage is not necessarily a statement about the image: Hölderlin merely speaks of words ("Worte"), not of images ("Bilder"). But the lines themselves contain the image of the flower in the simplest and most explicit of all metaphorical structures, as a straightforward simile introduced by the conjunction wie. That the words referred to are not those of ordinary speech is clear from the verb: to originate ("entstehn"). In everyday use words are exchanged and put to a variety of tasks, but they are not supposed to originate anew; on the contrary, one wants them to be as well-known, as "common" as possible, to make certain that they will obtain for us what we want to obtain. They are used as established signs to confirm that something is recognized as being the same as before; and re-cognition excludes pure origination. But in poetic language words are not used as signs, not even as names, but in order to name: "Donner un sens plus pur aux mots de la tribu" (Mallarmé) or "erfand er für die Dinge eigene Namen" (Stefan George): poets know of the act of naming—"nun aber nennt er sein Liebstes"—as implying a return to the source, to the pure motion of experience at its beginning.

The word "entstehn" establishes another fundamental distinction. The two terms of the simile are not said to be identical with one another (the word = the flower), nor analogous in their general mode of being (the word is like the flower), but specifically in the way they originate (the word originates like the flower). The similarity between the two terms does not reside in their essence (identity), or in their appearance (analogy), but in the manner in which both originate. And Hölderlin is not speaking of any poetic word taken at random, but of an authentic word that fulfills its highest function in naming being as a presence. We could infer, then, that the fundamental intent of the poetic word is to originate in the same manner as what Hölderlin here calls "flowers." The image is essentially a kinetic process: it does not dwell in a static state where the two terms could be separated and reunited by analysis; the first term of the simile (here, "words") has no independent existence, poetically speaking, prior to the metaphorical statement. It originates with the statement, in the manner suggested by the flower image, and its way of being is determined by the manner in which it originates. The metaphor requires that we begin by forgetting all we have previously known about "words" —"donner un sens plus pur aux mots de la tribu"—and then informing the term with a dynamic existence similar to that which animates the "flowers." The metaphor is not a combination of two entities or experiences more or less deliberately linked together, but one single and particular experience: that of origination.

How do flowers originate? They rise out of the earth without the assistance of imitation or analogy. They do not follow a model other than themselves which they copy or from which they derive the pattern of their growth. By calling them *natural* objects, we mean that their origin is determined by nothing but their own being. Their becoming coincides at all times with the mode of their origination: it is as flowers that their history is what it is, totally defined by their identity. There is no wavering in the status of their existence: existence and essence coincide in them at all times. Unlike words, which originate like something else ("like flowers"), flowers originate like themselves: they are literally what they are, definable without the assistance of metaphor. It would follow then, since the intent of the poetic word is to originate like the flower, that it strives to banish all metaphor, to become entirely literal.

We can understand origin only in terms of difference: the source springs up because of the need to be somewhere or something else than what is now here. The word "entstehn," with its distancing prefix, equates origin with negation and difference. But the natural object, safe in its immediate being, seems to have no beginning and no end. Its permanence is carried by the stability of its being, whereas a beginning implies a negation of permanence, the discontinuity of a death in which an entity relinquishes its specificity and leaves it behind, like an empty shell. Entities engendered by consciousness originate in this fashion, but for natural entities like the flower, the process is entirely different. They originate out of a being which does not differ from them in essence but contains the totality of their individual manifestations within itself. All particular flowers can at all times establish an immediate identity with an original Flower, of which they are as many particular emanations. The original entity, which has to contain an infinity of manifestations of a common essence, in an infinity of places and at an infinity of moments, is necessarily transcendental. Trying to conceive of the natural object in terms of origin leads to a transcendental concept of the Idea: the quest for the Idea that takes the natural object for its starting point begins with the incarnated "minute particular" and works its way upward to a transcendental essence. Beyond the Idea, it searches for Being as the category which contains essences in the same manner that the Idea contains particulars. Because they are natural objects, flowers originate as incarnations of a transcendental principle. "Wie Blumen entstehn" is to become present as a natural emanation of a transcendental principle, as an epiphany.

Strictly speaking, an epiphany cannot be a beginning, since it reveals and unveils what, by definition, could never have ceased to be there. Rather, it is the rediscovery of a permanent presence which has chosen to hide itself from us—unless it is we who have the power to hide from it:

> So ist der Mensch; wenn da ist das Gut, und es sorget mit Gaaben
> Selber ein Gott für ihn, kennet und sieht er es nicht.
> ("Brot und Wein," stanza 5)

Since the presence of a transcendental principle, in fact conceived as omnipresence (parousia), can be hidden from man by man's own volition, the epiphany appears in the guise of a beginning rather than a discovery. Hölderlin's phrase: "Wie Blumen entstehn" is in fact a paradox, since origination is inconceivable on the ontological level; the ease with which we nevertheless accept it is indicative of our desire to forget. Our eagerness to accept the statement, the "beauty" of the line, stems from the fact that it combines the poetic seduction of beginnings contained in the word "entstehn" with the ontological stability of the natural object—but this combination is made possible only by a deliberate forgetting of the transcendental nature of the source.

That this forgetting, this ignorance, is also painful becomes apparent from the strategic choice of the word "flower," an object that seems intrinsically desirable. The effect of the line would have been thoroughly modified if Hölderlin had written, for instance, "Steinen" instead of "Blumen," although the relevance of the comparison would have remained intact as long as human language was being compared to a natural thing. The obviously desirable sensory aspects of the flower express the ambivalent aspiration toward a forgotten presence that gave rise to the image, for it is in experiencing the material presence of the particular flower that the desire arises to be reborn in the manner of a natural creation. The image is inspired by a nostalgia for the natural object, expanding to become nostalgia for the origin of this object. Such a nostalgia can only exist when the transcendental presence is forgotten, as in the "dürftiger Zeit" of Hölderlin's poem which we are all too eager to circumscribe as if it were a specific historical "time" and not Time in general. The existence of the poetic image is itself a sign of divine absence, and the conscious use of poetic imagery an admission of this absence.

It is clear that, in Hölderlin's own line, the words do *not* originate like flowers. They need to find the mode of their beginning in another entity; they originate out of nothing, in an attempt to be the first words that will arise as if they were natural objects, and, as such, they remain essentially distinct from natural entities. Hölderlin's statement is a perfect definition of what we call a natural image: the word that designates a desire for an epiphany but necessarily fails to be an epiphany, because it is pure origination. For it is in the essence of language to be capable of origination, but of never achieving the absolute identity with itself that exists in the natural object. Poetic language can do nothing but originate anew over and over again; it is always constitutive, able to posit regardless of presence but, by the same token, unable to give a foundation to what it posits except as an intent of consciousness. The word is always a free presence to the mind, the means by which the permanence of natural entities can be put into question and thus negated, time and again, in the endlessly widening spiral of the dialectic.

An image of this type is indeed the simplest and most fundamental we can conceive of, the metaphorical expression most apt to gain our immediate acquiescence. During the long development that takes place in the nineteenth century, the poetic image remains predominantly of the same kind that in the Hölderlin passage we took for our starting point— and which, be it said in passing, far from exhausts Hölderlin's own conception of the poetic image. This type of imagery is grounded in the intrinsic ontological primacy of the natural object. Poetic language seems to originate in the desire to draw closer and closer to the ontological status of the object, and its growth and development are determined by this inclination. We saw that this movement is essentially paradoxical and condemned in advance to failure. There can be flowers that "are" and poetic words that "originate," but no poetic words that "originate" as if they "were."

Nineteenth-century poetry reexperiences and represents the adventure of this failure in an infinite variety of forms and versions. It selects, for example, a variety of archetypal myths to serve as the dramatic pattern for the narration of this failure; a useful study could be made of the romantic and post-romantic versions of Hellenic myths such as the stories of Narcissus, of Prometheus, of the War of the Titans, of Adonis, Eros and Psyche, Proserpine, and many others; in each case, the tension and duality inherent in the mythological situation would be found to reflect the inherent tension that resides in the metaphorical language itself. At times, romantic thought and romantic poetry seem to come so close to giving in completely to the nostalgia for the object that it becomes difficult to distinguish between object and image, between imagination and perception, between an expressive or constitutive and a mimetic or literal language. This may well be the case in some passages of Wordsworth and Geothe, of Baudelaire and Rimbaud, where the vision almost seems to become a real landscape. Poetics of "unmediated vision," such as those implicit in Bergson and explicit in Bachelard, fuse matter and imagination by amalgamating perception and reverie, sacrificing, in fact, the demands of consciousness to the realities of the object. Critics who speak of a "happy relationship" between matter and consciousness fail to realize that the very fact that the relationship has to be established within the medium of language indicates that it does not exist in actuality.

At other times, the poet's loyalty toward his language appears so strongly that the object nearly vanishes under the impact of his words, in what Mallarmé called "sa presque disparition vibratoire." But even in as extreme a case as Mallarmé's, it would be a mistake to assume that the ontological priority of the object is being challenged. Mallarmé may well be the nineteenth-century poet who went further than any other in sacrificing the stability of the object to the demands of a lucid poetic awareness. Even some of his own disciples felt they had to react against him by reasserting the positivity of live and material substances against the annihilating power of his thought. Believing themselves to be in a situation where they had to begin their work at the point where Mallarmé had finished his, they took, like Claudel, the precise counterpart of his attitudes or, like Valéry, reversed systematically the meaning of some of his key images. Yet Mallarmé himself had always remained convinced of the essential priority of the natural object. The final image of his work, in

Un Coup de Dés, is that of the poet drowned in the ubiquitous "sea" of natural substances against which his mind can only wage a meaningless battle, "tenter une chance oiseuse." It is true that, in Mallarmé's thought, the value emphasis of this priority has been reversed and the triumph of nature is being presented as the downfall of poetic defiance. But this does not alter the fundamental situation. The alternating feeling of attraction and repulsion that the romantic poet experiences toward nature becomes in Mallarmé the conscious dialectic of a reflective poetic consciousness. This dialectic, far from challenging the supremacy of the order of nature, in fact reasserts it at all times. "Nous savons, victimes d'une formule absolue, que certes n'est que ce qui est," writes Mallarmé, and this absolute identity is rooted, for him, in "la première en date, la nature. Idée tangible pour intimer quelque réalité aux sens frustes. . . ."

Mallarmé's conception and use of imagery is entirely in agreement with this principle. His key symbols—sea, winged bird, night, the sun, constellations, and many others—are not primarily literary emblems but are taken, as he says, "au répertoire de la nature"; they receive their meaning and function from the fact that they belong initially to the natural world. In the poetry, they may seem disincarnate to the point of abstraction, generalized to the point of becoming pure ideas, yet they never entirely lose contact with the concrete reality from which they spring. The sea, the bird, and the constellation act and seduce in Mallarmé's poetry, like any earthly sea, bird, or star in nature; even the Platonic "oiseau qu'on n'ouït jamais" still has about it some of the warmth of the nest in which it was born. Mallarmé does not linger over the concrete and material details of his images, but he never ceases to interrogate, by means of a conscious poetic language, the natural world of which they are originally a part—while knowing that he could never reduce any part of this world to his own, conscious mode of being. If this is true of Mallarmé, the most self-conscious and anti-natural poet of the nineteenth century, it seems safe to assert that the priority of the natural object remains unchallenged among the inheritors of romanticism. The detailed study of Mallarmé bears this out; the same is true, with various nuances and reservations, of most Victorian and post-Victorian poets. For most of them, as for Mallarmé, the priority of nature is experienced as a feeling of failure and sterility, but nevertheless asserted. A similar feeling of threatening paralysis prevails among our own contemporaries and seems to grow with the depth of their poetic commitment. It may be that this threat could only be overcome when the status of poetic language or, more restrictively, of the poetic image, is again brought into question.

The direction that such a reconsideration might take can better be anticipated by a reading of the precursors of romanticism than by the study of its inheritors. Assumptions that are irrevocably taken for granted in the course of the nineteenth century still appear, at an earlier date, as one among several alternative roads. This is why an effort to understand the present predicament of the poetic imagination takes us back to writers that belong to the earlier phases of romanticism such as, for example, Rousseau. The affinity of later poets with Rousseau—which can well be considered to be a valid definition of romanticism as a whole—can, in turn, be best understood in terms of their use and underlying concept of imagery. The juxtaposition of three famous passages can serve as an illustration of this point and suggest further developments.

The three passages we have selected each represent a moment of spiritual revelation; the use of semi-religious, "sacred," or outspokenly sublime language in all three makes this unquestionably clear. Rousseau is probably the only one to have some awareness of the literary tradition that stands behind the topos: his reference to Petrarch (*La Nouvelle Héloïse,* Part I, XXIII) suggests the all-important link with the Augustinian lesson contained in Petrarch's letter narrating his ascent of Mont Ventoux. A similar experience, in a more Northern Alpine setting, is related in the three passages. The Rousseau text is taken from the letter in *La Nouvelle Héloïse* in which Saint-Preux reports on his sojourn in the Valais:

Ce n'était pas seulement le travail des hommes qui rendait ces pays étranges si bizarrement contrastés; la nature semblait encore prendre plaisir à s'y mettre en opposition avec elle-même, tant on la trouvait différente en un même lieu sous divers aspects. Au levant les fleurs du printemps, au midi les fruits de l'automne, au nord les glaces de l'hiver: elle réunissait toutes les saisons dans le même instant, tous les climats dans le même lieu, des terrains contraires sur le même sol, et formait l'accord inconnu partout ailleurs des productions des plaines et de celles des Alpes. . . . J'arrivai ce jour là sur des montagnes les moins élevées, et, parcourant ensuite leurs inégalités, sur celles des plus hautes qui étaient à ma portée. Après m'être promené dans les nuages, j'atteignis un séjour plus serein, d'où l'on voit dans la saison le tonerre et l'orage se former au-dessous de soi; image trop vaine de l'âme du sage, dont l'exemple n'exista jamais, ou n'existe qu'aux mêmes lieux d'où l'on en a tiré l'emblême.

Ce fut là que je démêlai sensiblement dans la pureté de l'air où je me trouvais la véritable cause du changement de mon humeur, et du retour de cette paix intérieure que j'avais perdue depuis si longtemps. En effet, c'est une impression générale qu'éprouvent tous les hommes, quoiqu'ils ne l'observent pas tous, que sur les hautes montagnes, où l'air est pur et subtil, on se sent plus de facilité dans la respiration, plus de légèreté dans le corps, plus de sérénité dans l'esprit; les plaisirs y sont moins ardents, les passions plus modérées. Les méditations y prennent je ne sais quel caractère grand et sublime, proportionné aux objets qui nous frappent, je ne sais quelle volupté tranquille qui n'a rien d'âcre et de sensuel. Il semble qu'en s'élévant au-dessus du séjour des hommes on y laisse des sentiments bas et terrestres, et qu'à mesure qu'on approche des régions éthérées, l'âme contracte quelque chose de leur inaltérable pureté. On y est grave sans mélancolie, paisible sans indolence, content d'être et de penser. . . . Imaginez la variété, la grandeur, la beauté de mille étonnants spectacles; le plaisir de ne voir autour de soi que des objets tout nouveaux, des oiseaux étranges, des plantes bizarres et inconnues, d'observer en quelque sorte une autre nature, et de se trouver dans un nouveau monde. Tout cela fait aux yeux un mélange inexprimable, dont le charme augmente encore par la subtilité de l'air qui rend les couleurs plus vives, les traits plus marqués, rapproche tous les points de vue; les distances paraissent moindres que dans les plaines où l'épaisseur de l'air couvre la terre d'un voile, l'horizon présente aux yeux plus d'objets qu'il semble n'en pouvoir contenir: enfin le spectacle a je ne sais quoi de magique, de surnaturel, qui ravit l'esprit et les sens; on oublie tout, on s'oublie soi-même, on ne sait plus où l'on est . . .

Wordsworth's text is taken from book VI of *The Prelude* and describes the poet's impressions in crossing the Alps, after having taken part in one of the celebrations that mark the triumph of the French Revolution. Wordsworth begins by praying for the safeguard of the Convent of the Grande Chartreuse, threatened with destruction at the hands of the insurrection; his prayer is first aimed at God, then "for humbler claim" at nature:

> . . . and for humbler claim
> Of that imaginative impulse sent
> From these majestic floods, yon shining cliffs,
> The untransmuted shapes of many worlds,
> Cerulian ether's pure inhabitants,
> These forests unapproachable by death,
> That shall endure as long as man endures,
> To think, to hope, to worship, and to feel,
> To struggle, to be lost within himself
> In trepidation, from the blank abyss
> To look with bodily eyes, and be consoled.
> (VI.461–71)

Somewhat later in the same section, Wordsworth describes the descent of the Simplon pass:

> . . . The immeasurable height
> Of woods decaying, never to be decayed,
> The stationary blasts of waterfalls,

And in the narrow rent at every turn
Winds thwarting winds, bewildered and forlorn,
The torrents shooting from the clear blue sky,
The rocks that muttered close upon our ears,
Black drizzling crags that spake by the way-side
As if a voice were in them, the sick sight
And giddy prospect of the raving stream,
The unfettered clouds and region of the Heavens,
Tumult and peace, the darkness and the light—
Were all like workings of one mind, the features
Of the same face, blossoms upon one tree;
Characters of the great Apocalypse,
The types and symbols of Eternity,
Of first, and last, and midst, and without end.

(VI.624-40)

Hölderlin's poem "Heimkunft" begins with a description of a sun-rise in the mountains, observed by the poet on his return from Switzerland to his native Swabia:

Drinn in den Alpen ists noch helle Nacht und die Wolke,
Freudiges dichtend, sie dekt drinnen das gähnende Thal.
Dahin, dorthin toset und stürzt die scherzende Bergluft,
Schroff durch Tannen herab glänzet und schwindet ein Stral.
Langsam eilt und kämpft das freudigschauernde Chaos,
Jung an Gestalt, doch stark, feiert es liebenden Streit
Unter den Felsen, es gährt und wankt in den ewigen Schranken,
Denn bacchantischer zieht drinnen der Morgen herauf.
Denn es wächst unendlicher dort das Jahr und die heilgen
Stunden, die Tage, sie sind kühner geordnet, gemischt.
Dennoch merket die Zeit der Gewittervogel und zwischen
Bergen, hoch in der Luft weilt er und rufet den Tag.

Ruhig glänzen indess die silbernen Höhen darüber,
Voll mit Rosen ist schon droben der leuchtende Schnee.
Und noch höher hinauf wohnt über dem Lichte der reine
Seelige Gott vom Spiel heiliger Stralen erfreut.
Stille wohnt er allein und hell erscheinet sein Antliz,
Der ätherische scheint Leben zu geben geneigt. . . .

("Heimkunft," stanzas 1 and 2)

Each of these texts describes the passage from a certain type of nature, earthly and material, to another nature which could be called mental and celestial, although the "Heaven" referred to is devoid of specific theological connotations. The common characteristic that concerns us most becomes apparent in the mixed, transitional type of landscape from which the three poets start out. The setting of each scene is located somewhere between the inaccessible mountain peaks and the humanized world of the plains; it is a deeply divided and paradoxical nature that, in Rousseau's terms, "seems to take pleasure in self-opposition." Radical contradictions abound in each of the passages. Rousseau deliberately mixes and blurs the order of the seasons and the laws of geography. The more condensed, less narrative diction of Wordsworth transposes similar contradictions into the complexity of a language that unites irreconcilable opposites; he creates a disorder so far-reaching that the respective position of heaven and earth are reversed: ". . . woods decaying, never to be decayed . . . ," ". . . torrents shooting from the sky . . . ," ". . . the stationary blast of waterfalls. . . ." Hölderlin's text also is particularly rich in oxymorons; every word combination, every motion expresses a contradiction: "helle Nacht," "langsam eilt," "liebenden Streit," "toset und stürzt," "geordnet, gemischt," "freudigschauernde," etc. One feels everywhere the pressure of an inner tension at the core of all earthly objects, powerful enough to bring them to explosion.

The violence of this turmoil is finally appeased by the ascending movement recorded in each of the texts, the movement by means of which the poetic imagination tears itself away, as it were, from a terrestrial nature and moves toward this "other nature" mentioned by Rousseau, associated with the diaphanous, limpid, and immaterial quality of a light that dwells nearer to the skies. Gaston Bachelard has described similar images of levitation very well, but he may not have stressed sufficiently that these reveries of flight not only express a desire to escape from earth-bound matter, to be relieved for a moment from the weight of gravity, but that they uncover a fundamentally new kind of relationship between nature and consciousness; it is significant, in this respect, that Bachelard classifies images of repose with earth and not with air, contrary to what happens in the three selected texts. The transparency of air represents the perfect fluidity of a mode of being that has moved beyond the power of earthly things and now dwells, like the God in Hölderlin's "Heimkunft," higher even than light ("über dem Lichte"). Like the clouds described by Wordsworth, the poets become "Cerulian ether's pure inhabitants." Unlike Mallarmé's "azur" or even the constellation at the end of Un Coup de Dés which are always seen from the point of view of the earth by a man about to sink away, their language has itself become a celestial entity, an inhabitant of the sky. Instead of being, like the "flower" in Hölderlin's "Brot und Wein," the fruit of the earth, the poetic word has become an offspring of the sky. The ontological priority, housed at first in the earthly and pastoral "flower," has been transposed into an entity that could still, if one wishes, be called "nature," but could no longer be equated with matter, objects, earth, stones, or flowers. The nostalgia for the object has become a nostalgia for an entity that could never, by its very nature, become a particularized presence.

The passages describe the ascent of a consciousness trapped within the contradictions of a half-earthly, half-heavenly nature "qui semblait prendre plaisir à (se) mettre en opposition avec elle-même," toward another level of consciousness, that has recovered "cette paix intérieure . . . perdue depuis si longtemps." (It goes without saying that the sequel of the three works from which the passages have been taken indicate that this tranquillity is far from having been definitively reconquered. Yet the existence of this moment of peace in *La Nouvelle Héloïse*, in *The Prelude*, and in the poem "Heimkunft"—"*Ruhig* glänzen indes die silbernen Höhen darüber . . ."—determines the fate of the respective authors and marks it as being an essentially poetic destiny.) In the course of this movement, in a passage that comes between the two descriptions we have cited, Wordsworth praises the faculty that gives him access to this new insight, and he calls this faculty "Imagination":

> Imagination!—lifting up itself
> Before the eye and progress of my song
> Like an unfathered vapour, . . .
>   . . . In such strength
> Of usurpation, in such visitings
> Of awful promise, when the light of sense
> Goes out in flashes that have shewn to us
> The invisible world, doth Greatness make abode,
>
> The mind beneath such banners militant
> Thinks not of spoils or trophies, nor of aught
> That may attest its prowess, blest in thoughts
> That are their own perfection and reward—
> Strong in itself, and in the access of joy
> Which hides it like the overflowing Nile.
>
> (VI.525–48)

But this "imagination" has little in common with the faculty that produces natural images born "as flowers originate." It marks instead a possibility for consciousness to exist entirely by and for itself, independently of all relationship with the outside world, without being moved by an intent aimed at a part of this world. Rousseau stressed that there was nothing sensuous ("rien d'âcre et de sensuel") in Saint-Preux's moment of illumination; Wordsworth, who goes so far as to designate the earth by the astonishing periphrase of "blank abyss," insists that the imagination can only come into full play when "the light of sense goes out" and when thought reaches a point at which it is "its own perfection and reward"—as when Rousseau, in the Fifth *Rêverie*, declares himself "content d'être" and "ne jouissant de rien d'extérieur à soi, de rien sinon de soi-même et de sa propre existence."

We know very little about the kind of images that such an imagination would produce, except that they would have little in common with what we have come to expect from familiar metaphorical figures. The works of the early romantics give us no actual examples, for they are, at most, *underway* toward renewed insights and inhabit the mixed and self-contradictory regions that we encountered in the three passages. Nor has their attempt been rightly interpreted by those who came after them, for literary history has generally labeled "primitivist," "naturalistic," or even pantheistic the first modern writers to have put into question, in the language of poetry, the ontological priority of the sensory object. We are only beginning to understand how this oscillation in the status of the image is linked to the crisis that leaves the poetry of today under a steady threat of extinction, although, on the other hand, it remains the depository of hopes that no other activity of the mind seems able to offer.

GEOFFREY H. HARTMAN

The Romance of Nature
and the Negative Way

We know from "Tintern Abbey" that in certain "blessed" moods, the eye is quieted. Book XII of *The Prelude* relates that the tyranny of sight was, as well as "almost inherent in the creature," especially oppressive at a particular point in Wordsworth's life. This time coincided with an excessive sitting in judgment and may safely be identified with the period when the poet, disillusioned by the French Revolution and with Godwin, sought formal proof in everything till "yielding up moral questions in despair":

> I speak in recollection of a time
> When the bodily eye, in every stage of life
> The most despotic of our senses, gained
> Such strength in *me* as often held my mind
> In absolute dominion.
>
> (XII, 127 ff.)

He refuses to enter upon abstruse argument to show how Nature thwarted such despotism by summoning all the senses to counteract each other; but his reflections lead him somewhat later in the same book to think of those "spots of time" which preserved and renovated him. One of them is the famous episode of the young boy, separated from his companion on a ride in the hills, dismounting out of fear and stumbling onto a murderer's gibbet, mouldered down, and of which nothing remained except the murderer's name carved nearby and kept clean because of local superstition:

From *The Unmediated Vision*, copyright © 1954 by Geoffrey H. Hartman and from *Wordsworth's Poetry 1787–1814*, copyright © 1964 by Yale University.

> The grass is cleared away, and to this hour
> The characters are fresh and visible:
> A casual glance had shown them, and I fled,
> Faltering and faint, and ignorant of the road:
> Then, reascending the bare common, saw
> A naked pool that lay beneath the hills,
> The beacon on the summit, and, more near,
> A girl, who bore a pitcher on her head,
> And seemed with difficult steps to force her way
> Against the blowing wind. It was, in truth,
> An ordinary sight. . . .
>
> (XII. 244 ff.)

The nudity of such scenes has often been remarked and various hypotheses invented, for example that Wordsworth lacked sexual sensibility, saw in Nature a father substitute, etc. But a correct detailing of the characteristics of this moment would have to note first the cause of the faltering and fleeing, which is not so much the mouldered gibbet as the fresh and visible characters engraved by an unknown hand. The name evidently doesn't matter, only the characters as characters, and the effect on the boy is swift and out of proportion to the simple sight, a casual glance sufficing. Suggested first is the indestructibility of human consciousness, exemplified by the new characters, and after that the indestructibility of a consciousness in Nature, figured in the skeletal characters of a scene denuded of all color, sketched in a permanent black and white, yet capable of immense physical impact. The mystical chord is touched, and the eye overpowered by an intuition of characters affecting no single sense but compelling a comparison between the indestructibility of human consciousness and a physical indestructibility. The same effect will be found suggested in the second of the spots of time:

> I sate half-sheltered by a naked wall;
> Upon my right hand couched a single sheep,
> Upon my left a blasted hawthorn stood;
>
> (XII. 299 ff.)

and the description of the characters of the great Apocalpyse likewise starts with an intuition of indestructibility:

> the immeasurable height
> Of woods decaying, never to be decayed
> (VI. 623 ff.)

This, moreover, is coupled with a hint of the Last Judgment in the trumpeting of waterfalls that to the eye seem to possess the rigidity of rock,

The stationary blasts of waterfalls.

But before reaching a conclusion we should consider one more event, the most significant perhaps that enters through, yet overpowers, the eye. Wandering among London crowds the poet is smitten

> Abruptly, with the view (a sight not rare)
> Of a blind Beggar, who, with upright face,
> Stood, propped against a wall, upon his chest
> Wearing a written paper, to explain
> His story, whence he came, and who he was.
> Caught by the spectacle my mind turned round
> As with the might of waters; and apt type
> This label seemed of the utmost we can know,
> Both of ourselves and of the universe;
> And, on the shape of that unmoving man,
> His steadfast face and sightless eyes, I gazed,
> As if admonished from another world.
>
> (VII. 638 ff.)

As in the gibbet scene, the poet emphasizes that the sight was ordinary and sudden, that is, having no intrinsic claim on the mind, nor worked up by meditation. But a greater similarity obtains between the two, though it is by no means complete. Both events focus on a label written by an impersonal hand. But whereas the characters in the one case seem indestructible, here the label is a sign of human impotence. Yet the superficial label clearly points to a set of deeper and indestructible characters, for the suggestion is that the lost eyes of the beggar were only like a piece of paper, a visual surface, and that, being removed, they leave the man more steadfast, fixed, eternal. We rediscover Wordsworth's constant concern with denudation, stemming from both a fear of visual reality and a desire for physical indestructibility. And the fine image of the mind turned by the spectacle as if with the might of waters, refers to that vast identity established throughout the poems of Wordsworth, an identity against sight, its fever and triviality, and making all things tend to the sound of universal waters; subduing the eyes by a power of harmony, and the reason by the suggestion of a Final Judgment which is God's alone. The intuition of indestructibility in the midst of decay, and the identity of the power in light with the power of sound ("by form or image unprofaned") are the two modes of a vision in which the mind knows itself almost without exterior cause or else as no less real, here, no less indestructible than the object of its perceptions.

II

Nature, for Wordsworth, is not an "object" but a presence and a power; a motion and a spirit; not something to be worshiped and consumed, but always a guide leading beyond itself. This guidance starts in earliest childhood. The boy of *Prelude* I is fostered alike by beauty and by fear. Through beauty, nature often makes the boy feel at home, for, as in the Great Ode, his soul is alien to this world. But through fear, nature reminds the boy from where he came, and prepares him, having lost heaven, also to lose nature. The boy of *Prelude* I, who does not yet know he must suffer this loss as well, is warned by nature itself of the solitude to come.

I have suggested elsewhere how the fine skating scene of the first book (425–63), though painted for its own sake, to capture the animal spirits of children spurred by a clear and frosty night, moves from vivid images of immediate life to an absolute calm which foreshadows a deeper and more hidden life. The Negative Way is a gradual one, and the child is weaned by a premonitory game of hide-and-seek in which nature changes its shape from familiar to unfamiliar, or even fails the child. There is a great fear, either in Wordsworth or in nature, of traumatic breaks: *Natura non facit saltus.*

If the child is led by nature to a more deeply mediated understanding of nature, the mature singer who composes *The Prelude* begins with that understanding or even beyond it—with the spontaneously creative spirit. Wordsworth plunges into *medias res*, where the *res* is Poetry, or Nature only insofar as it has guided him to a height whence he must find his own way. But Book VI, with which we are immediately concerned, records what is chronologically an intermediate period, in which the first term is neither Nature nor Poetry. It is Imagination in embryo: the mind muted yet also strengthened by the external world's opacities. Though imagination is with Wordsworth on the journey of 1790, nature seems particularly elusive. He goes out to a nature which seems to hide as in the crossing of the Alps.

The first part of this episode is told to illustrate a curious melancholy related to the "presence" of imagination and the "absence" of nature. Like the young Apollo in Keats' *Hyperion*, Wordsworth is strangely dissatisfied with the riches before him, and compelled to seek some other region:

> Where is power?
> Whose hand, whose essence, what divinity
> Makes this alarum in the elements,
> While I here idle listen on the shores
> In fearless yet in aching ignorance?

To this soft or "luxurious" sadness, a more masculine kind is added, which results from a "stern mood" or "underthirst of vigor"; and it is in order to throw light on this further melancholy that Wordsworth tells the incident of his crossing the Alps.

The stern mood to which Wordsworth refers can only be his premonition of spiritual autonomy, of an independence from sense-experience foreshadowed by nature since earliest childhood. It is the 'underground' form of imagination, and *Prelude* II.315 ff. describes it as "an' obscure sense / Of possible sublimity," for which the soul, remembering *how* it felt in exalted moments, but no longer *what* it felt, continually strives to find a new content. The element of obscurity, related to nature's self-concealment, is necessary to the soul's capacity for growth, for it vexes the latter toward self-dependence. Childhood pastures become viewless; the soul cannot easily find the source from which it used to drink the visionary power; and while dim memories of a passionate commerce with external things drive it more than ever to the world, this world makes itself more than ever inscrutable. The travelers' separation from their guides, then that of the road from the stream (VI.568), and finally their trouble with the peasant's words that have to be "translated," express subtly the soul's desire for a *beyond.* Yet only when poet, brook, and road are once again "fellow-travellers" (VI.622), and Wordsworth holds to Nature, does that reveal—a Proteus in the grasp of the hero—its prophecy.

This prophecy was originally the second part of the adventure, the delayed vision which compensates for his disappointment (the "Characters of the great Apocalypse," VI.617–40). In its original sequence, therefore, the episode has only two parts: the first term or moment of natural immediacy is omitted, and we go straight to the second term, the inscrutability of an external image, which leads via the gloomy strait to its renewal. Yet, as if this pattern demanded a substitute third term, Wordsworth's tribute to "Imagination" severs the original temporal sequence, and forestalls nature's renewal of the bodily eye with ecstatic praise of the inner eye.

The apocalypse of the gloomy strait loses by this the character of a *terminal* experience. Nature is again surpassed, for the poet's imagination is called forth, at the time of writing, by the barely scrutable, not by the splendid emotion; by the disappointment, not the fulfillment. This (momentary) displacement of emphasis is the more effective in that the style of VI.617 ff., and the very characters of the apocalypse, suggest that the hiding places of power cannot be localized in nature. Though the apostrophe to Imagination—the special insight that comes to Wordsworth in 1804—is a real peripety, reversing a meaning already established, it is not unprepared. But it takes the poet many years to realize that nature's "end" is to lead to something "without end," to teach the travelers to transcend nature.

The three parts of this episode, therefore, can help us understand the mind's growth toward independence of immediate external stimuli. The measure of that independence is Imagination, and carries with it a precarious self-consciousness. We see that the mind must pass through a stage where it experiences Imagination as a power separate from Nature, that the poet must come to think and feel as if by his own choice, or from the structure of his mind.

VI–a (557–91) shows the young poet still dependent on the immediacy of the external world. Imagination frustrates that dependence secretly, yet its blindness toward nature is accompanied by a blindness toward itself. It is only a "mute Influence of the soul, / An Element of nature's inner self" (1805, VIII.512–13).

VI–b (592–616) gives an example of thought or feeling that came from the poet's mind without immediate external excitement. There remains, of course, the memory of VI–a (the disappointment), but this is an internal feeling, not an external image. The poet recognizes at last that the power he has looked for in the outside world is really within and frustrating his search. A shock of recognition then feeds the very blindness toward the external world which helped to produce that shock.

In VI–c (617–40) the landscape is again an immediate external object of experience. The mind cannot separate in it what it desires to know and what it actually knows. It is a moment of revelation, in which the poet sees not as in a glass, darkly, but face to face. VI–c clarifies, therefore, certain details of VI–a and seems to actualize figurative details of VI–b. The matter-of-fact interplay of quick and lingering movement, of up-and-down perplexities in the ascent (VI.567 ff.), reappears in larger letters; while the interchanges of light and darkness, of cloud and cloudlessness, of rising like a vapor from the abyss and pouring like a flood from heaven have entered the landscape bodily. The gloomy strait also participates in this actualization. It is revealed as the secret middle term which leads from the barely scrutable presence of nature to its resurrected image. The travelers who move freely with or against the terrain, hurrying upward, pacing downward, perplexed at crossings, are now led narrowly by the pass as if it were their rediscovered guide.

The Prelude, as history of a poet's mind, foresees the time when the "Characters of the great Apocalypse" will be intuited without the medium of nature. The time approaches even as the poet writes, and occasionally cuts across his narrative, the imagination rising up, as in Book VI, "Before the eye and progress of my Song" (version of 1805). This phrase, at once conventional and exact, suggests that imagination waylaid the poet on his mental journey. The "eye" of his song, trained on a temporal sequence with the vision in the strait as its final term, is suddenly obscured. He is momentarily forced to deny nature that magnificence it had shown in the gloomy strait, and to attribute the glory to imagination, whose interposition in the very moment of writing proves it to be a power more independent than nature of time and place, and so a better type "Of first, and last, and midst, and without end" (VI.640).

We know that VI–b records something that happened during composition, and which enters the poem as a new biographical event. Wordsworth has just described his disappointment (VI–a) and turns in anticipation to nature's compensatory finale (VI–c). He is about to respect the original temporal sequence, "the eye and progress" of his song. But as he looks forward, in the moment of composition, from blankness toward revelation, a new insight cuts him off from the latter. The original disappointment is seen not as a test, or as a prelude to magnificence, but as a revelation in itself. It suddenly reveals a power—imagination—that could not be satisfied by anything in nature, however sublime. The song's progress comes to a halt because the poet is led beyond nature. Unless he can respect the natural (which includes the temporal) order, his song, at least as narrative, must cease. Here Imagination, not Nature (as in I.96 ff.), defeats Poetry.

This conclusion may be verified by comparing the versions of 1805 and 1850. The latter replaces "Before the eye and progress of my Song" with a more direct metaphorical transposition. Imagination is said to rise from the mind's abyss "Like an unfathered vapour that enwraps, / At once, some lonely traveller." The (literal) traveler of 1790 becomes the (mental) traveler at the moment of composition. And though one Shakespearean doublet has disappeared, another implicitly takes its place: does not imagination rise from "the dark backward and abysm of time" (*The Tempest*, I.2.50)? The result, in any case, is a disorientation of time added to that of way; an apocalyptic moment in which past and future overtake the present; and the poet, cut off from nature by imagination, is, in an absolute sense, lonely.

The last stage in the poet's "progress" has been reached. The travelers of VI–a had already left behind their native land, the public rejoicing of France, rivers, hills, and spires; they have separated from their guides, and finally from the unbridged mountain stream. Now, in 1804, imagination separates the poet from all else: human companionship, the immediate scene, the remembered scene. The end of the *via negativa* is near. There is no more "eye and progress"; the invisible progress of VI–a (Wordsworth crossing the Alps unknowingly) has revealed itself as a progress independent of visible ends, or engendered by the desire for an "invisible world"—the substance of things hoped for, the evidence of things not seen. Wordsworth descants on the Pauline definition of faith:

> in such strength
> Of usurpation, when the light of sense
> Goes out, but with a flash that has revealed
> The invisible world, doth greatness make abode,
> There harbours; whether we be young or old,
> Our destiny, our being's heart and home,
> Is with infinitude, and only there;
> With hope it is, hope that can never die,
> Effort, and expectation, and desire,
> And something evermore about to be.
>
> (VI.599–608)

Any further possibility of progress for the poet would be that of song itself, of poetry no longer subordinate to the mimetic function, the experience faithfully traced to this height. The poet is a traveler insofar as he must respect nature's past guidance and retrace his route. He did come, after all, to an important instance of bodily vision. The way is the song. But the song often strives to become the way. And when this happens, when the song seems to capture the initiative, in such supreme moments of poetry as VI–b or even VI–c, the way is lost. Nature in VI–c shows "Winds thwarting winds, bewildered and forlorn," as if they too had lost their way. The apocalypse in the gloomy strait depicts a self-thwarting march and counter-march of elements, a divine mockery of the concept of the Single Way.

But in VI–c, nature still stands over and against the poet; he is still the observer, the eighteenth-century gentleman admiring a new manifestation of the sublime, even if the lo! or mark! is supressed. He moves haltingly but he moves; and the style of the passage emphasizes continuities. Yet with the imagination athwart there is no movement, no looking before and after. The song itself must be the way, though that of a blinded man, who admits, "I was lost." Imagination, as it shrouds the poet's eye, also shrouds the eye of his song, whose tenor is nature guiding and fostering the power of song.

It is not, therefore, till 1804 that Wordsworth discovers the identity of his hidden guide. VI–c was probably composed in 1799, and it implies that Wordsworth, at that time, still thought nature his guide. But now he sees that it was imagination moving him by means of nature, just as Beatrice guided Dante by means of Virgil. It is not nature as such but nature indistinguishably blended with imagination that compels the poet along his Negative Way. Yet, if VI–b prophesies against the world of sense-experience, Wordsworth's affection and point of view remain unchanged. Though his discovery shakes the foundation of his poem, he returns after a cloudburst of verses to the pedestrian attitude of 1790, when the external world and not imagination seemed to be his guide ("Our journey we renewed, / Led by the stream," etc.). Moreover, with the exception of VI–b, imagination does not move the poet directly, but always through the agency of nature. The childhood "Visitings of imaginative power" depicted in Books I and XII also appeared in the guise or disguise of nature. Wordsworth's journey as a poet can only continue with eyes, but the imagination experienced as a power distinct from nature opens his eyes by putting them out. Wordsworth, therefore, does not adhere to nature because of natural fact, but despite it and because of human and poetic fact. Imagination is indeed an *awe-full* power.

III

Wordsworth's attempt to revive the Romance mode for a consciously Protestant imagination had no issue in his own poetry, or even in English poetry as a whole, which will follow the freer romances of Keats, Shelley, and Scott. But in America, where Puritanism still questioned the sacred and also secular rights of imagination, a similar development is found. The possibility of a consciously Protestant romance is what inspires or self-justifies Hawthorne, Melville, and Henry James. If the Christian poets of the Renaissance wondered how they could use Pagan forms and themes, the neo-Puritan writers wonder how they can use the Christian superstitions. Not only do we find the often directly presented schism between an old-world and a new-world imagination, in which the old world is, sometimes nobly, under the spell of "superstitious fancies strong," but the action centers on the manner in which a strange central apparition, a romance phenomenon, is imaginatively valued. In the European society in which she moves, James' Daisy Miller is a white doe, and there are those who do the gentle creature wrong, who kill her, in fact, by knowing her wrongly. I have chosen, of course, a very simple case; but there is no need to ascend the scale of Jamesian or Melvillean fiction to the final white mystery. Wordsworth's scruples concerning the imagination are Puritan scruples even though they are gradually associated with Anglican thought.

That Wordsworth was seeking to develop a new kind of romance, one that would chasten our imaginations, is already suggested by the stanzas dedicating *The White Doe* to his wife. A moving personal document, they trace the history of his relation to romantic fiction. He describes his and Mary's love of Spenser, their innocent enjoyment of "each specious miracle." But then a "lamentable change"—the death of Wordsworth's brother—pierces their hearts:

> For us the stream of fiction ceased to flow,
> For us the voice of melody was mute.

Romance and realism are suddenly opposed. The truth is too harsh, and fiction is even blamed for deceiving the mind, for veiling reality with "the light that never was." Spenser, however, is so soothing, that he beguiles them once more, and the story of the Nortons, with its own "mild Una in her sober cheer," is composed.

But the death of Wordsworth's brother leaves its mark. Though Wordsworth returns to Spenser, the stream of fiction is troubled, it will never again flow lightly "in the bent of Nature." The poet seems to have interpreted his brother's death, like his father's, as a "chastisement" following an over-extension of imaginative hopes (cf. *Prelude* XII.309–16). The dream of happiness built on John's return was something *hyper moron*, secretly apocalyptic, or beyond the measure nature could fulfill. This is not to say that John's loss was the decisive cause for Wordsworth's decline as a poet—I have abjured speculation on this matter. Some speculations, however, are simply a way of describing the later poetry, and it is quite true that whether or not the decisive shock came in 1805, Wordsworth's mind is now much less inclined to "wanton" in "the exercise of its own powers . . . loving its own creation." If we compare his dedicatory stanzas to Mary with those Shelley wrote to *his* Mary and which preface "The Witch of Atlas," the distance between one poet's light-hearted espousal of "visionary rhyme" and the other's weight of scruples becomes fully apparent. It is as if Shelley and Wordsworth had polarized Spenserian romance, the former taking its *dulce*, the latter, its *utile*.

It might not seem possible that the later poetry could be beset by even more scruples, but this is what happens. Wordsworth's attitude toward his mind's "exercise of its powers" suffers a further restraint. He begins to watch on *two* fronts: to be deluded that "the mighty Deep / Was even the gentlest of all gentle things" is as dangerous as to gaze into the bottomless abyss. He is now as careful about an idealizing impulse as about the apocalyptic intimation. The presence of a Sympathetic Nature, which is the one supersitition for which he had kept his respect, for it is vital not only to poetry but also to human development, being a necessary illusion in the growth of the mind, this too is falling away. Yet the story of the white doe is his attempt to save the notion once more in some purer form. He knows that to give it up entirely is to return to a holy, but stern and melancholy, imagination.

Under the pressure of these many restraints, Wordsworth's mind has little chance to fall in love with or explore its own impressions. Self-discovery, which informs the meditative lyrics (the act of recall there is never a passive thing but verges on new and often disturbing intuitions) almost disappears. And, by a curious irony, the unpublished *Prelude,* which is his greatest testimony to the living mind, now discourages further self-exploration. Such later sentiments as:

> Earth prompts—Heaven urges; let us seek the light,
> Studious of that pure intercourse begun
> When first our infant brows their lustre won,

do not rely, in their weakness, on the external authority of the church, but on the internal authority of his own greatest poem, which is kept private, and as scripture to himself abets the flat reiteration of his ideas in a slew of minor poems. J. M. Murry is right in feeling that the later Wordsworth represents the process of self-discovery as much more ortho-dox from the beginning than it was; and Coleridge, severely disappointed by *The Excursion,* offers a similar diagnosis: Wordsworth's opinions, he said, were based on "self-established convictions" and did not have for readers in general the special force they had for the poet.

There are, nevertheless, strange happenings in the later poetry, which has a precarious quality of its own. Though Wordsworth no longer dallies with surmise, he cannot entirely forego apocalyptic fancies, or the opposite (if more generous) error which attributes to nature a vital and continuous role in the maturing of the mind. The old imaginative free-doms continue to rise up, like Proteus or Triton, against the narrow-minded materialism of his time—a living Pagan is better than a dead Christian spirit. He is not beyond being surprised by his imagination. It continues to defy his censorship, even if he queries every fancy, every moment of "quickened subjectivity." I shall conclude by considering certain incidents from the later poetry that show in what relation to his own mind Wordsworth stands.

In 1820, thirty years after his journey through the Alps, he takes Mary and Dorothy to the Continent. Dorothy keeps her usual journal, to which he probably turned in composing the "memorials" of that tour. While in the valley of Chamonix (a place sacred to the poet) the travelers hear voices rising from the mountain's base and glimpse below them a procession making its way to the church. Dorothy describes the scene for us:

> [we saw] a lengthening Procession—the Priest in his robes—the host, and banners uplifted; and men following two and two;—and, last of all, a great number of females, in like order; the head and body of each covered with a white garment. The stream continued to flow on for a long time, till all had paced slowly round the church. . . . The procession was grave and simple, agreeing with the simple decorations of a village church; the banners made no glittering shew; the Females composed a moving girdle round the Church; their figures, from head to foot, covered with one piece of white cloth, resembled the small pyramids of the Glacier, which were before our eyes; and it was impossible to look at one and the other without fancifully connecting them together. Imagine the *moving* Figures, like a stream of pyramids,—the white Church, the half-concealed Village, and the Glacier close behind, among pine-trees,— a pure sun shining over all! and remember that these objects were seen at the base of those enormous mountains, and you may have some faint notion of the effect produced upon us by that beautiful spectacle.

Wordsworth is inspired by this to a 'progress poem' entitled "Processions. Suggested on a Sabbath Morning in the Vale of Chamouny" which traces the spirit of religious ceremonies from ancient times to the present. The Alps, archaic strongholds, allow him to recognize in Pagan ritual the impure basis of Christian pageantry. Shrill canticles have yielded to sober litanies; silver bells and pompous decorations to "hooded vestments fair"; and noisy feasts to an assembly breathing "a Spirit more subdued and soft." Moreover, as he looks on, another archaic vestige suggests itself, which is hinted at in Dorothy's account: that the procession is born of the mountain, like the white pillars above it. Indeed, the glacier columns, juxtaposed with the moving column of white figures, bring to mind the theory of Creation by Metamorphosis. The mountain, in this Blakean insight, is "men seen afar."

Wordsworth is strangely frightened at this—not at the mere thought of metamorphosis but at a reflexive knowledge connected with it. He realizes he has viewed more than a transformed archaic ritual, or ancient truth: he has seen the *source* of that truth in his mind's excited and spontaneous joining of the living stream of people to the frozen of nature. As in his greatest poetry, the mind is moved by itself after being moved by something external. He writes a stanza similar in tenor and directness to the apostrophe to Imagination in the sixth book of *The Prelude*, similar at least in its magnificent opening:

Trembling, I look upon the secret springs
Of that licentious craving in the mind
To act the God among external things,
To bind, on apt suggestion, or unbind;
And marvel not that antique Faith inclined
To crowd the world with metamorphosis,
Vouchsafed in pity or in wrath assigned;
Such insolent temptations wouldst thou miss,
Avoid these sights; nor brood o'er Fable's dark abyss!

Wordsworth's reaction, visceral first, pontific later, differs from the usual religious decision to relinquish a profane subject or style. He does not say, in Herbert's sweet manner, farewell dark fables, or censor their use in Christian poetry. But he turns in the moment, and explicitly, from a power of his own mind without which poetry is not conceivable. It is not fabling merely, but "Fable's dark abyss"—the mind of man itself—he now fears to look on. He is afraid of fables because of their reaction on a mind that might brood too pregnantly on what they reveal of its power. Yet at the time of *The White Doe* he had still tried to 'convert' a fable by purifying its superstition and cleansing its mystery: the doe is not a metamorphosed spirit and her powers of sympathy are due to natural not supernatural causes. What a difference, also, between this sacred tremor and his earlier, almost cavalier attitude toward all mythologies! In 1798, and again in 1814, he professes to be unalarmed at their conceptions because of the greater "fear and awe" that fall on him when he regards "the Mind of Man— / My haunt, and the main region of my song." He did not fear his fear then as he does now, trembling before his own creative will.

Wordsworth's diffidence is no sudden thing; we found it at the beginning of his career, and related it to an extraordinary, apocalyptic consciousness of self. At that time religion seemed to him too much a product of that same apocalyptic consciousness. Nature had to be defended against a supernatural religion as well as against the barren eye of Science. Was it ever meant, he asks,

That this majestic imagery, the clouds
The ocean and the firmament of heaven
Should lie a barren picture on the mind?

In the later poetry, however, religion has changed its role. It now protects rather than threatens nature. He begins to identify with the Anglo-Catholic concept of the *via media* his ideal of Nature, of England, even of Poetry. The poet, he had said in 1802, is "the rock of defence for human nature;

an upholder and preserver, carrying everywhere with him relationship and love." He now sees the church as part of that rock: an *ecclesia* mediating by a divine principle of mercy the sterner demands of God, State, and Imagination, demands which have often threatened human nature, and led to individual or collective fanaticisms. Religion and imagination are intervolved (Wordsworth and Blake are in perfect accord on *this*), and whereas Catholicism incites an apocalyptic response:

> Mine ear has rung, my spirit sunk subdued,
> Sharing the strong emotion of the crowd,
> When each pale brow to dread hosannas bowed
> While clouds of incense mounting veiled the rood,
> That glimmered like a pine-tree dimly viewed
> Through Alpine vapours . . .

the Anglican Church, which is the *religio loci* corresponding to the *genius loci* of England, rejects such appalling rites in the hope that nature, man, and God constitute ultimately "one society":

> the Sun with his first smile
> Shall greet that symbol crowning the low Pile:
> And the fresh air of incense-breathing morn
> Shall wooingly embrace it; and green moss
> Creep round its arms through centuries unborn.

Covenant has replaced, as completely as possible, apocalypse: his emblem marries nature, time, and the spirit.

The *Ecclesiastical Sonnets,* from which the above extracts are taken, show Wordsworth is suspicious of everything that could rouse the apocalyptic passions. This is also an important clue to his later politics, which seem illiberal, apostate even; a failure of nerve like his poetry. The evidence against him is indeed black. "That such a man," cries Shelley, "should be such a poet!" Shelley did not know Wordsworth personally, but even the faithful Crabb Robinson, who made all the possible allowances, is compelled to address Dorothy in 1827: "I assure you it gives me a real pain when I think that some further commentator may possibly hereafter write: 'This great poet survived to the fifth decennary of the nineteenth century but he appears to have died in the year 1814, as far as life consisted in an active sympathy with the temporary [viz. temporal] welfare of his fellow-creatures.' " Only in matters of Church doctrine, as distinguished from Church or national politics, does something of Wordsworth's liberalism remain. His views, says H. N. Fairchild, praising where he thinks to blame, are "wholly consistent with modern Christian liberalism . . . very loose and vague, however, for a nineteenth-century High Churchman."

Wordsworth, it is clear, has passed from the idea that change (let alone revolutionary change) intends a repossession of the earth to the idea that it might cause a greater dispossession than ever. Harper has documented his panic fear of change. It is a deeply emotional and imaginative thing, and has almost no relation to his own very small prosperity. The Reform Bill of 1832, for instance, seems to him to herald a revolt of the masses. He prophesies ruin and destruction to England and thinks of having to leave it. His jeremiads indicate a soul which knows itself too well, and is still afraid in others of those "blasts of music" and "daring sympathies with power" to which he had given ear at the time of the French Revolution.

Dark thoughts—"blind thoughts" as he calls them in "Resolution and Independence"—certainly continue to impinge on him. Yet how deep they lie, almost too deep for notice. They come to the surface only in matters of politics, and in exceptionally self-conscious verses, like those in memory of Chamonix. The most famous of the River Duddon sonnets, the "After-thought" of the series, runs truer to course. The whole series, less conventional than it seems, participates in the poet's desire to bind together the powers of his mind and of nature; and to know this illumines the character of his final sonnet.

The "After-thought" begins very simply:

> I thought of Thee, my partner and my guide,
> As being passed away.

It makes us wonder, this quiet human directness, whom the poet is addressing, but then Willard Sperry's observation that "his brief for nature's morality was based upon her openness to our address" comes to mind. The more remarkable aspect of the verses is what Wordsworth can have meant by the river "passing away."

He must have recalled the prophecy of streams shrinking in the final fire, of "Old Ocean, in his bed left singed and bare." This must have come to him and threatened the entire basis of his sonnets, which is the partnership of mind and nature. Or is it his own death which he foresaw, as in "Tintern Abbey"? But why, in that case, would he talk of Duddon's death rather than of his own?

I suspect, in any case, that the personal fact of his dying seemed to him a small matter compared to the river's loss and the foreboded severing of the loves of man and nature. Duddon is mortal in that it may die in man or to him as he grows older, but especially in that it may die to the human imagination, generally, on Wordsworth's death. For if his special mission among poets is to marry nature to the mind, his death takes on a cosmic meaning. The rest of the poem, of course, dispels his strange fear concerning Duddon:

> —Vain sympathies!
> For, backward, Duddon! as I cast my eyes,
> I see what was, and is, and will abide;
> Still glides the Stream, and shall for ever glide;
> The Form remains, the Function never dies;
> While we, the brave, the mighty, and the wise,
> We Men, who in our morn of youth defied
> The elements, must vanish;—be it so!
> Enough, if something from our hands have power
> To live, and act, and serve the future hour;
> And if, as toward the silent tomb we go,
> Through love, through hope, and faith's transcendent dower,
> We feel that we are greater than we know.

This is pure consolation and too easy. His sympathies (for the stream!) are "vain" because nature outlives man and will continue to inspire him; and because man, too, has the promise, through religion, of an immortality that hopefully does not exclude the tie of nature.

Yet the distance between "Tintern Abbey" and the River Duddon "After-thought" is not great. The primary experience is one of nature, of the Wye or the Duddon or other great presences. In the earlier poems we are told directly of how the cataracts haunted the boy or how the objects of nature "lay upon his mind like substances" and "perplexed the bodily sense." The same kind of perplexity is produced by the appearance of the white doe. The mystery in nature is that of our relation to it, which is darkly sympathetic, so that Goethe calls it "das offenbare Geheimniss," an incumbent natural mystery. But this experience of relationship, open to all, is followed by the further mystery of its diminution, also shared by all. The poet who returns to Tintern Abbey knows his loss; he sees it in the glass of the landscape, darkly; and a prophetic fear, despite nature's continuing importance, leads him to envisage severance and even death. The conclusion that his death may mean the passing away of nature from the human mind is not yet drawn, for he prays that his sister may continue a relationship to which he is dying. But in the "after-thought" his fear touches the furthest point. It does so fleetingly, yet still bespeaks either a delusion of grandeur or a remarkable conviction that man and nature are growing irremediably apart, and that the gap between them, whether a historical error or a providential test, already verges on apocalypse. "The sun strengthens us no more, neither does the moon."

The burden of this secret consciousness in Wordsworth should not be underestimated. It is he who stands between us and the death of nature; and this is also the truest justification for the "egotistical sublime" in his poetry. He values his own lightest feeling for the sufficiencies of mother earth—

> The night that calms, the day that cheers;
> The common growth of mother-earth
> Suffices me—her tears, her mirth
> Her humblest mirth and tears

—because her call to him, unregarded, augurs a loss in our capacity to respond to nature, and hence the virtual opposite of that "great consummation" of which he sings in the verses that preface the 1814 *Excursion*. He feels that he must personally fasten or newcreate the links between nature and the human mind. The "Adonais" Shelley laments is strangely like his own conception of himself.

I may seem to exaggerate Wordsworth's sense of mission; but no one has yet explained the heart-sickness and melancholia of the aging poet. These are prompted, of course, by political fears (which are really imaginative fears) and by personal grief, yet do they differ, except in persistence, from earlier dejections? Is his "fixed despondency, uncorrected" human weakness merely, and the effect of old age, or may it not accord with his own younger picture of himself as a "meditative, oft a suffering man"? What his meditations were, and why linked intimately to a certain kind of suffering, may now be clear. The selfhood Wordsworth knew, and which is always related to a fear of the death of nature, is at first alleviated by his sense of special mission, then cruelly confirmed by what he takes to be his growing isolation. At the time of "Michael," he is still thinking "Of youthful Poets, who among these hills / Will be my second self when I am gone"; it is in hope of these that he spins his homely ballads. But he never recognizes Shelley or Keats or any of the following generation as his second self. He is a stubborn, old, opinionated man—perhaps; the fact remains that Shelley and Keats, though concerned with the humanizing of imagination, have greater affinities with the Renaissance poets and that these have greater affinities with one another than Wordsworth has with any of them. Milton, whose sense of mission is as strong as his, could turn to Spenser and even to Virgil; Blake, though almost unknown in his time, thought of himself as continuing or correcting Milton and the Bible; but Wordsworth, despite his love for the older writers, and especially for Milton, can turn to no one in his desire to save nature for the human imagination. He is the most isolated figure among the great English poets.

JOHN HOLLANDER

Wordsworth and the Music of Sound

In a strange little meditation written in 1919, Rainer Maria Rilke recalls his earliest schoolboy experiments with a then recently invented cylinder phonograph, and how what stayed with him longest were his belief that, as he put it, "independent sound, taken from us and preserved outside us, would be unforgettable," and the image later to work on his fancy—not the sound from the horn but the markings traced on the cylinder. This unassimilated impression lay dormant, Rilke suggests, until awakened in another context: while a student later on at the Beaux-Arts, he had become fascinated with skeletal anatomy and had procured a skull upon which to meditate at night (if as in a baroque emblem, he does not say). A passing glance seems to have precipitated an involuntary memory:

> By candlelight—which is often so particularly alive and challenging—
> the coronal suture had become strikingly visible, and I knew at once what
> it reminded me of: one of those unforgotten grooves, which had been
> scratched in a little wax cylinder . . .

and he goes on to outline a fancy:

> The coronal suture of the skull (this would first have to be investigated)
> has—let us assume—a certain similarity to the closely wavy line which
> the needle of a phonograph engraves on the receiving, rotating cylinder
> of the apparatus. What if one changed the needle and directed it on its
> return journey along a tracing which was not derived from the graphic

From *New Perspectives on Coleridge and Wordsworth*, edited by Geoffrey H. Hartman. Copyright © 1972 by Columbia University Press.

translation of a sound, but existed of itself naturally—well: to put it plainly, along the coronal suture, for example. What would happen? A sound would necessarily result, a series of sounds, music. . . .

Feelings—which? Incredulity, timidity, fear, awe—which of all the feelings here possible prevents me from suggesting a name for the primal sound which would then make its appearance in the world. . . ?

A subsequent expansion of technology and the evolution of musical institutions over fifty years allows us to identify Rilke's terrifying *Urgeraüsch*, his "primal sound," as nothing more awesome than the kind of *musique concrete* that is probably more to be described than heard. But this matter of technology is by no means trivial, I think, in the matter of the history of the Imagination; Rilke's childhood toy, which for the first time in history could can music, could thus provide a far more remarkable mechanical model of memory than previously envisioned, and initiated a deeper imaginative discontinuity with acoustical antiquity than any broached since, whether by tapes, happenings, or the solemnization of the aleatory, the playful, and the boring. Electronic technology might provide us with alternative emblems to Rilke's internalized *musica mundana*, his inaudible sounds of the heavenly vault inscribed in the arch of the human dome: we might think of an amplitude or frequency-modulated carrier wave, where the modulation by the imprinting of a sound transcription might stand easily for the imposition of consciousness of itself upon a mere act of hearing (or, by extension, for a humanization of an inert myth like the music of the spheres). We have grown up being able to flick a switch and thus plunge, *in medias res*, into the unprepared audibility of soundless music which has been going on unheard or suffering an Aeolian imprisonment; we can, with the twist of a knob, change the volume of musical sounds, or their enveloping timbre. We have, moreover, become accustomed to *underscoring*, to musical accompaniment of the visual beyond, and below, the projections of romantic desires for the *Gesammtkunstwerk*; and in a world increasingly flooded with piped-in sound, we have unwittingly had to accept the transformation of quiet music, magically coming from no visible source, into annoying noise.

There is an obvious parallel here with the imaginative status of the visual technologies—photographic, cinematic, projectional, and soon more available, perhaps, holographic—which have developed in the last century. Recent studies of Romantic imagery have underlined the ways in which visionary modes, at one moment in history, will anticipate the picturings of the as-yet-uninvented technologies of the visual. In a larger context, this is only part of the historical dialectic of science and poetry: discarded scientific models metamorphose into constellations of myth, and, in a recycling movement, industrial technolgies produce phenomena which unimaginatively duplicate some of the achieved visionary imagery in poetry of the past.

In this connection it might be remarked that the poetic treatment of the sounds of wind and water had achieved, by 1711, the full status of cliché; the great lullaby of eighteenth-century poetry is one of decorative words so emptied of their meaning that they have become musical sounds:

> Where-e'er you find "the cooling western breeze,"
> In the next line, it "whispers thro' the trees":
> If crystal streams "with pleasing murmurs creep,"
> The reader's threaten'd (not in vain) with "sleep":
> (Pope, *An Essay on Criticism*, ll. 350–53)

Or consider for a moment this instance, with which we also might have begun: Thomas Warton in his MS notes on Spenser comments on some lines about the harp of Philisides, or Sir Philip Sidney, in "The Ruines of Time." The harp is rising into the sky to become, like its Orphean predecessor, the constellation Lyra,

> Whilst all the while most heavenly noyse was heard
> Of the strings, stirred with the warbling wind
> That wrought both joy and sorrow in my mind

And Warton comments, "What Spenser's imagination here beautifully feigns, is actually brought into execution in the Aeolian harp, the effect of whose music is exactly what our poet describes: 'That wrought both joy and sorrow in my mind.'" Leaving aside the appalling standards of acoustical and musical description, we are faced with the relation between the eighteenth-century toy and the image it parodies.

There are moments—for Whitman, say, or Hart Crane—when these domestications of revelation appear to be fulfillments of a kind of modal, as opposed to a moral, prophecy. But in many ways the convenient reductions which invention affords—the overlaying of transparencies, for example, as a model of what must be accomplished, at the opening of "Tintern Abbey," by an intense mingling of terms drawn from landscape description and associationist psychology via the magical verb "connect"—such reductions will be read by poetic history as satanic parodies of the poetic process. Only Romanticism itself, actually, could react with answering energy to the notion of automata simulating will, perception, or utterance. Such contemporary phenomena are frequently functional in glossing eighteenth- and nineteenth-century poetic imagery (students need only be reminded of the Antonioni films to grasp the para-emblematic qualities of the image of the poplar tree's shadow falling across the face of Mariana in her moated grange); but perhaps to remark on this is only to confirm their reductive status.

We need hardly be reminded, however, that the auditory realm is ever secondary to the kingdom of sight; and in these observations on the treatment of sound in Wordsworth's poetry, we shall be continually re-ferred back to that secondariness by our want of a complementary term, in the aural dimension, to the word "visionary" in contrast with "visual." The records of Wordsworth's visionary hearing range from the formal "soundscapes" which Geoffrey Hartman has analyzed and named in the two long early topographical poems, through the imaginatively dangerous remythologizing of natural music in the interesting and problematic ode "On the Power of Sound." In a section of it, the poet addresses echoes as "Ye Voices, and ye Shadows / And Images of voice—" and these very shadows and images of the exhortation are as much a succedaneum and prop as that of invoking reflections as "echoes of vision" would be a fancy. A British linguistic scholar has put rather well one aspect of this phenom-enological commonplace: "sound stands more in need of external support than light, form or color; hence the greater frequency of the intrusion of outside elements into the description of acoustic phenomena." The "ex-ternal supports" here are those of metaphor. Shadow, and mirror-image in bronze or water, coexist in antiquity with echoes, and their personifications are parallel myths. But there is no analogue of painting or sculpture for the preservation of aural shades; until the invention of the phonograph, in fact, there is no way of recording sounds of discourse or music save by echoes or parrots. Nor can any dreams and imaginations of the ear save those of human discourse survive the feeble resources of the dreamer's reportage.

Thus, for example, while the afterimage of the daffodils can "flash upon" the inward eye, the immediate presence of the mountain echoes of a reciprocal poem composed two years later are "rebounds our inward ear/ Catches sometimes from afar," a kinetic characterization threatened, rather than elucidated, by the subsequent development of rubber balls. But the cultivation of this "inward ear" is nonetheless an important element in preparing for the representation of consciousness, and it is interesting to observe the parallels with, as well as the intersection of, the course of evolving an answerable diction which that element reveals. In 1802 Words-worth had addressed his brother John as a "*silent* Poet" who "from the solitude / Of the vast sea didst bring a watchful heart / Still couchant, an inevitable ear, / And an eye practised like a blind man's touch." But the openness of the sense of hearing is never the problem: crucial to the economy of the senses is the fact that we cannot close our ears as we do our eyes, and that vision is far more directional than hearing, which is not "To such a tender ball as th'eye confin'd" but, more like feeling, through all parts, at least of the head, "diffus'd." "A man, inasmuch as he has ears," said Emerson, "is accosted by the thunder and the birds." It is more a matter of the availability of appropriate conceptualization for representing the experience of hearing.

The poetic treatment of sound as such has a rather foreshortened history. Acoustic science distinguishes between the natures of noises and musical tones by demonstrating that the former result from vibrations at all frequencies within a band (and are thus, in a sense, more "general"), while the tones of music are produced by vibrations at a very few frequencies, carefully related mathematically. (It is this phenomenon, actually, which should inspire Pythagorean superstition, rather than the numerical ratios governing scales: the human ear performs what Leibniz called its "unconscious arithmetic" by distinguishing tone from noise as such. Ironically enough, an absolutely "pure" frequency, a concert-pitch a of 440 cycles per second, has only during the last fifteen years become, through the legitimization of electronic instruments, which alone can produce such sounds, a tone rather than a modern, industrial, electric *noise*, part of the humming and buzzing and beeping of machinery.) From classical times through the Renaissance, the imaginative distinction between tone and noise had a moral content. Music, as represented by Orphean myths and those of *musica mundana*, was the sound of Creation, of what had been organized; noise, whether the thundering which might be read as cracks in nature's structure, ambiguous sea-sounds, or whatever, was the sound of chaos in its eternal effort to creep further back into nature. Human speech (which, for the modern acoustician, is structured *noise*) was conceptually closer to music than to inanimate nonmusical sounds. This left only the noises which were to be read as belonging to music's realm—the sound of *nature* in the fullest sense, rather than merely a biological one, and these were assimilated through mythologizing. Echoes, the spirits inhabiting large natural concavities, were thus assimilated to musical spirits dwelling within the caves or shells of musical instruments (this becomes virtually a cliché of musical allusion in poetry from the seventeenth century on); the noise of moving water becomes an emblem of eloquence, and that sound, birdsong, and the rustling of foliage in the milder winds all enter, in pastoral tradition, into the conventional musical underscoring for the picture of the *locus amoenus.*

Good sound must be music or speech, then; and insofar as any sound at all is to be considered beneficial or pleasurable, it must be

metaphorically invoked as such. From this point of view, the catalogues of
outdoor sounds which are so ubiquitous in eighteenth-century poetry and
which are certainly derived from Renaissance descriptions of the *locus
amoenus* expand beyond the conventional lists as more and more kinds of
sound become part of the imaginative landscape. "Music to my ears," that
is, means not only "what I'm glad to hear," but at another level "what I
notice and what nourishes my aural attention." The sublime incorporates
what had been previously considered the noises of chaos into the rural
orchestra; torrents, the sounds of landslides, cataracts, thunder, and the
sounds of storm all come to signal the authenticity of the *locus terribilis*
even as the choir of birds and water and wind accompanies the lovely one,
and the mingling of piping or song and waterfall in pastoral eclogue
identifies a world in which poetry is creative and evocative force. There
are other aspects of this incorporation, of course. We must not neglect the
phenomenological consequences of the history of formal music itself; there
is certainly some connection between the developing taste for the piano-
forte, with its responsiveness to touch and its dynamic range, and the poetic
interest in the gradations of volume as a quality, and even a mode, of
sound. By the end of the eighteenth century, this is being reflected in
more general ways, and the so-called terraced dynamics of baroque music
give way to rolling ground. This is the musical context for the emergence
of the Romantic theme of auditory distancing as an aspect of the over-all
cliché: "Alles wird in der Entfernung Poesie: ferne Berge, ferne Menschen,
ferne Begebenheiten. Alles wird romantisch"—distancing makes everything
poetry, says Novalis, faraway hills, faraway humans, faraway happenings,
and although he does not add "ferne Laute"—faraway sounds—Romantic
tradition does so for him. Collins's Melancholy, in his ode "The Passions," to which I shall return, "from her wild sequester'd Seat, / In notes
by Distance made more sweet, / Pour'd through the mellow *Horn* her
pensive Soul." By 1806, Wordsworth can adduce, almost as if quoting a
received proverb, "sweetest melodies / Are those that are by distance made
more sweet"; both he and Collins imply a post-Renaissance meaning for
"sweet" in a musical context—in the seventeenth century it still means
only "in tune" (cf. modern residual "sour notes")—moving toward "dear."
It is as important to distinguish poetic conventions for the handling of
sound from the records of actual attentive listening, as it is to interpret
changing terminology correctly, though. Consider the following passage
from Coleridge's notebooks:

> . . . the moon is gone. The cock-crowing, too, has ceased. The Greta
> sounds on forever. But I hear only the ticking of my watch in the

pen-place of my writing-desk and the far lower note of the noise of the
fire, perpetual, yet seeming uncertain. It is the low voice of quiet
change, of destruction doing its work little by little.

A splendid sketch, perhaps, for an unrendered soundscape, and before
we can read its notations we must be assured that "low" refers to dynamic
and not to pitch. Coleridge is forever jotting down such sketches, as he is
continually raising questions about the possibilities of musical metaphor
and the limits of received language; this attentive interest is not uncon-
nected with his inability to write the ode on music which he occasionally
projected.

But here is Thomas Warton's figure of Melancholy:

> Raptur'd thou sitt'st, while murmurs indistinct
> Of distant billows sooth thy pensive ear
> With hoarse and hollow sounds

and again, with religious music in mind:

> . . . or let me sit
> Far in sequester'd isles of the deep dome,
> There lonesome listen to the sacred sounds
> Which, as they lengthen through the Gothic vaults,
> In hollow murmurs reach my ravish'd ear.

In both cases, the "hollow" quality of the sound has as little to do with an
act of listening, *en plein air,* as the "ravish'd ear"; it derives from the first
of Dryden's St. Cecilia's Day odes, and is about as accurate, in this
context, as a black shadow in a landscape by Claude. Instead, it authenti-
cates the sound by referring back to its source (the "hollow shell" of a lute
or a nymph's cave—these coalesce in neoclassical poetry) and by generat-
ing evocations like those of the desert music in Goldsmith's deserted
village:

> Along thy glades, a solitary guest,
> The hollow-sounding bittern guards its nest;
> Amidst thy desert walks the lapwing flies,
> And tires their ecchoes with unvaried cries.

The bittern's booming sounds hollow, and thus empty of meaning, in an
emptied world.

The hollow places give birth to music mythologized—the shell as
synecdoche for "lyre"; the literal, technically termed "shell" of the Renaissance lute; the caves; the labyrinths of the ear which gradually become
inevitable, as in Gray's lines from "The Progress of Poesy": "Or where

Maeander's amber waves / In Lingering Lab'rinths creep, / How do your tuneful Echo's languish, / Mute, but to the voice of Anguish?," where the "airy shell" has contracted into what suggests both the semicircular canals and the as-yet-unpoetized seashell of Wordsworth and Landor. The confusion between the shell-as-instrument of neoclassic cliché and the truly new Romantic image of the seashell is too elaborate to be discussed here. But the generative hollows tend to appear in the background of reference even when no formal invocation of them is made. Thus, toward the end of "Tintern Abbey":

> . . . when thy mind
> Shall be a mansion for all lovely forms,
> Thy memory be as a dwelling-place
> For all sweet sounds and harmonies

no skulllike cave of memory is openly described, but the recorded sounds will surely exist there forever as rebounding, undying echoes.

But these are hollows of potentiality. Goldsmith's hollow-sounding bittern announces the mockery of sublime ruin. Its solitariness distorts, rather than sensitizes, like that of Cowper's Selkirk for whom the tameness of the beasts around him must be shocking, who never hears "the sweet music of speech" and so can confess: "I start at the sound of my own." Conversely, the village music of what Goldsmith calls "the sounds of population" falls into the layered patterning of rural music that, throughout the seventeenth and eighteenth centuries, provided the model for the respresentation of sound listened-to out of doors:

> Sweet was the sound when oft at evening's close,
> Up yonder hill the village murmur rose;
> There as I past with careless steps and slow,
> The mingling notes came softened from below;
> The swain responsive as the milk-maid sung,
>
> The sober herd that lowed to meet their young,
> The noisy geese that gabbled o'er the pool,
> The playful children just let loose from school,
> The watch-dog's voice that bayed the whispering wind,
> And the loud laugh that spoke the vacant mind,
> These all in sweet confusion sought the shade,
> And filled each pause the nightingale had made.

"Responsive" usually occurs in pastoral to characterize the echoing phenomenon in nature which confirms the poetic character of the music of voice or instrument, and the ironies here emerge when we see how close this is to the antipastoral urban catalogues of Swift in a poem like "A

Description of the Morning." The point is that all the noises and voices enter into a polyphonic consort whose ancestry can be traced back to Spenser.

This is not the place to work out that genealogy; we shall simply recall the long tradition of soundscape accompanying the *locus amoenus* which was mentioned earlier. Classical and Renaissance traditions come together in the mingled vocal, instrumental, and natural music characterizing the Bower of Bliss. For Spenser, this mingling is sinister, mixing modes and systems and literary genres and betraying the pastoral conventions it sophisticatedly parodies, as the artificial vegetation betrays nature. But in his immediate seventeenth-century followers, the mixing of human and natural music becomes a positive presence in pastoral adaptation. Drayton, Browne, and Fletcher all convert traditional catalogues of birdsong into descriptions of contemporary broken-consort music, and provide a format for the quasi-visual representation of sounds, and eventually noises, in descriptive poetry.

The layering of the voices, whether in Spenserian stanza or in couplets, suggests the vertical format of polyphonic parts in score, and even when this has become minimal it still informs the way in which the sequence of reported sounds must be read. They are antiphonal, choral, or both: thus Gray again,

> The Attic Warbler pours her throat
> Responsive to the cuckow's note,
> The untaught harmony of spring

is rehearsing an old baroque theme of the bird-concert (reinforced in seventeenth-century Northern painting, by the way, by a minor genre that shows the brightly colored birds perched among green, unruined choirs of foliage, all singing from a book of musical notation held open by one of them). Aside from the literary convention, which helps to establish the manifest musical image, there is the almost unwitting involvement of one of the oldest prosthetic metaphors which aid our vestigial vocabulary of sound-description: *liquidity* is used as early as Lucretius to describe birdsong. In Renaissance pastoral, melody *pours* and sounds *fill* regions in such a way that the very imagery of the solo melodic line is "attuned" to that which literally describes the moving of water in brooks and streams which by convention *speak*, but in the lovely places, *sing*. Again, the problem of listening to nature seems to be one not of the inevitability of ear, or even the unmediated act of listening, but rather in the storage and retrieval of what has been heard.

Variations and extensions of this model abound in eighteenth-

century poetry. They range from orchestrations of village noises and
gothic echoes in Goldsmith and Blair, for example, to the almost paradigmatic preservation of the model that we should indeed expect to find in
Dyer's "Grongar Hill":

> While the wanton Zephyr sings,
> And in the vale perfumes his wings;
> While the waters murmur deep;
> While the shepherd charms his sheep;
> While the birds unbounded fly,
> And with musick fill the sky,
> Now, ev'n now, my joys run high.

Here are the harmonized delights of bucolic tradition, even to the juxtaposition of the sound and the smell of the moving air, a topos lurking
everywhere in the Renaissance *locus amoenus*. Wordsworth's more formal
musical orchestrations, in "An Evening Walk" and the "Descriptive
Sketches," are chiefly remarkable for the fine tuning of their auditory
attention, as well as for the way in which, in the former poem, they signal
and accompany the fading out of a scene. In the 1790s he can give
musical privilege, in that beautiful water-poem in remembrance of Collins, to the sound of "The dripping of the oar suspended," as he can in
another moment of silence (the silence that is audible when speech, rather
than sound, has ceased), a decade later, to "the flapping of the flame, / Or
kettle whispering its faint under-song." But if in the earlier poems the
music has become perfectly naturalized, the presentation of it has not.
There is the almost emblematic treatment of an instrumental consort in
the "Descriptive Sketches," mixing maids' voices, "twilight lute" (wisely
removed, in the 1849 revision—Wordsworth had never heard a lute in his
life), "village hum," fife, drum, and, finally, a wailing insect; this has a
distinct neoclassical flavor, in its implicit assumptions of a modality proper
to each instrument, rather in the manner, as shall be discussed shortly, of
the Augustan ode for music. But even the more characteristically natural
catalogues partake of this:

> An idle voice the sabbath region fills
> Of Deep that calls to Deep across the hills,
> Broke only by the melancholy sound
> Of drowsy bells for ever tinkling round;
> Faint wail of eagle melting into blue
> Beneath the cliffs, and pine-woods steady sigh;
> The solitary heifer's deepen'd low;
> Or rumbling heard remote of falling snow.

This catalogue, we are told at its beginning, is free of all "irreligious sound" save at the end now, where the avalanche demands that the sabbath be broken, and "the stranger seen below, the boy / Shouts from the echoing hills with savage joy." The "wail of eagle melting into blue" is masterful for the Miltonic syntax—the wail melts into the blue as the shrinking sight of the bird does—and the layers of sound, lowering in pitch while varying wildly in dynamic, timbre, and ordinary signification, are beautifully adapted to the part-song model. In the revision for the 1849 edition, Wordsworth adds a couplet, in this instance unwisely, for it destroys the effect of the original closure. But it is a significant, almost querulous reductive glossing, as if to remind the reader of the lost model: "All motions, sounds, and voices, far and nigh, / Blend in a music of tranquillity."

The "blending" here is that of vertical musical harmony, but another, older tradition lies behind it. The first musical sounds to request and receive "authentic comment" from the noises of nature are in Theocritus and Vergil, antiphonal at first and then, with the Renaissance, polyphonic. The alternative to the carefully orchestrated "layered" page of music is the blended duo of singing voice or instrument and the wind. For English poetry of the later eighteenth century and after, the only genuine music will be heard out of doors. For the poetry of the Renaissance, the richly mythologized world of music all took place, whether indoors or out, under the ordering, unifying, covering shell of the cosmos, a shell from which noise, like chaos, was excluded. Augustan thought and rhetoric tended to trivialize that musical mythology, and during the eighteenth century we can listen to chorded shells, lutes, harps, lyres, ravishing voices, and so forth creeping out into the generalized *locus amoenus* which all landscape becomes and reauthenticating themselves with what the traditions of speculative music from Aristotle on would have considered breaths of inanimate air. The voices of fair singers start blending with the wind, becoming sweetened by distance, and so forth; the aeolian harp, an eighteenth-century household toy, becomes the basis of a profound and widespread trope for imaginative utterance, and a kind of mythological center for images of combining tone and noise, music and sound.

There are moments in the history of this developing imagery when ambiguities and misunderstandings are possible. Dr. Johnson, for example, who is seldom generous toward the mythopoeic, seems to ignore the figurativeness of Gray's "rich stream of music" at the opening of "The Progress of Poesy," a stream that clearly starts "From Helicon's harmonious springs." Perhaps it is because the stream of imagery itself repeats its poetic phylogeny, moving from the classical allusion through the pastoral "laughing flowers" animated by the flow of eloquence, to the regions of the unpremeditated in the near-sublime landscape at the end of the strophe: "Now rowling down the steep amain, / Headlong, impetuous, see it pour: / The rocks, and nodding groves rebellow to the roar." "Gray," says Dr. Johnson,

> seems in his rapture to confound the images of spreading sound and running water. A "stream of music" may be allowed; but where does "music," however "smooth and strong," after having visited the "verdant vales" "rowl down the steep amain," so that "rocks and nodding groves, rebellow to the roar? If this be said of music, it is nonsense; if it be said of water, it is nothing to the purpose.

But it is said of the water-sound-music figure, still linked to poetry by the Heliconian origin. Just as there had to be, one feels, at least one poem in which the neoclassical term "shell" for "stringed instrument" would be confused even by the poet himself with the recently invented Romantic singing seashell, there appear to have to be these transitional passages from the stock emblem or epithet into the more modulated images. A fanciful figure for this might be the sounds of a harpsichord sonata by Arne, say, heard outside the house and across a brook amid a gentle fanning of leaves. A historical fact is the addition, in the 1770s and thereafter, of the so-called Venetian-swell mechanism to English harpsichords, in a vain attempt to compete with the piano's ability to control dynamics and thus analogically to invoke shades of feeling. Such a fact is figure enough.

Wordsworth never totally loses touch with conventions of musical imagery about natural noise, and such images keep reappearing long after more fully naturalized figures should have taken possession of the domain of sound. In the context of the musical ephithets, the aural experience of the bower, in "Nutting," "Where fairy water-breaks do murmur on / For ever" is astonishing, and more imaginatively than epistemologically revolutionary:

> I saw the sparkling foam,
> And—with my cheek on one of those green stones
> That fleeced with moss, under the shady trees,
> Lay round me, scattered like a flock of sheep—
> I heard the murmur and the murmuring sound

"The murmur *and* the murmuring sound"—as if the separation into two phenomena might begin to comprehend the interruption of actual stereophony occasioned by the one ear to the ground and the other upward. One hears the natural and one, the faery, one the literal water noises and the other the figurative bleatings of the rocks becoming sheep in the poem itself. This is one of the great anatomized acts of listening in Wordsworth, occurring at a moment of shaded, perhaps sated vision. It is the listening itself we are on the brink of hearing.

But consider for a moment a purportedly more casual report, a description of warblers in the *Guide to the Lakes:*

> . . . and their notes, when listened to by the side of broad still waters, or when heard in unison with the murmuring of mountain-brooks, have the compass of their power enlarged accordingly. There is also an imaginative influence in the voice of the cuckoo, when that voice has taken possession of a deep mountain valley . . .

There is an almost stepwise movement here from the acoustical fact that sound heard across still water is indeed amplified, to the *musical* phenomenon of the bird-brook duo (where the enlargement of the "power" is in the attention, the *listened-to* rather than the audible) and finally to the pure figure of the conclusion (the voice of the cuckoo only "takes possession" of the valley for the hearer who, in a special way, has lost possession of his senses). Even in glossing his own sound imagery, in the 1815 Preface, Wordsworth can move from mythological acoustics into the wider realm of acoustic mythology. He is commenting on the lines from the poem which reject the nightingale's fabulous, night-denying music for the internalized, self-hearing song of the stock dove, whose "voice was buried among trees, / Yet to be come at by the breeze."

> . . . a metaphor expressing the love of *seclusion* by which this bird is marked; and characterizing its note as not partaking of the shrill and the piercing, and therefore more easily deadened by the intervening shade; yet a note so peculiar, and withal so pleasing, that the breeze, gifted with that love of sound which the poet feels, penetrates the shade in which it is entombed, and conveys it to the ear of the listener.

The meta-language employs an image more complex than that of its object, for it is the listening, rather than the sound, which is being embraced. Not only is the pictorially operative word "shade" repeated twice (and in a context that calls only for the acoustically insulating "foliage"), but in the whole last part of the image it is caught up again and almost gothicized ("the shade in which it is entombed") by the near-pun on "shade = ghost." And finally, the breeze, which conventionally merely broadcasts, here becomes a fully realized form of the genius of listening, of the activity of the ear.

Here particularly, vision has come so much to the aid of hearing that it is tempting to move into a consideration of the bases, in the language of poetry, for eye-ear synesthesia. In many ways, the concept is itself misleading, for Wordsworth, at any rate. We are dealing neither with the isolated, almost ironic effect of a mixture of two conventional tropes (e.g., Coleridge: "Be the blind bard who on the Chian strand, / By those deep sounds possessed with inward light, / Beheld the Iliad and the Odyssey/ Rise to the swelling of the tuneful sea") nor with the violent Shelleyan interpenetration of sound and light occasioned by the interpenetration of tenor and vehicle in the metaphor; we are certainly always far removed from even an unsystematic disordering of the senses. In any event, these remarks are more concerned with language about sound than with strange reports about inner states; I should like only to consider momentarily the exemplary case of a rather attractive Romantic emblem. Carl Gustav Carus, friend of Goethe and imitator of Caspar David Friedrich, painted in 1823 a "Phantasie über die Musik." It shows the window of a chamber in a gothic building, looking out, at nightfall, on the moon rising over the sea, with a cathedral tower on the right; in the foreground is a bench, covered in dark blue drapery, with a harp resting on it. The harp fills most of the window—and the picture—and the moon shines through its strings. Subsequent commentators on the painting usually remarked that the moon-light "kissed" the strings, but the indoor scene is clearly a nocturnal version of the aeolian harp, with the moonlight playing the role of the wind. To invoke synesthesia in the reading of this picture would be, at very best, oblique. The light is as mythological a presence as the breeze that animates the poet who has become the instrument, in later versions of the theme. Carus's picture, in its hard-edged, emblematic manner, is a world apart from the painterly, atmospheric, diffuse scenes of indoor music at Petworth that Turner was doing at about the same time, in which the surface of the picture and the air in the room depicted both seem "filled," in an almost Wordsworthian way, with the sound of piano music.

Wordsworth's own metamorphoses of the aeolian harp figure follow interesting patterns. It will be remembered that the aeolian harp proper consists of strings of different diameters strung at different degrees of tensions across a flat, box-like sounding board so as to be tuned to unisons and octaves. Such an instrument, when set in an opened window, or suspended from a tree, generates full chords of the fundamental, up to the dominant seventh, as a function of the strength of the wind; that is, it does not play melodic lines nor does its fundamental pitch flatten, as in whistles and certain open flute pipes, when the wind's pressure decreases. Only the harmonies die down into the fundamental, and the over-all volume decreases. First described in Athanasius Kircher's musical encyclo-pedia in the seventeenth century, it became a sort of toy in the later decades of the eighteenth. Its appeal to the fancy is obvious: not only does the wind animating the strings combine the two genera of instrument, symbolic of the Apollonian and the Dionysian respectively in neoclassical tradition, but the aeolian harp comprises within itself the blending of instrumental sound and outdoor noise of wind which was becoming, in later eighteenth-century England, the imagination's authentic music.

The aeolian harp image is far more profound and prevalent, I think, than has been previously noted. Even to sketch out its history here is impossible, for one should have to start with two distant and distinct topoi, the harp hung on the willows *super flumina Babylonis* as an indication of a refusal to perform even laments for a conqueror, and the *fistula* or pipe hung on the pine tree, in order to reconsecrate the music to Pan, and thus help define the pastoral genre, in Vergil's seventh eclogue. The instrument refused, and the other one hung up in what Erwin Panofsky described as a rustic *ex voto*, fall together in Renaissance poetry as the instrument *abandoned*; it is an easy transition to the aeolian image, for the hand of the wind need only carelessly strike the neglected strings. There are many anticipations of this in Renaissance poetry, and the formal image is as frequent in German Romanticism as in England. (Indeed, the shift from instrument abandoned to aeolian harp is illustrated perfectly in such diverse passages as a major final speech in Grillparzer's *Sappho*, where the abandoned lyre, hanging on a column, sings in the wind; and the lyric "Pause" from *Die Schöne Müllerin*, where in a more homely context the same thing happens.)

The point is not that so many poets writing in English from James Thomson to Hart Crane make such different use of the aeolian harp image, but that it can appear in so many guises. Mörike writes a formal lyric about the aeolian harp, but Neitzsche, in *Ecce Homo*, uses it in an evolved form to describe how, while standing on a Venetian bridge, the sound of distant music over the canal blew through him as through the strings of an instrument, transforming everything he experienced. Emerson and Thoreau write poems manifestly directed to aeolian harps; but the latter, throughout his journals over many years, builds up an elaborate sequential prose-poem about what he calls his "telegraph-harp"—the aeolian harp effect (and, acoustically speaking, this is quite correct) of the wind blowing through telegraph wires along the railroad tracks, heard most clearly by putting one's ear to the resonating pole on which they are strung. Or take the following passage from *Walden*:

> Sometimes, on Sundays, I heard the bells, the Lincoln, Acton, Bedford, or Concord bell, when the wind was favorable, a faint, sweet and, as it were, natural melody, worth importing into the wilderness. At a suffi-

cient distance over the woods this sound acquires a certain vibratory hum, as if the pine needles were the strings of a harp which is swept. All sound heard at the greatest possible distance produces one and the same effect, a vibration of the universal lyre, just as the intervening atmosphere makes a distant ridge of earth interesting to our eyes by the azure tint it imparts to it. There came to me in this case a melody which the air had strained, and which had conversed with every leaf and needle of the wood, that portion of the sound which the elements had taken up and modulated and echoed from vale to vale. The echo is, to some extent, an original sound, and therein is the magic and charm of it. It is not merely a repetition of what was worth repeating in the bell, but partly the voice of the wood, the same trivial words and notes sung by a wood-nymph.

In one way, this is domesticated Wordsworth; but in the way in which it moralizes the image and expands it into the "universal lyre," immediately adducing a pictorial analogue in support of it, the passage is at once more Shelleyan and more German.

Wordsworth's versions of the figure never reach the proportions of Coleridge's avowed use of it. An early, gothicized parody shows up in "The Vale of Esthwaite"; at another extreme, the muse of "The White Doe of Rylstone," that invocation-figure of the Harp which is both what Wordsworth elsewhere calls "the romantic harp" and that of minstrelsy, becomes aeolian at the end of the first canto, in an image at first internalized and then remythologized again:

> Harp! we have been full long beguiled
> By vague thoughts, lured by fancies wild;
> To which, with no reluctant strings,
> Thou hast attuned thy murmurings;
> And now before this Pile we stand
> In solitude, and utter peace:
> But, Harp! thy murmurs may not cease—
> A Spirit, with his angelic wings,
> In soft and breeze-like visitings,
> Has touched thee—and a Spirit's hand

The "vague thoughts" are the surrogate wind, at first; but the increasingly difficult imaginative tasks, as the poem unfolds, demand a more powerful voice from the aeolianized harp, and the doubling of "Spirit" and the "Spirit's hand" reinforces this need for augmented power.

Sometimes the aeolian harp figure can totally vanish within its naturalized form. The fifth of the *River Duddon Sonnets* begins with a characteristic moment in which an image of sound will awaken visual impressions: "Sole listener, Duddon! to the breeze that played / With thy clear voice, I caught the fitful sound / Wafted o'er sullen moss and craggy ground. . . ." The breeze toys with the voice of the musical stream, playing *with* and almost *on* it; here the blending of music and noise occurs within the realm of natural noise itself, and the metaphorical musical voice here is naturalized even further by the breeze.

But perhaps the most problematic and revealing version of the image in Wordsworth comes from the Alfoxden notebook fragments. It should be quoted in its entirety; surely among the evocations of the ear as holding "A manifest communion with the heart," as being *inevitable,* this passage of all those sketches for *The Prelude* seems most fully realized:

> There was a spot,
> My favourite station when the winds were up
> Three knots of fir-trees, small and circular,
> Which with smooth space of open plain between
> Stood single, for the delicate eye of taste
> Too formally arrayed. Right opposite
> The central clump I loved to stand and hear
> The wind come on and touch the several groves
> Each after each, and thence in the dark night
> Elicit all proportions of sweet sounds
> As from an instrument. "The strains are passed"
> Thus often to myself I said, "the sounds
> Even while they are approaching are gone by,
> And now they are more distant, more and more.
> O listen, listen how they wind away
> Still heard they wind away, heard yet and yet,
> While the lost touch they leave upon the sense
> Is sweeter than whate'er was heard before,
> And seems to say that they can never die."

The instrument, activated by the wind, is a stringed one, and the overformal arrangement of the trees, like the "birch-trees risen in silver colonnade" in the sonnet from the *River Duddon* sequence just quoted, suggests an artifact. The wind-harp music from the trees, dissolving into itself, is composed into an animated emblem of the fleeting, the transitory; sound is heard (in the sense of "known" for which we often say "seen") as process here. The extended use of verbal doublings, ranging from the idiomatic "more and more" echoing and reechoing the "more distant," through the "listen, listen" and the repeated "wind away" with the ehoing senses of "blow," "twist," and almost "wend" (as of "way"), culminates in the last "yet and yet" of lingering audibility. The penultimate strain may indeed be the last accoustical one, echoed, at the very end, by memory's playback. The archaic musical meaning of "touch" for "musical phrase or passage" is intertwined with the tacticle image, and reinforced by the parallel older, strictly musical sense of "sweet"; all these doublings and amplifications are finally echoed in the literal sense of "die" which outlasts, at the end, the figurative one. Echoes first "die," in Pope's "Ode for Music on St. Cecilia's Day," through adaptation of an earlier musical term: "The strains decay, / And melt away, / In a dying, dying fall." The repetition is not only decorative but is meant to transfer the term to something like the famous Tennysonian usage, where the "flying-dying" rhyme is itself parallel to the animating, rising trumpet sound as opposed to the trailing, falling answer of the echoes. In the Wordworthian passage, it is the moment of expèrience itself, the transformed act of hearing which seems to become immortal.

Wordsworth's formal, public, and expository ode "On the Power of Sound" seems fully as interesting in its genre and rhetoric as in its doctrine; and in the light of the foregoing observations, the way in which both these aspects of the poem complete the metamorphosis of a neoclassical form seems an appropriate question with which to conclude. The ode poses critical problems which are not eased by the unduly high regard in which the poet himself held it: the same Vergilian phrase which he used as epigraph to the first printed version of the Immortality Ode appears in several MSS of the poem on sound: *Paulo majora canamus*, the announcement of a new, prophetic strain at the opening of the Fourth Eclogue. On the other hand, the genesis of the poem (from some lines of a canceled aside from "The Triad") and its rather uncommanding structure (it grew from a more promising five strophes in its first draft to the published thirteen, and with the order quite changed) confirm one's suspicion. It is a poem of the Will, despite the fact that Wordsworth deliberately placed it at the close of the *Poems of the Imagination.* But less so, in a way, than the 1806 poem on "The Power of Music," which tries almost paradigmatically to mythologize a street-corner fiddler as "An Orpheus! an Orpheus!" and which organizes the urban landscape around him, as around the full moon. All stop and watch him, and bend toward his playing like leaning towers and trees; the only image of real power is the final one, in which the urban street music is avowed to be the fully authentic counterpart of the rural outdoor noise, and the more trivial, literal counterpart of the murmurings of the brook is heard for what it is:

> Now coaches and chariots! roar on like a stream;
> Here are twenty souls happy as souls in a dream:
> They are deaf to your murmurs—they care not for you,
> Nor what ye are flying, nor what ye pursue!

The anapestic meter which this poem shares with "The Reverie of Poor Susan" is by no means accidental, nor is its placement directly after it in the 1850 edition. Both the fiddler and the caged thrush have the power to *accost* in the midst of the urban pressures that kill awareness, and in both instances the power of the music is momentary.

The poem on music is secondary in many ways to "The Reverie of Poor Susan"; the one on sound is anxiously conscious of the Immortality Ode at several places. Where it boldly takes on a tradition in order to modulate it, the poem is much more successful. I refer to its formal genre, the Augustan ode for music, as it descended from Dryden's two great St. Cecilia's Day odes, composed a decade apart. Dryden's first poem, "A Song for St. Cecilia's Day," is doctrinal: it rehearses mythology about the creative and affective power of harmony, devoting successive strophes to particular instruments as representatives of particular modalities and affections; and it ends with the continuing presence of music, even beyond apocalypse, when music will ring down the curtain on the *theatrum mundi* by being the signal of the last trumpet. In "Alexander's Feast," the affective power of music is demonstrated dramatically, rather than expounded and orchestrally imitated in the accompaniment: an anecdote about Alexander and Timotheus is expanded into an elaborate cantata-text which has the musical treatment much more in mind than did the earlier one, but which confirms the convention by allowing successive strophes to embody various moods and modalities. The poems by Congreve, Tate, and most importantly, Pope, which follow Dryden, maintain the tradition of deliberately allowing for variations in the setting, solo, tutti, chorus, and so forth, and for the use of particular instrumental obbligati; they also tend to combine the two Dryden prototypes, combining the expository *laus musicae* and the quasi-operatic treatment of an Orphean myth. Pope's "Ode for Music on St. Cecilia's Day" is most important in this connection. It was held up, with Dryden's, as a model of the form; Christopher Smart, when he translated Pope's poem into Latin in 1746, prefaced it with some observations on the genre, almost predictably remarking that "*Dryden's* is the sublime and magnificent; but *Pope's* is the more elegant and correct." More to the point, Martin Price has observed that Pope's use of Orpheus himself for a central figure, rather than Timotheus, is connected with the movement in Pope's ode "to the involvement in sensibility." Certainly music's power comes to be that of expressing, rather than, in a strictly neo-classic way, *eliciting* feelings, and in the echoic passage on the death of Orpheus, a cliché of pastoral becomes put, with its musical setting in mind, to expressive use:

> Yet ev'n in death Eurydice he sung,
> Eurydice still trembled on his tongue,
>   Eurydice the woods,
>   Eurydice the floods,
> Eurydice the rocks, and mountain hollows rung.

Christopher Smart's own "Ode on St. Cecilia's Day," also published along with his translation of Pope's, is a much more self-conscious and ambitious poem, for it manifestly turns the praise of music into the praise of English music and English poetry, in the specific figures of Waller and Purcell. It is a fully *literary* adaptation of the musical ode form, in that it is by no means attentive to the exigencies of a prospective musical setting, and in that the convention it follows—that of the Ode from Dryden to Pope—is modulated without regard for the original function of the structure, rhetoric, and mythology of the *laus musicae*. The most interesting sections for a reader in mind of the Wordsworth ode are the third, fourth, and fifth strophes. In the first of these, an astonishing night-scene is unveiled, possibly based on an Orphean image in one of Waller's own poems:

> In Penshurst's plains when Waller, sick with love,
> Has found some silent, solitary grove,
> Where the vague moon-beams pour a silver flood,
> Of trem'lous light athwart th'unshaven wood,
>   Within an hoary moss-grown cell,
> He lays his careless limbs without reserve,
> And strikes, impetuous strikes, each quer'lous nerve
>   Of his resounding shell.
> In all the woods, in all the plains
> Around a lively stillness reigns;
> The deer approach the secret scene,
> And weave their way thro' labyrinths green;
> While Philomela learns the lay
> And answers from the neighboring bay

In the pre-Keatsian silver of moonlight, the Ovidian nightingale story is inverted: it is the poet, the symbolic nightingale, who teaches the mere bird. The movement here is very much that of Robert Frost's "Never Again Would Birds' Song Be the Same" with its myth of the origins of nature's "voices" in the langauge and music of Eve's expressiveness. Smart's next two strophes are remarkable in their elaborate pictorial treatment of the story of Arion and the dolphin. Both he and Amphion are Orpheus-surrogates in Renaissance musical mythology, but the extended substitution of his story for those of Orpheus or Timotheus in the preceding major odes is introduced by the use of the river Medway, at the end of the Waller strophe, to waft the musical strains, as the wind might do, down to the sea. Arion is brought on theatrically thereafter. It may be that Words-worth's surprising use of Arion in his ode—rather than Amphion, builder of walls—drives from Smart.

But surely the most important stage in the untuning of the musical ode, in its transformation into a poem about language and feeling, and hence, about poetic tradition, comes with Collins. "The Passions: An Ode for Music," first performed, in one of the three musical settings it was to receive, in 1750, adapts the narrative format inherited from "Alexan-der's Feast" and the more purely historical and expository pattern of the first Dryden ode in a different way from Pope and Smart. The framing anecdote tells how, "When Music, Heav'nly Maid, was young," in antiq-uity, the Passions themselves "Throng'd around her magic Cell" to hear her; but variously affected by her music, moved to the emotions they themselves represented, fired up à la Alexander, they "snatch'd her Instruments of Sound" in order to perform themselves. What follows are the individual modal episodes, in which Fear, Anger, Despair, Hope, Revenge, Pity, Jealousy, Love, Melancholy, Cheerfulness, Joy, and Mirth are all momentarily represented as musicians. Each is afforded the appro-priate instrument, whether real or allegorical, so that lyre and pipe mix with viol, trumpet, drum, and horn; the shifting modality is underlined by the program for orchestration, as in all the odes. Most interesting are the episodes of Hope and of Melancholy. Hope is associated with echoing: "She call'd on Echo still thro' all the Song; / And where Her sweetest theme She chose, / A soft responsive Voice was heard at ev'ry Close." It is the rhythms of rising and falling hope that are suggested by the traditional pastoral figure of echoing landscape as nature applauding the poet; but by now we are far from the representation of music, or even of sound, and instead we are presented the arraying of the emotions on an orchestral model.

Melancholy and her music are heard over distant water:

And from her wild sequester'd Seat,
In Notes by Distance made more sweet,
Pour'd thro the mellow horn her pensive Soul:
    And dashing soft from Rocks around,
    Bubbling Runnels join'd the Sound;
Thro' Glades and Glooms the mingled Measure stole,
Or oe'r some haunted Stream with fond Delay,
    Round an holy Calm diffusing,
    Love of Peace and lonely Musing,
In hollow Murmurs died away.

Milton is here, not less in the confluence of music, darkness, and water from "Il Penseroso" than for the personification. The commonplace of distancing, as was observed earlier, is here; and an almost canonical instance of the expressive tone-sound *blending* is here as well. The mythology is almost parallel to Smart's anecdote of Waller informing the sound of the nightingale: it is Melancholy's aria with obbligato of *cor anglais* which gives its modality to the moving water resounding in the sublime landscape. The mingling is total and reciprocal, for the traditional authenticating force of the outdoor sound-scene is a necessary part of the personification itself.

Collins concludes with an encomium of "Caecilia's mingled World of Sound," by which he means the entire spectrum of the passions and the orchestrated array of music's effects, the inventory of modes which invoke moods. He adapts the traditional ode which praises music by submitting itself to setting (and for England in the eighteenth century, this is no small sacrifice) for an exposition of what is not inherently musical, and his mythology only needs to be carried a step further into the realm of outdoor sound to lose manifest contact with concert music. Wordsworth's "On the Power of Sound" owes as much to Collins and to Smart as to Dryden and Pope; but in a larger sense, Collins's use of music as a metaphor for more general expressiveness underlies all English Romantic tradition.

Wordsworth's ode abandons the irregular "Pindaric" pattern, with what Smart called its "vehemence of sudden and unlook'd for transitions" even within the microcosm of its versification, for fourteen strophes of sixteen lines each, all on the same pattern. Certainly the "turns" and "counterturns" of the inner rhetoric are minimized by this, and the structure is both more arbitrary and, nevertheless, more expository than the suggestions of self-generated form in the irregular Pindaric or even in Wordsworthian blank verse. The poem opens with an address to the ear:

> Thy functions are ethereal,
> As if within thee dwelt a glancing mind,
> Organ of vision! And a Spirit aerial
> Informs the cell of Hearing, dark and blind
>
> (1–4)

But the ear is avowedly *le deuxième sens*—the dependence upon vision as a comparative and even a metaphorical base is unquestioned; nevertheless, the implicit contrast between the elements of *ether* and *air* (the "And" has almost the force of "but") invokes the latter as more concrete, more natural. Wordsworth continues:

Intricate labyrinth, more dread for thought
To enter than oracular cave;
Strict passage, through which sighs are brought,
And whispers for the heart, their slave
(5–8)

and a catalogue of unplesant sounds of pain and anguish concludes with "Hosannas pealing down the long-drawn aisle, / And requiems answered by the pulse that beats / Devoutly, in life's last retreats." The *auricular* cave which Blake envisioned as a great, spiral labyrinth leading upward (but collapsed, in its fallen state, into the constricting tiny windings of the *cochlea*) here is connected with the gothicized image of the cave of horrid sounds through the near-pun. And if groans and moans from Blair and Young are humanized in this passage, so are the images of sound-effects appearing in other Wordsworthian contexts. Thus, the overhanging echoes in the fan vaulting of King's Chapel, Cambridge, "that branching roof / Self-poised, and scooped into ten thousand cells, / Where light and shade repose, where music dwells / Lingering—and wandering on as loth to die" in one of the *Ecclesiastical Sonnets*, are absorbed into the great corporeal expansion of the ear in this strophe.

The following ones continue to catalogue, on the model of musical odes but without any of the rhetoric of self-dramatization, the sounds of life. Echoes, the "Shadows / And Images of voice," are described as

to hound and horn
From rocky steep and rock-bestudded meadows
Flung back, and, in the sky's blue caves, reborn—
(34–37)

and paired with "a careless quire" which, in the convention of pastoral concert, would have been of birds:

Happy milk-maids, one by one
Scattering a ditty each to her desire,
A liquid concert matchless by nice Art,
A stream as if from one full heart.
(45–48)

With a shift of context, the last couplet could be Crashaw; the point about all these scattered fancies is that they keep pointing toward a primal presence and power behind the phenomena. Recapitulations of intensely musical moments in past poetry abound: "For the tired slave, Song lifts the languid oar, / And bids it aptly fall, with chime / That beautifies the fairest shore," and the musical oars of Cleopatra, Canute, and perhaps Marvell's Bermuda-bound pilgrims somehow blend with the naturalized music of water dripping from the blades of more domestic rowers. The "Lydian airs" of "L'Allegro" are specifically invoked. But almost at the center of the poem, the focus is manifestly shifted:

> Point not these mysteries to an Art
> Lodged above the starry pole;
> Pure modulations flowing from the heart
> Of divine Love, where Wisdom, Beauty, Truth
> With Order dwell, in endless youth?
>
> (108–12)

—Not sounds, in short, but Sound.

The following strophes enact the search for the spirit of Sound, leaving the ear behind. With unambiguous echoes of Dryden's cadences, we follow "Orphean Insight" through "the first leagues of tutored passion," where

> Music deigned within this grosser sphere
> Her subtle essence to enfold,
> And voice a shell drew forth a tear
> Softer than Nature's self could mould.
>
> (117–20)

We are led through the realms of medieval and Renaissance speculative music, through the mythologies of world order and healing and persuasion; "Hell to the lyre bowed low; the upper arch / Rejoiced that clamorous spell and magic verse / Her wan disasters could disperse." It is all the more remarkable how the ninth strophe, after a casual mention of Amphion, devotes itself totally to Arion and the dolphin, praising him as the musician who would "humanize the creatures of the sea, / Where men were monsters." Wordsworth would seem to be following Smart in his concentration on what is usually a peripheral story, and to be thinking of the Immortality Ode in his attention to the redemptive memoriousness of sound moving over water toward a final shore. Certainly the Ovidian conclusion suggests this: "And he, with his preserver, shine star-bright / In memory, through silent night" (ll. 143–44).

Hard upon this comes the wilder myth of panic piping: "the eyeballs of the leopards, / That in high triumph drew the Lord of vines, / How did they sparkle to the cymbal's clang!" And with a masterful shift of dynamic and tonality, the poem moves out of the epochs of musical mythology into the Romantic world of sound: "To life, to *life* give back thine ear" seems still part of the Dionysian revelry in the first half of the strophe. But the movement away from the sound of music, in the mythological sections, to the sound of sound is almost programmatic for Wordsworth:

Ye who are longing to be rid
Of fable, though to truth subservient, hear
The little sprinkling of cold earth that fell
Echoed from the coffin-lid

(154–57)

The whole eighteenth century had been listening for the music of sound; Wordsworth had sought in many ways to escape the bondage of the ear to "laboured minstrelsies" of musical language itself. In "Peter Bell," the continued pattern of de-spooking the terrifying noises is part of a larger program of humanizing romance. On the top of Mount Snowdon, the resounding of the bottom of consciousness occurs as a complementary phase of the moment of vision. From time to time Wordsworth plays with the music, if not the sound, of silence. But only in the sound ode does he try to abstract in a systematic way a higher fiction.

The concept of "harmony" in its general sense flickers intermittently, over the centuries, with an array of latent musical meanings. Wordsworth wishes to free the "one pervading spirit / Of tones and numbers" by which all is controlled from some of the more deadened conventions; the ode's whole movement from ear to music to a harmony beyond has been to prepare for the splendid conclusion of the antepenultimate strophe, with its reminders of the cadences of the Immortality Ode:

The heavens, whose aspect makes our minds as still
As they themselves appear to be,
Innumerable voices fill
With everlasting harmony;
The towering headlands, crowned with mist,
Their feet among the billows, know
That Ocean is a mighty harmonist;
Thy pinions, universal Air,
Ever waving to and fro,
Are delegates of harmony, and bear
Strains that support the seasons in their round;
Stern Winter loves a dirge-like sound.

(181–92)

The final fiction of the ode will be that of the sound which created light, and its signals a rondure in the poem from the secondariness of the aural sense at the opening to the primacy, not of the ear, but to the disturbances of air to which it responds. Sound pierces darkness, whereas light seems to have no effect upon silence. It is sounds, rather than illuminations, which seem to awaken us from sleep, and which can invade our dreams. Alarms release visions, and in poetic tradition the beginning of

Pindar's first Pythian ode, its golden Apollonian lyre releasing a flurry of brilliant images, figures the sounds of beginnings, of creations. The final strophe of Wordsworth's ode returns to this:

> A Voice to Light gave Being;
> To Time, and Man his first-born chronicler;
> A Voice shall finish doubt and dim foreseeing,
> And sweep away life's visionary stir
>
> (209–12)

The model from Dryden, of music as order creating the world and music as the last trump undoing it, lies far behind this return. The Logos, as Sound, will outlast all the silences of eternity. Wordsworth's image of sound itself progresses through the crisis of the challenge of silence, the silence occasioned by switching culture off that the intermittences of nature may be audible. But at the end of the poem, again recapitulating the Immortality Ode, "the WORD, that shall not pass away" is restored to eternal life. A remythologizing of the music of the spheres, the *musica mundana* of ancient fiction, has been accomplished, *via, but not terminating in,* the fabulous power of what is, in the more domestic sense, mundane. Even the fancies of eighteenth-century poetry which celebrate this mundane sounding by calling it music are part of the fiction. And even the *musica mundana* of Rilke's *Ur-geraüsch,* the music of one sense, or even of all senses, becoming another; even "the still, sad music of humanity" become, for the sound that lies as far behind language as it does beyond music, but phonetic shadows. If the largest shadow of all, that of the biblical fiction, looms over the conclusion, it is not one that the Wordsworth of 1828 would be in any position to avoid.

M. H. ABRAMS

Two Roads to Wordsworth

The first critic of Wordsworth's poetry was Wordsworth himself, and in his criticism, as in his poetry, he speaks with two distinct voices. The first voice is that of the Preface to *Lyrical Ballads,* in which Wordsworth powerfully applies to his poetry some humanistic values of the European Enlightenment. In his Preface the controlling and interrelated norms are the essential, the elementary, the simple, the universal, and the permanent. The great subjects of his poetry, Wordsworth says, are "the essential passions of the heart," "elementary feelings," "the great and simple affections," "the great and universal passions of men," and "characters of which the elements are simple . . . such as exist now, and will probably always exist," as these human qualities interact with "the beautiful and permanent forms of nature." His aim is a poetry written in a "naked and simple" style that is "well-adapted to interest mankind permanently." And the poet himself, as "a man speaking to men," both affirms and effects the primal human values: the joy of life, the dignity of life and of its elemental moving force, the pleasure principle, and the primacy of the universal connective, love. The poet "rejoices more than other men in the spirit of life" both within him and without, pays homage "to the grand elementary principle of pleasure, by which he knows, and feels, and lives, and moves," and is "the rock of defence of human nature . . . carrying everywhere with him relationship and love."

Wordsworth's second critical voice has been far less heeded by his readers. It speaks out in the "Essay, Supplementary to the Preface" of his *Poems* of 1815, and reiterates in sober prose the claims he had made, years before, in the verse "Prospectus" to *The Recluse* (first printed with his Preface to *The Excursion*) and in the opening and closing passages of *The Prelude:* claims that it is his task to confront and find consolation in human suffering—whether the "solitary agonies" of rural life or the "fierce confederate storm / Of sorrow" barricadoed within the walls of cities—since he is a poet who has been singled out "for holy services" in a secular work of man's "redemption." In his "Essay" of 1815, Wordsworth addresses himself to explain and justify those aspects of novelty and strangeness in his poetry that have evoked from critics "unremitting hostility . . . slight . . . aversion . . . contempt." He does so by asserting that he, like every "truly original poet," has qualities that are "peculiarly his own," and in specifying his innovations, he does not now take his operative concepts from eighteenth-century humanism, but imports them from theology; that is, he deliberately adapts to poetry the idiom hitherto used by Christian apologists to justify the radical novelty, absurdities, and paradoxes of the Christian mysteries. For Wordsworth claims in this essay that there are "affinities between religion and poetry," "a community of nature," so that poetry shares the distinctive quality of Christianity, which is to confound "the calculating understanding" by its contradictions:

> For when Christianity, the religion of humility, is founded upon the proudest quality of our nature [the imagination], what can be expected but contradictions?

In the "Essay" of 1815, accordingly, Wordsworth does not represent poetry as elemental and simple, but stresses instead its "contradictions" —that is, its radical paradoxicality, its union of antitheses, its fusion of the sensuous and the transcendent, its violation of the customary, and its reversal of status between the highest and lowest. Poetry, for example, imitates the supreme contradiction of the Incarnation itself: it is "ethereal and transcendent, yet incapable to sustain [its] existence without sensuous incarnation." The higher poetry unites the "wisdom of the heart and the grandeur of imagination" and so achieves a "simplicity" that is "Magnificence herself." Wordsworth's own poems manifest "emotions of the pathetic" that are "complex and revolutionary." As for "the sublime"—he is specifically a poet "charged with a new mission to extend its kingdom, and to augment and spread its enjoyments." For as one of the poets who combine the "heroic passions" of pagan antiquity with Christian wisdom he has produced a new synthesis—an "accord of sublimated humanity." And his chief enterprise as a poet is expressed in a Christian paradox—he must cast his readers down in order to raise them up: their spirits "are to be humbled and humanized, in order that they may be purified and exalted."

Wordsworth as primarily the simple, affirmative poet of elementary feelings, essential humanity, and vital joy, and Wordsworth as primarily the complex poet of strangeness, paradox, equivocality, and dark sublimities— these diverse views, adumbrated by Wordsworth himself, were established as persistent alternative ways to the poet by Matthew Arnold and by A. C. Bradley. The cause of Wordsworth's greatness, Arnold said, taking his cue from Wordsworth's Preface to *Lyrical Ballads*, "is simple, and may be told quite simply. Wordsworth's poetry is great because of the extraordinary power" with which he feels and renders and makes us share "the joy offered to us in nature, the joy offered to us in the simple, primary affections and duties." And from the naturalness of his subject and the sincerity of his feeling, his characteristic and matchless style is that of "the most plain, firsthand, almost austere naturalness." Wordsworth's great boon to us in "this iron time," Arnold says in his verses, is that he has restored our lost capacity for spontaneous and uncomplicated responsiveness, "the freshness of the early world." He adds, however, that Wordsworth achieved his "sweet calm" only by the expedient of averting his ken "from half of human fate."

Although Bradley did not publish his great essay on Wordsworth until 1909, thirty years after Arnold's appeared, he set out explicitly to supplement what he regarded as Arnold's valid but incomplete view of the poet by specifying other qualities without which "Wordsworth is not Wordsworth." His challenge to Arnold's way to Wordsworth is direct and uncompromising: "The road into Wordsworth's mind must be through his strangeness and his paradoxes, and not round them." In pursuing this road Bradley follows the lead, not of Wordsworth's Preface, but of his vatic poetic pronouncements, which Arnold had noted only to derogate as the style "more properly . . . of eloquent prose." As Bradley's other essays make evident, his critical concepts, and his sensitiveness to negative and paradoxical elements in literature, also owe a great deal to the philosophy of Hegel. As Hegel himself had noted, however, his categories of negation, contradiction, and synthesis are (like Wordsworth's concept of the "contradictions" in the products of the modern poetic imagination) the conceptual equivalents of the paradoxes and the *coincidentia oppositorum* of the Christian mysteries. In the Hegelian cast of his critical concepts, then, Bradley is in broad accord with the spirit of Wordsworth's own "Essay, Supplementary to the Preface" of 1815.

In Bradley's view, that which is most distinctive in Wordsworth's poetry is "peculiar," "audacious," "strange," and Wordsworth's characteristic attitudes are a complex of contraries or contradictions. Although

Wordsworth sang of joy and love, "he did not avert his eyes" from anguish or evil, but often represented "a dark world"; and though he undertook to show that suffering and misery can in fact be the conditions of happiness, strength, and glory, he did not pretend that this possibility solved "the riddle of the painful earth"—"the world was to him in the end 'this unintelligible world.' " Wordsworth is "preeminently the poet of solitude," yet "no poet is more emphatically the poet of community." His native bent was not to simplicity, but to "sublimity"; and in this "mystic" or "visionary" strain "there is always traceable a certain hostility to 'sense,' " an intimation of something illimitable, eternal, infinite, that is "in some way a denial" of the limited sensible world, "contradicting or abolishing the fixed limits of our habitual view." As Bradley describes the paradoxical qualities of a Wordsworthian spot of time, using a portentous term, "Everything here is natural, but everything is apocalyptic."

Twentieth-century critics of Wordsworth have tended to follow either Arnold's or Bradley's road to the poet, and the diverse approaches have yielded two Wordsworths. One Wordsworth is simple, elemental, forthright, the other is complex, paradoxical, problematic; one is an affirmative poet of life, love, and joy, the other is an equivocal or self-divided poet whose affirmations are implicitly qualified (if not annulled) by a pervasive sense of mortality and an ever-incipient despair of life; one is the great poet of natural man and the world of all of us, the other is a visionary or "mystic" who is ultimately hostile to temporal man and the world of sense and whose profoundest inclinations are toward another world that transcends biological and temporal limitations; one is the Wordsworth of light, the other the Wordsworth of chiaroscuro, or even darkness. Criticism since mid-century continues to manifest, and often to sharpen, this division, although the commentators who take either the one or the other of the old roads to Wordsworth have introduced new critical concepts that make their work seem, in the 1970s, distinctively "modern." I shall try to identify a few of the more conspicuous innovations within each of the traditional perspectives.

THE SIMPLE WORDSWORTH

In *The Poet Wordsworth* (1950) Helen Darbishire is an unqualified Arnoldian: Wordsworth is a poet whose motive power was "the depth and force of his feeling for humanity," who vindicated "sense-experience as the foundation of knowledge" and represented "simple men and women who are moved by the great emotions." John F. Danby's poet, in a book published a decade later, is also, as his title asserts, *The Simple Wordsworth;* the innovative element is Danby's view that Wordsworth is a craftsman whose simplicity has been achieved by "an alert and conscious artist," who controls the reader's responses by his management of the narrative personae, "tones of voice," and "masks." Danby's critique of *The Idiot Boy* is a belated recognition that Wordsworth is an accomplished comic poet. Its focus is on the interplay of the narrative voice, the voices of the characters, and the poet's own voice in sustaining the fine balance of humor and human warmth in the evolving story.

Danby expressly opposes his treatment of Wordsworth as intentional artificer to the New Critical approach to a poem as a free-standing and autonomous structure of meanings, to be judged without recourse to the artist or his intention. Cleanth Brooks's essay on Wordsworth's *Ode: Intimations of Immortality* demonstrates what can be achieved by such a close reading of the poem "as an independent poetic structure," interrogated for what it "manages to say" entirely "in its own right" as a primarily ironic and paradoxical deployment of thematic imagery. Having assimilated the insights made possible by this strict limitation of perspective in the New Criticism, many critics in the last decade or two have undertaken, like Danby, to rehumanize poetry by viewing the poet, in Wordworth's phrase in the Preface, as "a man speaking to men," and by exploiting concepts such as "voice," "persona," "tone," and "point of view," which emphasize the poet's own involvement, as well as his management of the reader's participation, in the fictional process.

Such a revitalized rhetoric of poetry is prominent in many recent writings about Wordsworth. In the third chapter of *The Music of Humanity*, for example, Jonathan Wordsworth demonstrates the essential role, in *The Ruined Cottage,* of the interplay between Wordsworth's two "poetic selves," the Pedlar and the Poet, in effecting the reader's imaginative consent to the author's own attitudes toward the tragic story. In an essay that has been much debated, Stephen Parrish reads *The Thorn* not as a quasi-supernatural story, but as an artful dramatic monologue, in which the controlling principle is the revelation of the mental workings of its credulous narrator, the old sea captain. Neil Hertz's essay "Wordsworth and the Tears of Adam"—with a shift of emphasis from Wordsworth's rhetorical artistry to the characteristic disjunction of consciousness in his poetry—discriminates "the transformation of the voice" in a short verse passage, and details the interaction among three "aspects of Wordsworth's self" and a fourth subjectivity, that of the responding reader.

THE PROBLEMATIC WORDSWORTH

In the 1960s there appeared a new mode of criticism in America whose appeal to younger critics presages its growing importance in studies of Romantic literature. The primary terms of this criticism are "consciousness" (or "self-consciousness") and the "dialectic" of its dealings with what is not-consciousness, and its characteristic procedure is to find something "problematic" in the surface meaning of single passages and to regard this as a clue to a deep structure manifesting an unspoken preoccupation of the poet. The proximate sources of this critical procedure are the diverse movements in European thought loosely classified as "phenomenology," "existentialism," and "structuralism," but its central idiom and concerns derive ultimately from Hegel; so that, when applied to Wordsworth, it can be regarded as a revived form of Bradley's neo-Hegelian approach to that poet. The focus, however, is much sharper than Bradley's, and the chief operative concepts are much more restricted. For as Hegel in his *Phenomenology of Spirit* translated the manifold particularities of human and individual history into diverse moments of the transactions between consciousness and its alienated other, so these critics view the manifold surface particularities of Romantic poems as generated primarily by a single submerged plot: the sustained struggle of the poet's consciousness (operating in the mode often called "imagination") to achieve "autonomy," or absolute independence from that adversary which is not itself—namely, "nature," the world of sensible objects.

In his influential essay "Intentional Structure of the Romantic Image," first published in 1960, Paul de Man sets out from the observation that there is a "dialectic" that is "paradoxical"—a "fundamental ambiguity" or "tension" that "never ceases to be problematic"—in Romantic attempts to link the polarities of consciousness, or imagination, and nature. De Man's paradigmatic instance is Mallarmé, who is represented as a revealing point of reference because he is a late Romantic who took over what had hitherto been an implicit tension of polar attitudes, "the alternating feeling of attraction and repulsion that the romantic poet experiences toward nature," and made it explicit as a "conscious dialectic of a reflective poetic consciousness." Mallarmé, unlike earlier Romantic poets, "always remained convinced of the essential priority of the natural object," so that his writings as an extreme "anti-natural poet" are a defiantly hopeless struggle by consciousness (or by the language in which consciousness manifests itself) to annihilate, by reducing to its own self, a nature that Mallarmé knows to be ultimately indefeasible. Wordsworth's poetry, on the other hand, with its "radical contradictions" in the representation of landscape (de Man's example is the passage on crossing the Alps in *The Prelude*, Book VI), puts into question "the ontological priority of the sensory object," by recourse to the faculty he calls "imagination," which "marks . . . a possibility for consciousness to exist entirely by and for itself, independently of all relationship with the outside world."

Geoffrey Hartman also finds that Wordsworth's treatment of nature is "problematic," and that a number of passages in *The Prelude* which "overtly celebrate nature" in fact "share a motif opposed to the overt line of argument." Hartman's repeated reference, however, is not to Mallarmé but to Blake, the extreme representative of a deliberate commitment to a visionary and anti-natural imagination. "Blake," says Hartman, "would snap . . . that Wordsworth is of his party without knowing it." The difference is that Wordsworth, when he comes face to face with his "autonomous imagination," fears it, shies from it, or veils it. In consequence, his poetry constitutes "a series of evaded recognitions" of imagination and "an avoidance of apocalypse"—where imagination is defined by Hartman as "consciousness of self raised to apocalyptic pitch" and apocalypse signifies "any strong desire to cast out nature and to achieve an unmediated contact with the principle of things," hence as "involving a *death* of nature." It is this "unresolved opposition between Imagination and Nature"—through Wordsworth's "fear of the death of nature"—that "prevents him from becoming a visionary poet."

Two other essays represent an approach to Wordsworth that emphasizes the duplicity and the strain between contradictions in his writings; the major operative concept, however, is not a revived Hegelian opposition between consciousness and an alien other, but the post-Freudian distinction between Manifest and latent, conscious and unconscious content. The basic claim is that Wordsworth's overt or surface meaning often overlies a covert countermeaning that expresses what the poet profoundly felt and believed, as against what he rationalized himself into believing.

David Perkins' *The Quest for Permanence* undertakes to "go beneath the surface" of Wordsworth's poetry in order to explore the "negative implications" that are sometimes "contrary to his overt intentions and obiter dicta"; for any interpretation that concentrates on Wordsworth's obiter dicta "is not touching what is deepest in him." Under Wordsworth's overt claims that certitude and peace attend upon "the union of mind with nature," Perkins finds a contrary sense that there is a "gulf between human nature . . . and the rest of nature," and that man is doomed to be an isolated being, estranged from both nature and other men. There are symptoms also of "a kind of schizoid retreat" from situations that threaten the poet's composure, which in its extreme form manifests itself in Wordsworth as an attraction to the ultimate security of the grave.

In *The Limits of Mortality*, published in the same year as Perkins' *Quest for Permanence* (1959), David Ferry's aim is to discover in Wordsworth "ideas and feelings which can in some way be related to our own deepest feelings and ideas." Ferry penetrates to this modern element, as he says, by "a special way of reading his poems." This way to Wordsworth is to strike a sharp dichotomy between the " 'surface' of his poems" and the "deeper" and "hidden" meanings which are in "tension" or "conflict" with the surface meanings, and to assert the prepotency of the hidden and antithetic meanings as constituting the "ultimate subject matter" of a poem. As Ferry formulates this semantic peripety:

> [The] apparent subject matter is a kind of cipher or hieroglyph for meanings which reject or devaluate the very experiences which express them. . . . The symbolic meanings of [Wordsworth's] poems tend to reject their sensuous, dramatic surfaces.

Like A. C. Bradley a half-century earlier, Ferry sets out, as he says, to correct Arnold's "tendency to take Wordsworth's vocabulary of feeling at face value," hence to evaluate him as "the poet of the primary affections and simple feelings." By Ferry's interpretative strategy, however, the paradoxical Wordsworth works free from Bradley's careful qualifications to become the polar opposite of Arnold's Wordsworth. The sophisticated modern reader is now enabled to look right through Wordsworth's surface assertions of reverence for a "sacramental" nature, love for elemental man, and esteem for the simple affections and ordinary experience, in order to discern a countermeaning of which the poet himself remained unaware—that is, a "mystical" yearning for an eternal and unchanging realm of being to which nature and man and even the articulations of poetry itself (since all are alike trapped in the conditions of time, space, and vicissitude) are an intolerable obstruction, an offense against the purity of eternity. Hence to the knowing reader Wordsworth's "sacramentalist" poems, far from being simple and natural in style, often turn out to be "contradictions of themselves" and to express a yearning "for their own destruction," and Wordsworth's "mystical imagination" is recognized to be "a hater of temporal nature" and "the enemy of poetry as of all distinctively human experience." Ferry's closing summation of the Wordsworth of the great decade is that "his genius was his enmity to man, which he mistook for love, and his mistake led him into confusions which he could not bear. But when he banished his confusions, he banished his distinctive greatness as well."

Even the confirmed Arnoldian must admit the plausibility of some of the insights achieved by the recent critics who premise their reading of Wordsworth on the paradoxical strains and equivocal attitudes in his poetry. And it is a measure of the range and magnitude of Wordsworth's achievement that he continues to speak to us and our interests when interpreted by neo-Hegelian concepts, or when viewed as a proto-Mallarmé, or as a Blake manqué, or as, under the brave surface, really one of us in our age of alienation, anguish, and existential absurdity. An inveterate under-reading of the textual surface, however, turns readily into a habitual over-reading. The problem is, to what extent do these recent critical perspectives on Wordsworth simply bring into visibility what was always, although obscurely, there, and to what extent do they project upon his poems the form of their own prepossessions?

This is not the place to argue out the difficult issue. Instead, I shall cite some contemporary critics who, like A. C. Bradley, believe that Arnold described what is really there, but enlarge the scope of their vision to encompass the half of Wordsworth from which Arnold averted his ken. In their work, as in Bradley's essay, Wordsworth stands as a complex but integral poet, rather than as a radically divided one whose deepest inclinations, known to the modern critic but not to the poet himself, undercut or annul his repeated affirmations.

Like the recent explorers of the problematic Wordsworth, Lionel Trilling points to an aspect of his poetry that is strange, remote, even chilling to us. His account of it, however, is not psychoanalytic (Wordsworth's unconscious revulsion from life) but historical—Wordsworth's participation in a persistent strain of Hebrew and Christian culture which, at odds with the modern preoccupation with heroic struggle and apocalyptic violence, is committed to quietism, peace, and a wise passiveness. Wordsworth's quietism, however, "is not in the least a negation of life, but . . . an affirmation of life so complete that it needed no saying"; Trilling in fact uses Wordsworth as the positive standard by which to define the negatives of our adversary culture. Wordsworth has an "acute sense of his own being" that sharpens his awareness of other beings, and his intention is "to require us to acknowledge" the being of his narrative personae and so "to bring them within the range of conscience" and of "natural sympathy." It is not Wordsworth but we moderns who "do not imagine being . . . that it can be a joy" and who "are in love, at least in our literature, with the fantasy of death." Writing also in the affirmative tradition of Arnold, Jonathan Wordsworth nonetheless identifies in *The Ruined Cottage* a dimension of poetic genius that Arnold had denied to Wordsworth: the power to reconcile us imaginatively with an instance of seemingly pointless suffering, futile courage, and meaningless death in a way that manifests both the poet's artistry and his "humanity"—"an insight into emotions not his own"—and with a success that places him "among the very few great English tragic writers."

The position of Harold Bloom in the critical division about Words-worth's poetry is a complex one. Citing Geoffrey Hartman, he concurs in the latter's distinction between surface and covert meaning and in the associated claim that, as Bloom puts it, "the inner problem of *The Prelude*, and of all the poetry of Wordsworth's great decade, is that of the autonomy of the poet's creative imagination," hence of a "hidden conflict between Poetry and Nature." But Bloom's reading of Wordsworth, taken overall, is different from Hartman's. He accepts Wordsworth's own statement, most notably in the "Prospectus" to *The Recluse*, that his high argument is the possibility of a union, by means of imagination, between mind and nature, in a reciprocity that redeems the world of ordinary experience. Instead of regarding Wordsworth as an all-but-Blake, he expressly differentiates his poetry from Blake's and parallels it instead to that of Wallace Stevens, as a "naturalistic celebration of the possibilities inherent in our condition here and now." Bloom accordingly reads *Tintern Abbey* as representing the poet in the act of discovering the theme of all his best poetry, a "reciprocity between the external world and his own mind" in which the two agents are equal in initiative and power. *The Old Cumberland Beggar*, in Bloom's analysis, registers a correlative aspect of Wordsworth's genius, his rever-ence for essential human life, seemingly alienated and "stripped to the nakedness of primordial condition," yet "still powerful in dignity, still infinite in value." And though he believes that Wordsworth's confidence in an imaginative communion of mind, nature, and man later weakened and failed, Bloom pays tribute to the novelty and magnitude of the enterprise. Wordsworth "personified a heroic mode of naturalism, which even he then proved unable to sustain." "No poet since," he declares, "has given us more." Such a view is consonant with that of the present writer, who has explored *The Prelude*, and the opening book of *The Recluse* into which it leads, as Wordsworth's attempt to save the traditional design and values of human life, inherited from a Christian past, but to translate them to a naturalistic frame of reference—that is, to represent them as generated by a reciprocity between the natural world and the minds of men, "as natural beings in the strength of nature."

Wordsworth criticism is in a flourishing condition these days, and its vigorous internal disputes testify to the poet's continuing vitality and pertinence. We are rediscovering what a number of Wordsworth's major contemporaries acknowledged—that he has done what only the greatest poets do. He has transformed the inherited language of poetry into a medium adequate to express new ways of perceiving the world, new modes of experience, and new relations of the individual consciousness to itself, to its past, and to other men. More than all but a very few English writers, Wordsworth has altered not only our poetry, but our sensibility and our culture.

THOMAS WEISKEL

Wordsworth and the Defile of the Word

Nearing the end of the first book of the poem on his own life, Wordsworth confesses to some uncertainty. He fears that already he may have been misled "By an infirmity of love for day / Disowned by memory," and he counts on Coleridge's sympathy to see him through (*P* 1.612 ff.). His project in this loving reclamation of childhood had been frankly therapeutic:

> . . . my hope has been, that I might fetch
> Invigorating thoughts from former years;
> Might fix the wavering balance of my mind,
> And haply meet reproaches too, whose power
> May spur me on, in manhood now mature,
> To honorable toil.
>
> (1.620–25)

Yet his original project is fast receding before an enterprise more tentative and promising. Even if his hope should be "but an impotent desire," he has made a discovery, which now solicits him with the charm of the visionary and displaces the reproaches he had anticipated to a new quarter:

> Yet should these hopes
> Prove vain, and thus should neither I be taught
> To understand myself, nor thou to know
> With better knowledge how the heart was framed
> Of him thou lovest; need I dread from thee

From *The Romantic Sublime: Studies in the Structure and Psychology of Transcendence.*
Copyright © 1976 by The Johns Hopkins University Press.

> Harsh judgments, if the song be loth to quit
> Those recollected hours that have the charm
> Of visionary things, those lovely forms
> And sweet sensations that throw back our life,
> And almost make remotest infancy
> A visible scene, on which the sun is shining?
>   (1.625–35)

It is difficult to know how open is this question addressed to Coleridge.
For Coleridge, we feel, is not the real addressee; he stands, like a neutral
alienist, sympathetic but mute, for an agent or element in Wordsworth
himself that would judge harshly the enterprise now in view. As if an
answer to his question scarcely mattered—he is picking up confidence—
Wordsworth continues:

> One end at least hath been attained; my mind
> Hath been revived, and if this genial mood
> Desert me not, forthwith shall be brought down
> Through later years the story of my life.
> The road lies plain before me;—'tis a theme
> Single and of determined bounds; and hence
> I choose it rather at this time, than work
> Of ampler or more varied argument,
> Where I might be discomfited and lost.
>   (1.636–44)

We note that Wordsworth's "genial mood" depends upon neither his own
self-understanding nor the successful communication of his history in the
terms of "knowledge." This cure, if such it is, comes about almost
incidentally, as a side effect in his rehearsal of the past. By settling for less
in the way of theme and argument, he gains more, a genial state of mind
which cannot be sought directly, only received gratuitously.

It is true that Wordsworth will later seem to be educated by the
visible scenes of childhood, as if their rememoration indeed constituted a
kind of knowledge. Certain episodes seem especially instructive, imbued
with a latent message now to be decoded:

> There are in our existence spots of time,
> That with distinct pre-eminence retain
> A renovating virtue, whence, depressed
> By false opinion and contentious thought,
> Or aught of heavier or more deadly weight,
> In trivial occupations, and the round
> Of ordinary intercourse, our minds
> Are nourished and invisibly repaired;
> A virtue, by which pleasure is enhanced,

That penetrates, enables us to mount,
When high, more high, and lifts us up when fallen.
This efficacious spirit chiefly lurks
Among those passages of life that give
Profoundest knowledge to what point, and how,
The mind is lord and master—outward sense
The obedient servant of her will.

(12.208–23)

One can have much of Wordsworth by heart and still be surprised, notably by the submerged metaphors. Here, "lurks," with its suggestion of the hidden and even the sinister, makes one pause only to find that resonance picked up by "passages": a spirit lurks in a passage. "Passages" refers presumably to events that involved a passing from one state to another and also to the passing back and through of retrospection; in this sense, "passages of life" are equivalent to "spots of time." But a "passage" is also a text; one reads these texts or signifiers by passing into and through them. Such passages "give" knowledge but conceal the efficacious spirit; at the very least this spirit, lying as it were in ambush, is to be distinguished from knowledge of the mind's sovereignty. (Actually, "knowledge" is a late idea here; Wordsworth first wrote that the spirit lurks among passages "in which / We have had deepest feeling that the mind / Is lord and master" (1805, 11.270–71), and this phrase evolved through "Profoundest feeling" to become "Profoundest knowledge.") The knowledge or feeling of the mind's great power is often given to Wordsworth, but the spirit comes not as a consequence of this insight but as if in response to it. If *The Prelude* is an indirect quest for the efficacious spirit or genial mood, that quest is fulfilled in a hidden and somewhat unpredictable concomitance.

What then was Wordsworth's discovery? His undeniable claim to originality can be advanced in many directions—he aggrandized the everyday; he virtually destroyed the-poem-which-is-*about*-something by taking the subject out of poetry; he naturalized the archaic, daemonic, and divine sources of power. What must orient us here is his discovery of a mode of conversation, now most easily recognized outside of poetry in the domains of the authentic psychoanalyst and a certain kind of expert teacher too tentative to know or say for sure what he "really" thinks. This conversation is not a "communication" (the cant word of our social world); its aim is not the transmission of knowledge or a message but the springing loose of an efficacious spirit which haunts the passages of self-knowledge, however shallow or deep. Yet to describe *The Prelude* as any kind of conversation seems perverse. Its apparent form is closer to monolithic monologue; it drifts, gets lost, peters out now and then, and generally proceeds without the dramatic constraints a stricter form or a genuine auditor would compel. The ostensible interlocutor has no chance to reply, and indeed it might be said that Coleridge's assumption of this role presupposed his own subsidence as a poet. Worst of all, this "conversation" has for its exclusive theme the inner history of the speaker, and it is thus a discourse apparently exempt from the veridical testing conversation normally entails.

Nevertheless, in its deeper lineaments *The Prelude* has the shape and structure of a dialogue. Wordsworth's real interlocutor is not Coleridge but himself, a part of himself, archaic or prospective but in any case alienated from his present, who beckons to him across a "vacancy." "Often do I seem," he says, "Two consciousnesses, conscious of myself / And of some other Being" (2.31–33). That "other Being" is in part a remembered state of mind, a previous consciousness, and in part the inferred protagonist of visible scenes of whom he is now conscious for the first time. For the first time because that other Being did not exist in the past; though he now exists there, he is a creation of the present. Freud regarded the appearance of a subject as an active character in his own memory as decisive evidence that the original experience had been worked over.

> It may indeed be questioned whether we have any memories at all *from* our childhood: memories *relating to* our childhood may be all that we possess. Our childhood memories show us our earliest years not as they were but as they appeared at the later periods when the memories were revived. In these periods of revival, the childhood memories did not, as people are accustomed to say, *emerge*; they were *formed* at that time.

The radical reading of *The Prelude* must begin with this insight, which no one who has tried the experiment of recollection needs an analyst to confirm. So Wordsworth is to be found forming his significant other Being even as he searches for his signature in recollected hours, perhaps finding him truly only "in that silence while he hung / Listening" like the boy at Winander in conversation with the owls (5.364–88).

In general, the other Being or consciousness implied by Wordsworth's speech remains inaccessible except through the immensely mediated languages of memory and desire. The whole series of representations—images, thoughts, ideas, words—function as the signifiers in this dialogue, and they cannot be short-circuited in an unmediated intuition because that Other is defined, as locus or possibility, only by these signifiers. Insofar as Wordsworth is a speaker, that Other is the being to whom his speech is unconsciously directed; but the Other is also the one to whom he listens, and it is in fact mainly as a listener that Wordsworth overtly construes his identity in *The Prelude*. For there is and has been an evident continuity in his listening. Even as a child, he says, amid "fits of vulgar joy" and "giddy bliss,"

> . . . even then I felt
> Gleams like the flashing of a shield;—the earth
> And common face of Nature spake to me
> Rememberable things
>
> (1.581–88)

and they are still so speaking because "The scenes which were a witness of that joy / Remained in their substantial lineaments / Depicted on the brain" (1.599–601). If he fails to understand this speech, and he often does, sometimes egregiously, the fact of being spoken to remains, and its aim and value depend in no way on the accurate reception of a message. It may even be that Wordsworth's misconstructions, his significant *méconnaissances*, are the essential pivots of this dialogue, for they enable him to change from listener to speaker; they enable him to be cured. We appreciate in any case that these failures are not the result of a faulty archeology, as if the past could indeed be unearthed by consciousness. They are liberating evasions, obscurities which preserve both the mystery (and hence the power) of his interlocutor and the authenticity of his own speech, which otherwise might slide toward the vain repetition or imitation of an alienated self. We might even suppose, as the point of an ideal cure no doubt hypothetical, a moment of pure speech in which the Other is so entirely obscured as not to exist, and Wordsworth knows only a presence uncompounded by the absence which makes speech necessary.

We may have the vague impression that it is Nature with whom Wordsworth is speaking. In one sense this is true, for "the earth / And common face of Nature" is the predominant locus of the signifier. But Nature herself exhibits a paradoxically fugitive omnipresence in *The Prelude*. Wordsworth rarely speaks directly to Nature, more often of or about her; we find a more or less consistent differentiation between Nature and "the language of the sense":

> Ye Presences of Nature in the sky
> And on the earth! Ye Visions of the hills!
> And Souls of lonely places! can I think
> A vulgar hope was yours when ye employed
> Such ministry, when ye through many a year
> Haunting me thus among my boyish sports,
> On caves and trees, upon the woods and hills,

> Impressed upon all forms the characters
> Of danger or desire; and thus did make
> The surface of the universal earth
> With triumph and delight, with hope and fear,
> Work like a sea?
>
> (1.464–75)

Nature is generally two or more ontological degrees removed from the "characters" that can be perceived or intended, listened to or read. Nature hovers in the background as the sum or ground of the intermediary personifications ("Powers," "genii," "Presences," "Visions," "Souls") who are supposed as actual agents of articulation. Nature is thus the guarantor of the dialogue, at once the principle assumed to cover and redeem its discontinuities and a kind of screen on which the multiplicity of representations is projected. When "forms" begin to assume the shape and function of "characters," Nature's significant absence (or "negative presence") is already presupposed, for characters are symbols standing in for something no longer immediately there. Behind every symbol is an absence, the death of the thing (form or image) whose place the symbol takes. Hence speech itself is founded on the withdrawal of the primordial object, in which we find as well the essential formula of anxiety.

It is in this passage from forms to characters, from image to symbol, that the efficacious spirit lurks, and it is the intricate turnings of this passage that I propose to follow and hope to map. We may conceive two domains, an order of imagination or memory and an order of symbol or speech, though the content of these opposed domains ought to be educed from the analysis and not out of an hypothesis. *The Prelude* as a whole is an attempt to negotiate the strait leading from remembered images, and from the power of mind to which these images continue to testify, to capable speech. "I have seen such things—I see them still (memory)—and see moreover deeper into them, as if anew (imagination)—I therefore was and am a favored being (identity)—and I can speak (be a poet)." This argument, here abstractly reduced and overemphasized, presides over each rememoration in the poem, as if this poem were in fact a prelude, achieving its unforeseen finalities only under propaedeutic pretense. In a way the argument serves as "profoundest knowledge" to orient and occasion the "efficacious spirit" which is the poem itself. Moreover, the passage discernible in the project of *The Prelude* emerges with strange and almost literal insistence in the poem's crucial episodes and at the heart of its recurrent figures.

We use the notion of poetic imagination loosely to gloss over the mysterious gap between a power of perception and a power of articulation or composition. Keats says that "every man whose soul is not a clod / Hath visions, and would speak, if he had loved / And been well nurtured in his mother's tongue," but that can't possibly be true; a mute inglorious Milton is no Milton at all. At times it seems as if the Romantic poets (Blake, of course, apart) were engaged in a conspiracy of occultation concerning the Word, as if to acknowledge that its enjoining power involved the betrayal of a dangerous secret.

The fact is that the passage from imagination to symbol was occluded for Wordsworth, and yet the essential moment of his greatest poetry is right in the midst of this occlusion. He halts or is halted right at the point where the image is eclipsed—where it is on the verge of turning into a "character" in a higher, nonvisual discourse. This moment—and it is an experience as well as a dialectical locus—is the sole province of what he calls "visionary power," and it is the very type of the sublime moment. Here is one of Wordsworth's first attempts to formulate its liminal significance:

> . . . for I would walk alone,
> Under the quiet stars, and at that time
> Have felt whate'er there is of power in sound
> To breathe an elevated mood, by form
> Or image unprofaned; and I would stand,
> If the night blackened with a coming storm,
> Beneath some rock, listening to notes that are
> The ghostly language of the ancient earth,
> Or make their dim abode in distant winds.
> Thence did I drink the visionary power;
> And deem not profitless those fleeting moods
> Of shadowy exultation: not for this,
> That they are kindred to our purer mind
> And intellectual life; but that the soul,
> Remembering how she felt, but what she felt
> Remembering not, retains an obscure sense
> Of possible sublimity, whereto
> With growing faculties she doth aspire,
> With faculties still growing, feeling still
> That whatsoever point they gain, they yet
> Have something to pursue.
>
> (2.302–22)

The mood of shadowy exultation lies beyond the profane domain of form or image, and yet the subject is here not quite integrated into the order of symbolic sound. The notes to which he listens remain a "ghostly language," a pattern of signifiers without signifieds, a language without semantic dimension. The signifier precedes the signified, which may indeed never arrive; or in terms closer to Wordsworth's, the subject is initiated into the *how* of the discourse but not the *what,* and the affective exaltation depends precisely on this halting at a threshold. The "power in sound / To breathe an elevated mood" is here being listened to, but that slight personification ("breathe") refers us obliquely to Wordsworth's situation as a speaker who knows how he wants to sound but not quite what he has to say.

Wordsworth was not a symbolic poet and not a descriptive poet either, if indeed a poet can be descriptive. His landscapes hover on the edge of revelation without revealing anything, and so the very moment of hovering, of glimpsed entry into the beyond, when "the light of sense / Goes out, but with a flash that has revealed / The invisible world" (6.600–602), usurps the missing climax of symbolic revelation. In the Snowdon vision, for example, the salient elements of that magnificent scene—the suspended moon, the sea of hoary mist, the blue chasm in the vapor—refuse to harden into symbolic equation with the imagination or anything else, as Geoffrey Hartman has observed. And this is so despite the fact that Wordsworth is there working explicitly with notions of analogy, type, and emblem. So too with that spot of time when the young boy, having lost his way while riding near Penrith, sees a naked pool, the beacon on the summit, and the girl with a pitcher forcing her way against the wind—salient images which are less than symbols and all the more powerful for that. Or the schoolboy in his mountain lookout, waiting to be fetched home for a holiday that turned into a funeral, who later finds himself returning to certain "kindred spectacles and sounds"—

> . . . the wind and sleety rain,
> And all the business of the elements,
> The single sheep, and the one blasted tree,
> And the bleak music from that old stone wall,
> The noise of wood and water, and the mist
> That on the line of each of those two roads
> Advanced in such indisputable shapes
> (12.317–23)

—thence to drink as at a fountain. Many instances of such salience could be adduced, but this feature of Wordsworth's landscapes is widely appreciated and is here evoked only to suggest the scope of the moment we wish to isolate. If the images so projected into the field of Wordsworth's past were to lose their opacity and become the transparent signifiers of an invisible world, the soul would "remember" what she felt and have nothing left to pursue. The conversation, propelled as it is by the baffled misconstruction of the signifier, would be over; Wordsworth would understand himself. Indeed, as the poem goes on Wordsworth is less and less disposed to interrogate the images that rise upon him. The gestures of self-inquisition become the mere feinting of a mind learning how knowledge is opposed to efficacious power.

Visionary power is associated with the transcendence of the image and in particular with the "power in sound"; yet it depends upon a resistance within that transcendence of sight for sound. In the Wordsworthian moment two events appear to coalesce: the withdrawal or the occultation of the image and the epiphany of the character or signifier proper. A form or image may be installed in either the imaginative or symbolic domains. There is a world of difference between the two, but the differentiation can never be found within the image itself. If an image is symbolic, that fact is signaled by what we loosely call "context"—its inscription in an order or language whose structure is prior to its meaning (signifieds) and so determines it. On the other hand, an image (fantasy or perception) may fall short of the symbolic, in which case it remains opaque and meaningless in itself. Earlier we spoke of rememoration as a confrontation with a signifier, but strictly speaking, an image becomes a signifier only when it is recognized as such, and this may involve imputing an intentionality to the image. (A homely example: a child responds to pictures or the type in a book only as colors and shapes until the magical moment when he discerns that they are representations; it is the displaced recapitulation of this moment that is in question here.) There is implicit in the passage from imagination to symbol a confrontation with symbolicity—the very fact of structure in its priority and independent of its actual organization. Hence the signifier may be misconstrued in two possible ways. It may be simply misread, or—and this is in point with Wordsworth—there may be a resistance or a barrier to its recognition as a signifier, a resistance to reading itself as opposed to seeing. I think the resistance may be identified with what Wordsworth calls imagination.

Death and the Word

The spots of time give to the mind the knowledge or feeling of its own sovereignty and occasion the gift of efficacious spirit as well. "Life with me," says Wordsworth, "As far as memory can look back, is full / Of this beneficent influence" (1805, 11.277–79). It is curious that these remembered events should have therapeutic power, since the two memories Wordsworth goes on to present are of a kind we should normally call traumatic, and they each contain intimations of death.

In fact, however, the whole idea of spots of time is installed in a line of associations concerning death. In the first manuscripts containing the bulk of books 1 and 2 (MSS. V, U), the passage "There are in our existence spots of time . . ." follows Wordsworth's account of the drowned man at Esthwaite, later assigned to book 5 (426–59). He had seen a heap of garments on the shore and watched for half an hour to see if a bather would emerge. But no one did, and the next day—"(Those unclaimed garments telling a plain Tale)"—the body was recovered:

> At length, the dead Man, 'mid that beauteous scene
> Of trees, and hills and water, bolt upright
> Rose with his ghastly face. . . .
>
> (1805, 5.470–72)

Why Wordsworth hadn't run for help the night before isn't clear, since surely the "Tale"—or at least the suspicion of something wrong—would have been plain enough to a boy of eight. In any case, MS. V continues with a meditation on disasters that later proved full of beneficent influence:

> . . . bolt upright
> Rose with his ghastly face. I might advert
> To numerous accidents in flood or field
> Quarry or moor, or 'mid the winter snows
> Distresses and disasters, tragic facts
> Of rural history that impressed my mind
> With images to which in following years
> Far other feelings were attached; with forms
> That yet exist with independent life
> And, like their archetypes, know no decay.

And then follows "There are in our existence spots of time. . . . " The sequence suggests that the spots of time were in their origin "tragic facts" for which time has provided a kind of redemption, permitting their association with "Far other feelings." We might find the tragic (or deathly or traumatic) associations clustering around "spots," whereas "of time" suggests the curative efficacy of a supervening continuity. Here the misconstruction of a memory-representation—entering, we must always assume, into the representation itself—and in particular the poet's indifference to the role of death in his most valuable memories, would seem to lie at the heart of the cure.

In the first spot of time Wordsworth is a very young boy of five or so riding with a trusted family servant on the moors near Penrith.

> We had not travelled long, ere some mischance
> Disjoined me from my comrade; and, through fear
> Dismounting, down the rough and stony moor

I led my horse, and, stumbling on, at length
Came to a bottom, where in former times
A murderer had been hung in iron chains.
The gibbet-mast had mouldered down, the bones
And iron case were gone; but on the turf,
Hard by, soon after that fell deed was wrought,
Some unknown hand had carved the murderer's name.
The monumental letters were inscribed
In times long past; but still, from year to year,
By superstition of the neighbourhood,
The grass is cleared away, and to this hour
The characters are fresh and visible:
A casual glance had shown them, and I fled,
Faltering and faint, and ignorant of the road:
Then, reascending the bare common, saw
A naked pool that lay beneath the hills,
The beacon on the summit, and, more near,
A girl, who bore a pitcher on her head,
And seemed with difficult steps to force her way
Against the blowing wind.

(12.231–53)

The emotional pivot of this episode is a word, a name, a group of characters suddenly glimpsed. One kind of fear, not knowing where one is, is violently superseded by the virtual panic of another kind of fear, being in a terrible place or spot. Losing its way, the ego is exposed involuntarily to a death, for the characters mean "a murderer was executed at this spot": death for a death, the law of sacrifice which is the simplest formula of justice. The custom in the background here is the execution of a murderer at the spot of the crime, so that the spot becomes charged with the ritual significance of atonement. It is a place in nature but not of it, the very point of contiguity between the natural order and the order of law; hence "By superstition of the neighbourhood, / The grass is cleared away" lest the stark exigencies of the law should be mitigated by natural process. The centrality of spot-ness here—migrating, subliminally, into the idea of spots of time—is even clearer in the 1805 version:

Faltering, and ignorant where I was, at length
I chanced to espy those characters inscribed
On the green sod: forthwith I left the spot.
(1805, 11.300–302)

In one sense the spot is an image with a continuum of images, just as the spots of time are salient memory representations within the vaguer continuum structured by a linear idea of time. But the text insists, with an emphasis as extraordinary as it is literal, on this spot as a signifier: characters, "monumental letters," or "writing" (1805). This it is which mediates the meaning of the spot, turning faltering confusion "forthwith" into panic and headlong flight. The order of law is inserted into the order of nature by means of writing. Precisely parallel to the point of contiguity between law and nature—that is, the idea of death and the logic of death for death—is the point of contiguity between image and signifier or symbol. We arrive, by no doubt too great a jump as yet, at the equation writing = death, or more exactly, the recognition of a signifier = the intimation of death.

Here we are greeted by a curious fact. In the first manuscript version we have, the characters that were to be given such prominence are unmentioned:

> A man, the murderer of his wife, was hung
> In irons, moulder'd was the gibbet mast,
> The bones were gone, the iron and the wood,
> Only a long green ridge of turf remained
> Whose shape was like a grave. I left the spot.

Evidently in revision (between 1802 and 1805) Wordsworth brushed up on the facts. He would have learned that the victim was a man and learned too, possibly for the first time, of the characters, and that they were still extant. (This is the kind of genetic detail that renders unacceptably naive that reading of The Prelude which would accept Wordsworth's myth of memory at face value and evade the origination of the memories in the present tense of a grown man.) In revision, the "long green ridge of turf . . . Whose shape was like a grave" turns into the portentous characters, which suggests that the representations of a secondary anxiety were being retrospectively superimposed upon the memory trace of a grave. If this is "association," it is deeper than what we usually mean by association, for the revision enables the poet Wordsworth to concentrate and perhaps to discover the emotional center of the memory. The element of panic enters the text with the appearance of the characters, as if they constituted the deep meaning of the grave, and not vice versa. At any rate, we have underlined in the very genesis of the passage a deep connection between death and the word.

Yet the point of the episode and its justification as a spot of time lies not in the epiphany of characters but in the subsequent vision:

> It was, in truth,
> An ordinary sight; but I should need
> Colours and words that are unknown to man,

> To paint the visionary dreariness
> Which, while I looked all round for my lost guide,
> Invested moorland waste, and naked pool,
> The beacon crowning the lone eminence,
> The female and her garments vexed and tossed
> By the strong wind.
>
> (12.253–61)

Things are invested with a "visionary" aspect as if in recompense for the prior fear; though for the boy it is a dubious consolation, for he must contend with "dreariness," an involuntary perceptional alienation from the "ordinary" (hence he doesn't think to hail the girl). This is a liminal state in which mediations have fallen away. The common that he ascends is "bare," the pool "naked," the moorland a "waste," and even the beacon crowns a "lonely Eminence" (1805). The features of the landscape by which he might expect to orient himself are remote, withdrawn in an unapproachable stasis. The girl, however, "more near" in more ways than one, is an image not of stasis but of difficulty, of forces locked in contrariety. There is a play on clothing beneath the surface: dreariness invests the landscape by divesting it until it is naked, just as the wind whips at the girl's garments. The girl proceeds "with difficult steps to force her way" against the visionary divestment which threatens her with the fate of the denuded, static landscape. As object ("outward sense") to the boy's mind she yet retains her motion and her humanizing garments against the involuntary, dehumanizing strength of that mind, and she thereby images the boy's own difficult struggle against his imagination.

How should the imagination—that is, the literal, perceptional imagination—come to have such withering strength? Both the intensity and the alienating effect of the imagination in its phase of lordship and mastery seem to derive from the terror that has gone before. We need to put the two halves of the spot of time back together. Vision occurs in flight from the characters and appears to realize the deathly intimations read in the characters. But the proportions of seeing to reading, of image to symbol, have been reversed. "A casual glance had shown them, and I fled": the briefest sight, surcharged with meaning, while visionary dreariness is drawn out seeing, twice rendered by the poet—as if there were indeed a hidden message threatening to emerge in the pool, the beacon, and the girl—which yet falls short of symbolic revelation. An extended seeing replaces reading in this flight; it is a "backward" displacement or regression from the order of symbol to that of image, and it functions to defend the ego against the death which has been signified. That death is displaced or projected (and thereby diffused) into the denuded landscape where the fixating spot is doubled as the naked pool and the beacon on the summit. The wind against which the girl—and by extension the boy—are struggling represents not death but the obscure power we have found inextricably associated with death, a power for which we have as yet no name. For in truth, as strange and indeed academic as it sounds, it is against the fact that things may come to signify that the boy is forcing his difficult way.

The uncontrollable intensity of the imagination is often rendered as a strong wind in *The Prelude*, as M. H. Abrams showed long ago. In the preamble, for example, the inner breeze is creative up to a certain point:

> For I, methought, while the sweet breath of Heaven
> Was blowing on my body, felt within
> A corresponding mild creative breeze,
> A vital breeze which travell'd gently on
> O'er things which it had made, and is become
> A tempest, a redundant energy
> Vexing its own creation.
>
> (1805, 1.41–47)

Here too is evidently a threshold after which the wind becomes de-creative, "vexing" (as with the garments of the girl) what has been brought to birth in perception. In composition as in reading, winds attend the threshold of the word, for wind is the image of the invisible, the representation of the peculiar power of signifying within the perceptional order of the imagination. In book 5 Wordsworth brings the liminal concept of the visionary into connection with the works of mighty poets:

> Visionary power
> Attends the motions of the viewless winds,
> Embodied in the mystery of words:
> There, darkness makes abode, and all the host
> Of shadowy things work endless changes,—there,
> As in a mansion like their proper home,
> Even forms and substances are circumfused
> By that transparent veil with light divine,
> And, through the turnings intricate of verse,
> Present themselves as objects recognised,
> In flashes, and with glory not their own.
>
> (5.595–605)

Wordsworth had a gift for phrasing that defies analysis. Power attends motions of winds which are embodied in a mystery: a series of quasi-metaphorical displacements away from words, compounded by indefinite reference ("there," "that transparent veil"). The passage is evoking the penumbra of words, the power inherent not in what they mean but in that they mean; or, in what they are, independent of their meaning—in an earlier language, the *how* and not the *what* of sublimity. When a "form" or a "substance" is taken up by a signifier, it receives a super-added power and a divine glory immanent in the circumfusing veil of the signifier. Power inheres not in the perceptual form but in language or symbolicity itself; we remember that the boy drank the visionary power listening to a language devoid of forms and substances ("by form / Or image unprofaned"),

> . . . notes that are
> The ghostly language of the ancient earth,
> Or make their dim abode in distant winds.
> (2.308–10)

But there is in "ghostly language" a ghost to be confronted; our spot of time has shown us that in the passage to the visionary power of signification lurks the thought of death. There, "darkness makes abode" and "shadowy things" as well as "light divine." In order to arrive "As in a mansion like their proper home," forms and substances must die out of the imaginary or perceptual order and into the symbolic order of verse. For the speaker or poet this passage appears to involve the intimation of sacrifice and the assumption of guilt.

In the next spot of time, the fact of guilt is explicitly focused in relation to the visionary moment. Wordsworth is remembering his vigil on a crag where he waited for a pair of horses to bear him home from school for the Christmas holidays:

> . . . 'twas a day
> Tempestuous, dark, and wild, and on the grass
> I sate half-sheltered by a naked wall;
> Upon my right hand couched a single sheep,
> Upon my left a blasted hawthorn stood;
> With those companions at my side, I watched,
> Straining my eyes intensely, as the mist
> Gave intermitting prospect of the copse
> And plain beneath.
> (12.297–305)

Before the holidays were over, his father was dead:

> The event,
> With all the sorrow that it brought, appeared
> A chastisement; and when I called to mind
> That day so lately past, when from the crag
> I looked in such anxiety of hope;

> With trite reflections of morality,
> Yet in the deepest passion, I bowed low
> To God, Who thus corrected my desires;
> And, afterwards, the wind and sleety rain,
> And all the business of the elements,
> The single sheep, and the one blasted tree,
> And the bleak music from that old stone wall,
> The noise of wood and water, and the mist
> That on the line of each of those two roads
> Advanced in such indisputable shapes;
> All these were kindred spectacles and sounds
> To which I oft repaired, and thence would drink,
> As at a fountain.
>
> (12.309–26)

There are several suggestions of dissonance in this retrospection. The salient features of the landscape are rehearsed twice, as in the Penrith passage, and the secondary emphasis is upon the features themselves rather than upon their incidental discovery in an ulterior seeing, a looking for a lost guide or a pair of horses. The mist, for example, is at first an interposed obstacle, giving "intermitting prospect of the copse / And plain beneath" on which the boy's expectant eyes are focused; when the memory is re-formed, the mist advances in "indisputable shapes," itself a signifier. More striking, however, is the dissonance surrounding the matter of guilt. If the "desires" corrected by God were simply the boy's eagerness to go home, it is at least odd that his father's death should be felt as a chastisement of that most natural and filial wish. For a boy of thirteen to feel ambivalent upon the occasion of his father's death is perfectly normal, and the ambivalence that may be presumed to be original has made its way into the phrasing—in the "anxiety of hope" and that curious uncertainty about the decorum of grief: "With trite reflections of morality, / Yet in the deepest passion, I bowed low / To God. . . ." We begin to suspect that there is more to those desires than the boy's wish to go home for Christmas.

Editor de Selincourt finds in the "indisputable shapes" of the mist an echo of Hamlet's confrontation with his father's ghost: "Thou com'st in such a questionable shape / That I will speak to thee." Hamlet means "a shape that can be questioned" as well as "an uncertain shape": in contrast on both counts, the shapes of Wordsworth's ghost-mist are "indisputable." Again we have the *how*—in a way that can't be questioned—but not the *what*: the liminal moment when the signifier appears, *apparently* without a signified. But could it be that Wordsworth on the crag had a premonition of his father's death, that this is the signified of those signifying shapes? In fact, he could not have known of his father's fatal illness while waiting to go home, but the first formation of this memory, in the very early *Vale of Esthwaite*, makes this very premonition explicit:

> Long, long, upon yon naked rock
> Alone, I bore the bitter shock;
> Long, long, my swimming eyes did roam
> For little Horse to bear me home,
> To bear me—what avails my tear?
> To sorrow o'er a Father's bier.
>
> (422–27)

Of course, we have no way of knowing what the boy on the crag felt, and I might add, no need to know. We have insisted all along that it is a question of "creative" retrospection, of memories formed at the time they seem merely to emerge. The whole theme of guilt may well be a "later" addition, a reworking of the original impression, as indeed the *Vale* text goes on to imply:

> Flow on, in vain thou hast not flow'd,
> But eased me of a heavy load;
> For much it gives my heart relief
> To pay the mighty debt of grief,
> With sighs repeated o'er and o'er,
> I mourn because I mourned no more.
>
> (428–33)

The ground of our speculation is but the firmer if we assume that the guilt—incurred by an unconscious desire for his father's death—is retrospectively associated, through the premonition, with visionary salience. It is as if that "indisputable" premonition, like the characters on the turf, were the cost of vision, the price of salience. At first, when he "called to mind / That day so lately past," he experienced not renovating power, but a feeling of guilt, so that he bowed low to God. It is only "afterwards" that the "kindred spectacles and sounds" come to be a source of power—after, that is, the power has been paid for by the ritual gestures of expiation and correction.

    For what is striking about this spot of time is not the presence in it of a commonplace oedipal ambivalence but the deeper evasion of the oedipal "correction." God ironically corrects the filial desire for reunion (to go home) by fulfilling the unconscious desire signified in the premonitory "indisputable shapes." Hence the guilt. More important, however, is the question, In what sense does Wordsworth stand corrected? Far from repenting—or repressing—the spectacles and sounds which are linked to his desires, Wordsworth repairs often to them, "and thence would drink / As at a fountain":

> . . . and on winter nights,
> Down to this very time, when storm and rain
> Beat on my roof, or, haply, at noon-day,
> While in a grove I walk, whose lofty trees,
> Laden with summer's thickest foliage, rock
> In a strong wind, some working of the spirit,
> Some inward agitations thence are brought.
> (12.326–32)

The inner or correspondent breeze has its source in a deep affiliation with a visionary moment whose ambivalent burden or message of death has been unconsciously repudiated even as it is consciously expiated. Hence the importance of his ritual chastisement; it covers (from himself) a deeper refusal to bow low. Hence, too, the division in his mind, which intends on the one hand "deepest passion" in its bowing low and yet is aware of the triteness and the ritual conventionality of the gesture. "I mourn *because* I mourned no more": as in the *Vale* text, grief is a "mighty debt"—something owed, not felt, or felt only because it is owed. Lest it seem too schematic to speak here of conscious and unconscious, we have in a draft Wordsworth's own intuitive attribution of the "working of the spirit" to an inner conflict, unconscious and unresolved:

> When in a grove I walk whose lofty trees
> Laden with all their summer foliage, rock
> High over head those workings of the mind
> Of source and tendency to me unknown,
> Some inward agitations thence are brought
> Efforts and struggles tempered and restrained
> By melancholy awe or pleasing fear.

The last line of the draft employs the very diction of the negative sublime in its third, or resolution, phase. But the "inward agitations" derive from a source, the locus of visionary power, which is prior to that resolution and in fact resists it, so that these agitations must be "tempered and re-strained" as by a God who awes and corrects.

We are now perhaps in need of drawing back and assuming a perspective from which the pattern exhibited in the spots of time can be seen in relief. Both spots of time locate the visionary—the phase in which the mind is lord and master—just "this side" of the order of the signifier ("characters," "indisputable shapes") in the liminal space where the signi-fier appears but is not yet fully—consciously—read. Yet the spatial metaphor may distract us; in so crucial a matter it is wise to guard against being traduced by the specious simplicity of a diagram. For the liminal space of the visionary is also a liminal moment, and a moment not before but *after* the threshold has been recrossed in retreat. In the first case, the flight from the word and the extraordinary seeing attending it are represented quite literally, though it is the figurative flight which we have now in view. (According to Freud, flight is the prototype of repression.) The signified of those characters—death—is repressed in this flight, but it thereupon reappears in the imaginary order, in the landscape as invested by "visionary dreariness." In the case of the holiday vigil, the flight is much subtler: it is both revealed and covered by the acceptance of a guilt for which the cause remains obscured and unacknowledged. This permits a return to the "kindred spectacles and sounds," as if the intimations of death with which they were imbued could be detached and exorcised through a ritualized guilt.

We may now return to our initial perplexity with some chance of enhanced understanding. How is it that the spots of time retain a "renovating virtue," a therapeutic efficacy? Not, it would appear, because they "give / Profoundest knowledge" of the mind's great power—that feature of them merely marks those "passages of life" in which the spirit is likely to be found lurking. The spots of time revive the mind because through them the ego returns, in retrospection, to the liminal place where "some working of the spirit, / Some inward agitations" still are active. It is true that the liminal place is the very locus of the visionary, but we have seen that visionary salience is itself a dialectical response to the order of symbol. The symbol—the image as symbol or signifier—is glimpsed, and the power of the subsequent visionary state depends upon the repression of the signified, which reappears, as by a profound logic or economy, in the protective domain of things seen. It follows that the reviving of the imaginative power which the spots of time effect depends upon the continued repression of the signified. If the "source and tendency" of those "workings of the mind" were to become known to Wordsworth, no "inward agitations," no "Efforts and struggles" could thence be brought; there would be no correspondent breeze answering the "strong wind" without. Both within themselves, as coherent memory-fantasies, and within the poem, as episodes in the project of recollection, the spots of time dramatize a saving resistance to the passage from image to symbol. This resistance *is* the imagination—a higher, "visionary" seeing whose very intensity, either as salience or as "redundant energy," occludes the symbol.

HAROLD BLOOM

The Scene of Instruction:
"Tintern Abbey"

I start with Nietzsche, as perhaps the least Wordsworthian of interpretative theorists. This is one of his note-book jottings, of 1855, urging a revisionary view of "memory":

> One must revise one's ideas about *memory*: here lies the chief temptation to assume a "soul," which, outside time, reproduces, recognizes, etc. But that which is experienced lives on "in the memory"; I cannot help it if it "comes back," the will is inactive in this case, as in the coming of any thought. Something happens of which I become conscious: now something similar comes—who called it? roused it?

Nietzsche demystifies and desubjectivizes memory; Wordsworth so mystified memory as to make of it the one great myth of his antimythological poetry.

I set against both this demystification and this spiritualization the vast expansion of the concept of memory that took place in Freud. The empirical model for memory, before Freud, was an easy target for Nietzsche's deconstructive energies, since memory was seen as a mechanically causal process, based upon the association of ideas. One idea associated itself with another pretty much as the motion of one entity affected another. But here is the philosopher Stuart Hampshire's perceptive brief summary of the conceptual change that Freud accomplished:

> For the simple machinery of the association of ideas, Freud substitutes complex activities of projection, introjection and identification in the

From *Poetry and Repression*. Copyright © 1976 by Yale University. Yale University Press, 1976.

solution of conflicts. The importance of this substitution, from the philosophical point of view, is just that these activities are represented as activities; and because they are so represented, the underlying motives of them can be investigated. Within this scheme, the question of "Why?" —the demand for an explanation in any particular case—does not call for a universally valid psychological law and a statement of initial conditions. Since these processes are represented as activities of mind, the question "Why" asks for a description of the situation or situations, and therefore of the given problem, to which these continuing activities were the solution adopted. The effect of the substitution of the active for the passive mood is that the subject is required to search in his memory for the past situation, as it survives in his mind, and to acknowledge or to disclaim its superimposition on the present.

One impulse that rises in me, as I read this lucid philosophical comment on Freud, is to remember Freud's remark that "The poets were there before me," since Hampshire's observation would be a perfectly commonplace and accurate enough description of the difference between a pre-Wordsworthian memory poem, like Gray's Eton Ode, and a poem like *Tintern Abbey*. The difference between Wordsworth and Freud is that while both greatly expanded the concept of memory, Wordsworth very nearly made it into a Kabbalistic hypostasis, a new *sefirah* or magical attribute of Divine Influence, while Freud set it overtly in the context of anxiety, repression, and defense. I revert to my analogical and antithetical principle; a composite trope and a composite defense are different faces of the same ratios of revision. "Memory," for Wordsworth, is a composite trope, and so in Wordsworth what is called memory, or treated as memory, is also a composite defense, a defense against time, decay, the loss of divinating power, and so finally a defense against death, whose other name is John Milton.

In *The Ego and the Id* (1927), Freud suggests as a model of our mental apparatus the vision of an organism floating in water. As the surface of this organism is molded, internally and externally, into differentiation, what results as a difference Freud called the "ego," the "ich." Beneath this surface, and going down to the depth of the organism, is what Freud called the "id," the *it*, a naming in which Freud ultimately followed Nietzsche. The model is complex and subtle, and I cannot give an adequate account of it here. But one feature of it is crucial as part of Freud's concept of memory. The ego is visualized as broadening out from a layer of memory-traces, called the preconscious. These memory-traces are defined as remnants of perceptions, and only through an accumulation of memory-traces is there a growth in consciousness.

A memory-trace is a very tricky notion, one that I myself do not understand, and while Freud doubtless understood it, he never explained it adequately. Freud's word is *Erinnerungsspur*, which could be interpreted psychologically *or* physiologically. Laplanche and Pontalis, the Lacanian authors of *The Language of Psychoanalysis*, do not help clarify this notion when they say that "memory-traces are deposited in different systems, and subsist permanently, but are only reactivated once they have been cathected," that is, invested with psychic energy. A trace that subsists permanently, while waiting for a heavy psychic investor to come along, is a vision of the mind that all great poetry, including Wordsworth's, refutes. Dr. Samuel Johnson, who darkly knew that the mind is above all a *ceaseless activity*, could have taught these current psychoanalytic linguistifiers a little more respect for the power of the mind over itself, as well as over nature and language. But Freud also, of course, knew what the great moral psychologists from Pascal and Montaigne to Dr. Johnson and Coleridge have known, which is that memory is active mind, always dangerous, always at work misreading the predicaments of consciousness. Here are Laplanche and Pontalis at their most hilarious, reducing Freud to a kind of Chaplin or Buster Keaton of the memory-machine:

> The memory-trace is simply a particular arrangement of facilitations [path-breakings], so organized that one route is followed in preference to another. The functioning of memory in this way might be compared to what is known as "memory" in the theory of cybernetic machines, which are built on the principle of binary oppositions.

Jacques Derrida, as usual, is a much more adequate and perceptive interpreter of the relation of memory to language in Freud. Derrida tells us that the psyche is a kind of text and that this text is constituted of what Derrida calls "written traces." Early Freud (1895) speaks of memory as if it is a composite trope rather like influence; memory is defined as "the capacity to be altered in a lasting way by events which occur only once." Derrida assimilates Freud to Nietzsche by finding "the real origin of memory and thus of the psyche in the difference between path-breakings" or sensory excitations as they encounter resistances in consciousness. What Derrida calls "the trace as memory" is the impalpable and invisible difference between two path-breaking forces impinging upon what becomes the individual mind. With Derrida's more complex and subtle Hiedeggerean notion of the *trace* proper, as opposed to Freud's memory-trace, I am not concerned here, because I wish to talk only about one text, Wordsworth's *Tintern Abbey*, and the intrusion of a concept of memory into the meaning of that poem. This concept is essentially Wordsworth's own, and can be illuminated by juxtaposition with Freud's, and with Derrida's brilliant exegesis of Freudian memory. But even the Wordsworthian concept of memory is very secondary to my aims in this discourse. I want to offer an antithetical reading of Wordsworth's *Tintern Abbey*, employing my map of misprision and some aspects of a larger scheme of what I have called the Scene of Instruction in chapter 3 of *A Map of Misreading*. In that scheme the study of a poem as misprision or a revisionary text is only the sixth and final phase of a complex attempt at complete interpretation, in which a text is fully related to a precursor text or texts.

I do not believe that Wordsworth meant this poem to be "about" memory; I think he intended what he called "restoration" to be the subject of the poem. He seems to have wanted a far more positive, hopeful, even celebratory poem than the one he actually wrote. As with the *Intimations* Ode, the poet desired to emphasize restitution, compensation, gain rather than loss. But his revisionary genius intended otherwise or, if we want to select Freudian terms, the defensive process of repression gave Wordsworth a very different poem than the one he set out to write. I am going to suggest that the Sublime tropes or strong hyperboles of *Tintern Abbey* work to repress the still-haunting presence of Milton's texts, particularly of the invocations to Books III and VII of *Paradise Lost*. Because of the preternatural strength of Wordsworth's unconsciously purposeful forgettings of Milton, the true subject of *Tintern Abbey* becomes memory rather than spiritual or imaginative renovation. Indeed, I will go so far as to argue not only that the meaning of *Tintern Abbey* is in its relationship to Milton's invocations, but that the poem becomes, despite itself, an invocation of Milton. Memory deals with absence, and the crucial or felt absence in *Tintern Abbey* is Milton's.

As with my antithetical account of Blake's *London*, which uncovered an opposition in that poem between prophetic voice and demonic writing, *Tintern Abbey* Kabbalized will show some similar patterns of a struggle between voicing and marking, and between hearing and seeing, a struggle in which visible traces usurp the hopeful murmur of prophetic voice. But Blake warred always against the bodily eye, and overtly aspired towards the status and function of the *nabi* or visionary orator. Wordsworth and Coleridge, as their better scholars have shown us, longed for a composite, originary sense that combined rather than opposed seeing and hearing. If memory-traces and their implicit metaphor of script usurp a greater dream in *Tintern Abbey*, then it is not so much the Hebraic dream of divine voice as it is the complex synaesthesia of a more culturally mixed idea of the poetic vocation. Thomas McFarland and M. H. Abrams have traced Coleridge's images of "A light in sound, a sound-like power in light" to the theosophist Boehme and the metaphysician Schelling, both of whom were aware of the more ultimate source of these images in Kabbalah. Like most Kabbalist images, these in turn go back to Neoplatonic speculative origins. Wordsworth's source for such images was invariably Coleridge, whose "conversation" poems provided an immediate model for *Tintern Abbey*. Yet we do not feel either Coleridge's presence or absence in the poem, for Coleridge induced in the much stronger Wordsworth no anxieties of poetic influence.

The joy of what they considered to be a fully active imagination expressed itself for both poets in a combined or synaesthetic sense of seeing-hearing. Wordsworth seems to have believed, quite literally, that he had retained this combined sense much later into childhood than most people do. The phenomenon is overtly an element in the *Intimations* Ode, and has little explicitly to do with *Tintern Abbey*. Yet *Tintern Abbey* is at once the most enigmatic and perhaps the most influential of modern poems. Among much else it begins that splendidly dismal tradition in which modern poems intend some merely ostensible subject, yet actually find their true subject in the anxiety of influence.

The most defiantly Wordsworthian of modern critics, Geoffrey Hartman, says that "in Wordsworth, it is always a sound or voice that must 'grow with thought,' as well as a person. As if when voice broke, identity itself were in danger of breaking." Hartman, commenting on the "Boy of Winander" fragment, asserts a remarkable freedom for Wordsworth from the burden of influence-anxiety. Though Hartman, in my judgment, idealizes Wordsworth, his formidable summary here is another antagonist that must be met:

> Now the one kind of echo missing from Wordsworth's poetry, or very carefully used when used at all, is the echo we call a literary allusion. The literary echo, in Wordsworth, is "reduced" to experience by a "cure of the ground"; and when it does occur it is so internalized that it points to the *phenomenology* of literary allusion. This grounding of allusion in experience—in the personal and mortal experience of time—has an unexpected result. Take away the play of allusion, the comforting ground of literary-historical texture, and you place the burden of responsiveness directly on the reader.

My first response to this is to marvel at the miracle of a cure of the ground so thorough that "literary-historical texture" has disappeared. Hazlitt spoke what he knew to be a relative truth when he said of Wordsworth's poetry that in it we *seem* to begin anew on a *tabula rasa* of poetry.

Hazlitt's relativism has become Hartman's absolutism, but then Hartman loves Wordsworth more than Hazlitt did, but then again Hazlitt had the mixed blessing of knowing Wordsworth personally. Hartman's true point is Wordsworth's characteristic *internalization* of allusion. Internalization is at once the great Wordsworthian resource and the great Wordsworthian disaster, and it is never enough to praise Wordsworth for a process in which he was indeed, as Keats saw, the great poetic inventor and, as Keats also saw, the great poetic villain; indeed as much a hero-villain, I would say, as his true precursor, Milton's Satan. In *The Borderers*, Milton's Satan is Oswald, but elsewhere in Wordsworth he becomes a much subtler and finer figure, the Solitary of *The Excursion*, and even finer, the really dangerous element in Wordsworth's own poetic ego, or what Blake would have called Wordsworth's own Spectre of Urthona, the anxiety-principle that usurps voice in all the great poems, and substitutes for voice various memorial inscriptions, various traces of a Miltonic anteriority.

Something richer and more mature in Wordsworth wins out over even this spectral blocking-agent in *The Prelude*, but I am uncertain as to who wins in the greatest and most influential of Wordsworth's shorter poems, the grand triad of *Resolution and Independence*, the *Intimations of Immortality* Ode, and *Tintern Abbey*. I myself love *Tintern Abbey* more than any other poem by Wordsworth, but the love is increasingly an uneasy one. I do not see how any poem could do more or do better; it dwarfs Yeats or Stevens when they write in the same mode. I suspect that *Tintern Abbey* is *the* modern poem proper, and that most good poems written in English since *Tintern Abbey* inescapably repeat, rewrite, or revise it. If there is something radically wrong with it, something radically self-deceptive, then this radical wrongness at last will not be seen as belonging to *Tintern Abbey* alone.

The language of *Tintern Abbey* centers upon the interplay of hearing and of seeing. To "hear" goes back to an Indo-European root (*ken*) which means to pay attention, watch, observe, beware, guard against, as well as to listen. To "see" goes back to a root (*sekw*) that means to perceive. *To hear is thus also, etymologically, to see, but to see is not necessarily to hear.* This etymological oddity holds, in a Kabbalistic kernel, the deepest anxiety of Wordsworth's poem, which is an anxiety about Wordsworth's relation to his precursor-of-precursors, that mortal god, John Milton. Of all Milton's poetic descendants, including even Blake, Wordsworth was the strongest, so strong indeed that we must face a dark truth. Wordsworth's greatest poem, *The Prelude*, was finished, in its essentials, a hundred and seventy years ago, and no subsequent poetry written in English can sustain a close comparison with it, no matter what fashionable criticism tries to tell us to the contrary. There is an Emersonian law of compensation in literary history as there is in any other history, including the life of each individual. Nietzsche and Emerson, more than any other theorists, understood that other artists must pay the price for too overwhelming an artist. Wordsworth, like Milton, both enriches and destroys his sons and daughters. Wordsworth is a less dramatic destroyer, because of the program of internalization that he carried out, but he may have been the greatest Tamerlane of the two.

Let me reduce my own hyperboles, which seem to have been rather unacceptable to my own profession, the scholars of poetic tradition. The problem of surpassing Wordsworth is the fairly absurd one of going beyond Wordsworth in the process of internalization. But what, in a poem, is internalization? I will compare two passages of poetry, and then ask which of these has gone further in the quest towards internalizing what we still like to call the imagination.

Here is the first:

> I am still completely happy.
> My resolve to win further I have
> Thrown out, and am charged by the thrill
> Of the sun coming up. Birds and trees, houses,
> These are but the stations for the new sign of being
> In me that is to close late, long
> After the sun has set and darkness come
> To the surrounding fields and hills.
> But if breath could kill, then there would not be
> Such an easy time of it, with men locked back there
> In the smokestacks and corruption of the city.
> Now as my questioning but admiring gaze expands
> To magnificent outposts, I am not so much at home
> With these memorabilia of vision as on a tour
> Of my remotest properties, and the eidolon
> Sinks into the effective "being" of each thing,
> Stump or shrub, and they carry me inside
> On motionless explorations of how dense a thing can be,
> How light, and these are finished before they have begun
> Leaving me refreshed and somehow younger.

This is the opening of John Ashbery's beautiful *Evening in the Country*, one of the most distinguished descendants of *Tintern Abbey*. Contrast it to the ancestral passage:

> . . . that blessed mood
> In which the burthen of the mystery,
> In which the heavy and the weary weight

Of all this unintelligible world,
Is lightened:—that serene and blessed mood,
In which the affections gently lead us on,—
Until, the breath of this corporeal frame
And even the motion of our human blood
Almost suspended, we are laid asleep
In body, and become a living soul:
While with an eye made quiet by the power
Of harmony, and the deep power of joy,
We see into the life of things.

I will revisit these lines later, as I attempt a full reading of the poem. Here I am concerned only with the poetry of the growing inner self. Whose poetic self is more inner, Ashbery's or Wordsworth's? Both poets are experiencing a blessed mood that is at work repairing a previous distress, and both poets are seeing into the life of things. But are there still things for them to see into? Can we distinguish, whether in Wordsworth, or Emerson, or in all of their mixed progeny, between internalization and solipsism? It is palpable, to me, that there is a touch more externality to the world of things in Ashbery's lines than there is in Wordsworth's. In Wordsworth's supreme moments, as in Emerson's, things become transparent, and the inner self expands until it introjects not less than everything, space and time included. At least Ashbery still knows and says "how dense a thing can be," however motionless or quiet the exploring eye of the poet may have become.

No one is going to manage, ever, to accomplish the delightful absurdity of writing the *history* of the perpetually growing inner self. This helps one to see why the phrase "the history of poetry" is, at best, an oxymoron. If a friend came to me and declared that he was about to embark upon a history of consciousness, then I would weep for him. But it *is* possible to write the more limited history of a few changes in historical psychology, which is what the Dutch psychiatrist J. H. Van den Berg admirably accomplished in a book called *Metabletica*, translated into English under the title of *The Changing Nature of Man*. It is also possible to work out some, at least, of the relationship between philosophy's struggles with the idea of solipsism, and literature's rather more desperate struggles with the same notion. A disputable but provocative book by a British literary scholar, A. D. Nuttall, has attempted just this, quite recently, under the title of *A Common Sky: Philosophy and the Literary Imagination.* Van den Berg does not discuss Wordsworth, but he centers upon Rousseau and upon Freud, both of them relevant to any account of Wordsworthian internalization. Nuttall does not like Wordsworth, whom he oddly compounds with Nietzsche, because to Nuttall the Wordsworthian innerness is essentially a solipsism. Here is a cento of Nuttall on Wordsworth:

Wordsworth remains a philosophically inarticulate member of the school of Locke. . . .

. . . Wordsworth is plainly bewildered. He is afraid that his insights are merely projections, hopes that they are telling him about external reality. But the important thing is that, whatever the final decision . . . the categories of his thought are Lockian. But Wordsworth, unlike Locke, has a distinctive psychology, a peculiar cast to his mind, and is therefore afraid, as Locke was not, that his ideas are not truly representative of the world. . . .

. . . It was almost inevitable that the slow progress of subjective isolation should have, as one of its psychological consequences, a compensatory obsession with the objective condition. The poet, inhabiting an increasingly mental world, grows hungry for "thinghood." For the Cartesian rationalist, articulate thought is the foundation of our confidence in reality. For Wordsworth one suspects that articulate thought and reality are in some way inimical to one another. This may partly be traced to Wordsworth's own strange spiritual development in which articulateness was attained at the very time when his grip on the object became infirm.

I think that Nuttall, in these comments, has mixed up two closely related but still separate states: highly self-conscious extreme subjectivity, and solipsistic fear that there is nothing beyond the subject. He is correct in observing Wordsworth's curious nostalgia for the object, which after all became the tradition that led from Wordsworth to Ruskin to Pater to Proust to Beckett, and also from Wordsworth to Emerson to Whitman to Stevens to Hart Crane to Ashbery. But this nostalgia for nature, this sense of the estrangement of things, finds a more convincing explanation in Van den Berg's formulations, who distinguishes the historical changes that caused the inner self to expand so alarmingly. Here is a rather full cento of passages from Van den Berg:

The theory of repression . . . is closely related to the thesis that there is sense in everything, which in turn implies that everything is past and there is nothing new. . . .

. . . The factualization of our understanding—the impoverishment of things to a uniform substantiality—and the disposal of everything that is not identical with this substantiality into the "inner self" are both parts of one occurrence. The inner self became necessary when contacts were devaluated. . . .

. . . A pure landscape, not just a backdrop for human actions: nature, nature as the middle ages did not know it, an exterior nature closed within itself and self-sufficient, an exterior from which the human element has, in principle, been removed entirely. It is things-in-their-farewell, and therefore is as moving as a farewell of our dearest. . . .

. . . The inner self, which in Rousseau's time was a simple, soberly filled, airy space, has become ever more crowded. Permanent residents have even been admitted; at first, only the parents, who could not stand being outside any longer, required shelter, finally it was the entire ancestry. . . . The inner life was like a haunted house. But what else could it be? It contained everything. Everything extraneous had been put into it. The entire history of mankind had to be the history of the individual. Everything that had previously belonged to everybody, everything that had been collective property and had existed in the world in which everyone lived, had to be contained by the individual. It could not be expected that things would be quiet in the inner self.

. . . Almost unnoticed—for everybody was watching the inner self—the landscape changed. It became estranged, and consequently it became visible. . . .

. . . the estrangement of things . . . brought Romanticism to ecstasy.

These passages are the background to Van den Berg's formidable critique of Freud, for Freud is viewed as the prophet of the complete inner self and the completely estranged exterior:

Ultimately the enigma of grief is the libido's inclination toward exterior things. What prompts the libido to leave the inner self? In 1914 Freud asked himself this question—the essential question of his psychology, and the essential question of the psychology of the twentieth century. His answer ended the process of interiorization. It is: the libido leaves the inner self when the inner self has become too full. In order to prevent it from being torn, the I has to aim itself on objects outside the self; [Freud]: ". . . ultimately man must begin to love in order not to get ill." So that is what it is. Objects are of importance only in an extreme urgency. Human beings, too. The grief over their death is the sighing of a too-far distended covering, the groaning of an overfilled self.

It is clear to me that Van den Berg's analysis, rather than Nuttall's, is precisely relevant to Wordsworthian internalization, including what Hartman calls the internalizing of the phenomenology of literary allusion. Nuttall sees Wordsworth as another victim of the hidden solipsism inherent in British empiricism from Locke onwards. Thus, the key-formula of British literary solipsism would be the most celebrated sentence in Locke's *Essay Concerning Human Understanding:*

Since the mind, in all its thoughts and reasonings, hath no other immediate object but its own ideas, which it alone knows or can contemplate, it is evident that our knowledge is only conversant about them.

There are poets who followed Locke, and perhaps an aspect of Wordsworth did, but this is to discount entirely the Coleridgean element in Wordsworth's vision of the imagination. Wordsworth's mind asserted, *contra* Locke and Nuttall, that it had also an immediate object in nature, or rather an answering subject in nature. But I think it correct nevertheless to say of Wordsworth what Van den Berg says of Rousseau, that the love of that answering subject, nature, is a love that distances and estranges nature. Internalization and estrangement are humanly one and the same process.

I turn to the text of *Tintern Abbey*, and to the interpretation of the poem as a Scene of Instruction. I begin with the last phase of this scene, the application to *Tintern Abbey* of my map of misprision, in order to uncover the pattern of revisionism in the poem, to trace the network of ratios, tropes, defenses, and images that are the final consequences of Wordsworth's struggle with Milton.

Let us map *Tintern Abbey* together. The poem consists of five verse-paragraphs, of which the first three (lines 1–57) form a single movement that alternates the ratios of *clinamen* and *tessera*. The fourth verse-paragraph is the second movement (lines 58–111) and goes from the ratio of *kenosis* to a *dæmonization* that brings in the Sublime. The fifth and final verse-paragraph is the third and last movement (lines 112–159), and alternates the ratios of *askesis* and *apophrades*. To abandon my own esoteric shorthand, lines 1–57 shuttle back and forth between dialectical images of presence and absence and representing images of parts and wholes. Lines 58–111 alternate images of fullness and emptiness, of gain and loss, with images of height and depth. Finally lines 112–159 move from inside/outside juxtapositions of the self and nature to an interplay of images of earliness and lateness. This is of course merely a very rough revisionary pattern, but it is there all right, in *Tintern Abbey* as in hundreds of good poems afterwards, down to the present day. What is unique to each poem is the peculiar balance between tropes and defenses in these ratio-structures or patterns-of-images. It will be seen that in *Tintern Abbey* the intricate dance of substitutions between tropes and defenses of limitation and of representation exposes the problematics of the Wordsworthian motives for so thoroughly internalizing literary allusion as to give the effect of the first thoroughly original stylistic breakthrough in British poetry since Milton's *Penseroso*. But the price of this breakthrough is considerable, and can be traced up the interpretative ladder of a scene or scheme of Instruction.

In *A Map of Misreading*, I cited Kierkegaard as the Theorist of the Scene of Instruction, this being the Kierkegaard of the *Philosophical Fragments*.

Perhaps I should have cited earlier Kierkegaard, particularly the remark-able brief essay in volume I of *Either/Or* called "The Rotation Method." In some sense, Wordsworth's *Tintern Abbey* is a "rotation method," and it may be illuminating to interpret Wordsworth's opening lines with a few Kierkegaardian excerpts firmly in mind:

> My method does not consist in change of field, but resembles the true rotation method in changing the crop and the mode of cultivation. Here we have at once the principle of limitation, the only saving principle in the world. The more you limit yourself, the more fertile you become in invention. . . .
>
> The more resourceful in changing the mode of cultivation one can be, the better; but every particular change will always come under the general categories of *remembering* and *forgetting*. Life in its entirety moves in these two currents, and hence it is essential to have them under control. It is impossible to live artistically before one has made up one's mind to abandon hope; for hope precludes self-limitation. . . . Hope was one of the dubious gifts of Prometheus; instead of giving men the foreknowledge of the immortals, he gave them hope.
>
> To forget—all men wish to forget, and when something unpleasant happens, they always say: Oh, that one might forget! But forgetting is an art that must be practiced beforehand. The ability to forget is con-ditioned upon the method of remembering. . . . The more poetically one remembers, the more easily one forgets; for remembering poetically is really only another expression for forgetting. . . .
>
> . . . Forgetting is the true expression for an ideal process of assimilation by which the experience is reduced to a sounding-board for the soul's own music. Nature is great because it has forgotten that it was chaos; but this thought is subject to revival at any time. . . .
>
> . . . Forgetting and remembering are thus identical arts.

We cannot apply Kierkegaard to the opening of *Tintern Abbey*, or Van den Berg to its close, without de-idealizing our view of this great poem. Wordsworthian criticism at its best has overidealized *Tintern Abbey*. To this day I would judge the account of *Tintern Abbey* in Hartman's early book, *The Unmediated Vision*, the strongest reading the poem has received, but it is a canonical reading, and an apocalyptically idealizing one. The experience that Wordsworth had five years before writing *Tintern Abbey* is indeed, as Kierkegaard said, "reduced to a sounding-board for the soul's own music," but Hartman follows Wordsworth's own idealization of his supposed experience. Who is right, Kierkegaard or Wordsworth? Shall we believe the poet in his own self-presentation?

Wordsworth's title for the poem is deceptively casual, or rather this immensely ambitious poem is deceptively left untitled, since the title proper is the throw-away, *Lines*. But the generations of readers who have canonized the poem have given it the mistitle that has stuck, *Tintern Abbey*, which is not even the place of the poem's composition and vision, but gratuitously happens to be the nearest landmark. The place *does* matter, at least to Wordsworth, and so does the time:

> Five years have passed; five summers, with the length
> Of five long winters! and again I hear
> These waters, rolling from their mountain-springs
> With a soft inland murmur. —Once again
> Do I behold these steep and lofty cliffs,
> That on a wild secluded scene impress
> Thoughts of more deep seclusion; and connect
> The landscape with the quiet of the sky.
> The day is come when I again repose
> Here, under this dark sycamore, and view
> These plots of cottage-ground, these orchard-tufts,
> Which at this season, with their unripe fruits,
> Are clad in one green hue, and lose themselves
> 'Mid groves and copses. Once again I see
> These hedge-rows, hardly hedge-rows, little lines
> Of sportive wood run wild: these pastoral farms,
> Green to the very door; and wreaths of smoke
> Sent up, in silence, from among the trees!
> With some uncertain notice, as might seem
> Of vagrant dwellers in the houseless woods,
> Or of some Hermit's cave, where by his fire
> The Hermit sits alone.

That exclamation point in the middle of line 2 indicates surprise that it should have been as long as five years since the poet's last visit, a surprise that must indicate an overwhelming sense of the past recaptured, of everything at first being or at least seeming much the same as it had been. Every interpreter has noted, surely correctly, the importance of the more comprehensive sense, hearing, having the primacy over sight, here at the outset of the poem. Wordsworth does not commence talking about the renewal of vision in any literal sense. Once again he hears *these* waters, with their murmur that to his ears oddly marks them as inland. Wordsworth attached a lame note to this "inland murmur" as to just how many miles in along the Wye you could still hear the sea. But his literalism misinterprets his own figuration, and his "soft murmur" prophesies his own *Intimations* Ode:

> Hence in a season of calm weather
> Though inland far we be,
> Our Souls have sight of that immortal sea
> Which brought us hither,

> Can in a moment travel thither,
> And see the children sport upon the shore,
> And hear the mighty waters rolling evermore.

Though twenty-eight years inland from his birth, Wordsworth hears again the particular intimation of his own immortality that he first heard five years before on the banks of the Wye. This is what the opening figuration of *Tintern Abbey* means, but hardly what it says, for the poem's opening *illusio* speaks of an absence in order to image a hoped-for presence. Rhetorically, Wordsworth emphasizes the length of the five years that have gone by, but his meaning is not in how long the absence of the "soft inland murmur" has been felt, but how vividly the presence of the hearing is revived. Psychologically, the phenomenon is the primary defense of reaction-formation, the opposition of a particular self-limitation to a repressed desire by manifesting the opposite of the desire. The desire repressed here is the ultimate, divinating desire to live forever, and the reaction-formation is the awareness, breaking through repression, of the passage of five long winters, despite the renewal of hearing and subsequently of vision.

Hartman and others have written usefully of the reciprocity that is renewed in the opening passage between Wordsworth's mind and the presence of nature. I want to emphasize instead the transition throughout the poem's first movement, up through line 57, from the initial reaction-formation or rhetorical irony to a psychic turning-against-the-self on Wordsworth's part, which as a figural representation is a remarkable instance of thinking-by-synecdoche. In line 42 of the poem, Wordsworth suddenly switches from "I" and "me" to "us" and "we." He is the part, and all people capable of imaginative experience become the whole. This plural subject is sustained until the magnificent "We see into the life of things" in line 49, after which in lines 50–57, Wordsworth is back to "I" and "me," to being a solitary or mutilated part of a universal whole, and a note of the vicissitudes of instinct, of psychic reversal, enters into the text again. This passage into and out of the universal is determined, in my interpretation, by the poem's largely hidden, revisionary struggle with two great precursor-texts, the invocations to Books III and VII of *Paradise Lost*. I want now to review the first fifty-seven lines of *Tintern Abbey* in the particular context of poetic misprision, of Wordsworth's relation to Milton, which centers upon the curiously placed figuration of the Hermit.

Hartman relates the Hermit of *Tintern Abbey* to the Leech Gatherer of *Resolution and Independence* and both to the vision and voice of St. John in Revelation. I would use Hartman's own description of the Hermit to suggest a more radical and poetically dangerous identification, in which the Hermit stands, through the fixation of a primal repression, for the blind contemplative Milton of the great invocations. Here is Hartman's account of the Hermit:

> The Hermit of *Tintern Abbey* is an image of transcendence: he sits fixed by his fire, the symbol, probably, for the pure or imageless vision. . . .
>   . . . the Hermit appears, fixed near his fire, freed in his perception from the forms of the external world, a relic of eternity and prophet of the immortal sea's return.

Milton's presentation of himself, in his maturity, is certainly not as a Hermit, I would admit. But the Miltonic Solitary or *Penseroso*, the true start for Wordsworth as Pilgrim and Wanderer, appears at the close of *Il Penseroso* as a Hermit. This Hermit first *hears* an immortal music and only then has a vision of heaven. But the dialectic of Milton's presence and absence begins earlier in *Tintern Abbey* than in the epiphany of the Hermit, and continues long after the vision of the Hermit has faded.

Hartman does not view the traces, hidden and visible, of Milton in *Tintern Abbey* as evidence of Wordsworth's anxiety, but rather of his strength. Hartman does not overestimate the strength, for it is indeed beyond estimation, but he discounts the anxiety that pervades the poem, an anxiety that mixes worries about imaginative priority with more overt worries about the continuity of imagination between the younger and the older Wordsworth. But to discount the anxiety of influence is to commit oneself to the idealizing process that is canonization, and that leads to canonical misreading, so that strong readers become weaker than they need be. Here is Leslie Brisman, very much in Hartman's tradition, writing of the Milton-Wordsworth influence-relation in his sensitive and brilliant book, *Milton's Poetry of Choice and Its Romantic Heirs*:

> Throughout *The Prelude,* Wordsworth labors to create moments where an arrest of time at the "uncreated" opens into a sense of the re-created, of imaginative alternatives imagined anew. . . . But in expressing a longing for a voice like that of nature, Wordsworth achieves a moment of voice: "Spring returns,— / I saw the Spring return." Appealing for poetic voice in the invocation to *Paradise Lost,* Book III, Milton also expressed the failure of voice when he acknowledged that the seasons return, "but not to me returns / Day." Wordsworth cannot be said to echo Milton—"spring" is just the word for which Milton could not at that moment find voice. But Wordsworth has the power of sight, the power of relationship with nature, and can gather from that relationship the voice with which to proclaim, and rest on the claim, "Spring returns,— / I saw the Spring return." The return of the word "Spring" makes poetry participate in the renewal, taking on the authority of the natural world.

This seems to me a beautiful idealism, but sadly counter to the truths and sorrows of poetic misprision, and particularly to the sorrowful truth of Wordsworth's deep anxieties as to whether his power of relationship with nature can compensate him for his failures to rise to as much as he could have risen of Milton's more antithetical visionary power. For Wordsworth as well as Milton knows that poetry cannot take on the authority of the natural world, but must assault the supposed priority of the natural object over the trope. The old paradoxes of poetic influence are at work here; Brisman shows us Wordsworth consciously, overtly alluding to the Invocation of Book III. I will proceed now to show Wordsworth unconsciously, repressively alluding to the same invocation in *Tintern Abbey*, with this repression in turn leading to a greater, more daemonic, precisely Sublime repressive alluding to the invocation to Book VII of *Paradise Lost.*

Book III of *Paradise Lost* begins by hailing the Holy Light. Milton speaks of himself as revisiting the Light, and of hearing again the "warbling flow" of Divine waters. But Milton is like the nightingale, and sings darkling. Seasons return, but not to Milton, for the Day does not return. Milton therefore prays to the "Celestial light" to purge and disperse all mist from his mind, that he may see and tell of invisible things. Lines 9–18 of *Tintern Abbey* are a misprision or reversed epiphany of this Miltonic passage, and are resumed in the opening lines of the *Intimations* Ode, where the "Celestial light" is absent though all the glories of nature are present. For Wordsworth, unlike Milton, "the day is come," and the season is seasonally bestowing its fruits to the seeing eyes. The mist that Milton prays be purged from his mind is sent up, to Wordsworth's sight, from the fire of the Hermit's cave. And if all this transposition seems far-fetched, then examine the very strangely phrased opening of the poem's very next verse-paragraph:

> These beauteous forms,
> Through a long absence, have not been to me
> As is a landscape to a blind man's eye:

Need we question who this blind man is?

Let us, for now, pass rapidly over the great second movement of the poem (lines 58–111), concentrating in it only upon the major interplay between tropes and defenses. There are a series of metonymic reductions—thought half-extinguished to gleams, recognitions to dimness and faintness, joys and raptures to aches and dizziness. This emptying-out psychically is less a regression or even an undoing than it is an isolation—the reduction from fullness to emptiness is a loss of context. The enor-

mous restitution for this loss is in the magnificent series of hyperboles that
dominate lines 93–111.

> And I have felt
> A presence that disturbs me with the joy
> Of elevated thoughts; a sense sublime
> Of something far more deeply interfused,
> Whose dwelling is the light of setting suns,
> And the round ocean and the living air,
> And the blue sky, and in the mind of man:
> A motion and a spirit, that impels
> All thinking things, all objects of all thought,
> And rolls through all things. Therefore am I still
> A lover of the meadows and the woods,
> And mountains; and of all that we behold
> From this green earth; of all the mighty world
> Of eye, and ear,—both what they half create
> And what perceive; well pleased to recognize
> In nature and the language of the sense
> The anchor of my purest thoughts, the nurse,
> The guide, the guardian of my heart, and soul
> Of all my moral being.

   If an antithetical criticism of poetry is in any way useful, then it
must illuminate this major instance of the Sublime. If the Sublime depends upon repression, as I insist it does, then where shall we find repression in these remarkably expressive and emphatic lines? How can there be
meaningful repression where so much emerges, where it seems surely that
Wordsworth must be having his whole say, must be bringing his whole soul
into activity?
   I would reply to these questions by indicating how problematic this
passage is, and how deeply a repressed element is at work in it. Despite
the hyperbolic language, Wordsworth makes only a measured assertion of
the power of his mind over the universe of sense, and also over language.
The hyperboles make it difficult for us to realize, at first, how guarded the
passage is. The poet's thoughts are touched to sublimity by a presence that
dwells in nature and in the mind, but is identified with neither. The
monistic presence is clearly more allied to Hebrew than to Greek thought,
but this pervasive motion and spirit is not identified with the Hebrew-
Christian *ruach,* or breath-of-Jehovah. And though this presence/motion/
spirit appears to be monistic in its aims, the poet stops well short of
asserting that it reconciles subject and object. It impels both, it rolls both
through things and through the poet's mind, but it does not abolish the
differences between them. Nor is the poet's reaction to the spirit what we

might expect, for instead of declaring his love for or worship of the spirit, he proclaims instead the continuity of his love for natural sights and sounds. Having invoked directly his eye and his ear, he makes, even more surprisingly, a deep reservation about his own perpetual powers, or rather an almost hyperbolical admission of limitation. The mighty world of eye and ear is not a balance of creation and of perception, but of half-creation and full-perception. Having acknowledged such a shading of imagination, it is no surprise that Wordsworth should then be happy to recognize anchor, nurse, guide, and guardian in powers not his own—in nature and the language of the self.

What *is* being repressed here is Wordsworth's extraordinary pride in the strength of his own imaginings, his preternatural self-reliance, as we find it, say, in the verse "Prospectus" to *The Excursion* or in Book XIV of *The Prelude.* An unconsciously purposeful forgetting is at work in the depths of Wordsworth's own spirit, and what it forgets is a ferocity of autonomy and strength unequalled in British poetry since Milton. Are these the accents of one whose eye and ear only half-create?

> For I must tread on shadowy ground, must sink
> Deep—and, aloft ascending, breathe in worlds
> To which the heaven of heavens is but a veil.
> All strength—all terror, single or in bands,
> That ever was put forth in personal form—
> Jehovah—with his thunder, and the choir
> Of shouting Angels, and the empyreal thrones—
> I pass them unalarmed. Not Chaos, not
> The darkest pit of lowest Erebus,
> Nor aught of blinder vacancy, scooped out
> By help of dreams—can breed such fear and awe
> As fall upon us often when we look
> Into our Minds, into the Mind of Man—
> My haunt, and the main region of my song.

That is Wordsworth, taking on Jehovah and Milton together, only a few months before writing *Tintern Abbey.* That is not a poet whose eye and ear "half-create." *Power* is being repressed in *Tintern Abbey,* a power so antithetical that it could tear the poet loose from nature, and take him into a world of his own, restituting him for the defense of self-isolation by isolating him yet more sublimely. Wordsworth defends himself against his own strength through repression, and like all strong poets he learns to call that repression the Sublime.

What are we to do with the phrase "half-create"? Can we keep memory out of it? I think not. For you cannot have repression without *remembering to forget*, and the price of repression in *Tintern Abbey* is that memory largely usurps the role of subject in the poem. But memory of what? I return to an earlier formula in this discourse—there is a struggle in *Tintern Abbey* between voicing and marking, in which Wordsworth wants to rely upon voice and the memory of voice, and somewhat fears relying upon sight and the memory of sight. There is a hidden but quite definite *fear of writing* in *Tintern Abbey*, or perhaps rather a fear of being delivered up to a potential fear of writing.

It is in Dorothy's voice that Wordsworth first recaptures his own former language, and only then does he read his own lost ecstasies in the shooting lights of her wild eyes. All through the poem, the poet says he is being *taught*, indeed he explicitly affirms that he has returned to a Scene of Instruction. But it becomes clearer as the poem proceeds that he wants to be taught or retaught primarily through the ear (as the later Milton was), though he knows that this is not really possible, since the eye is the most despotic of our senses. *And Nature will not stop writing*, though he would prefer her to keep to oral composition. For consider the vocabulary of the poem: it opens with a murmur, but then nature begins to write when the cliffs *impress* thoughts upon the scene, and when they connect landscape and sky. Whatever the source of the Hermit's fire, the silent wreaths of smoke are also a writing, and so are the beauteous forms that have been held as memory-traces. Wordsworth, like his scholarly disciple, Hartman, prefers the after-image to the spoken-trace, but his own poem keeps forcing him to read nature and not just to hear her. The world is not intelligible without writing, not even the natural world, and this is a sorrow to Wordsworth. Though his eye is chastened and made quiet by a power of sound, he still is constrained to say not that he *hears* the life of things, but that he *sees* into them. This pattern persists throughout the poem; the gleams and dim recognitions are visual, and when he does *look* on nature, in his mature phase, he *hears* loss, however beautifully, in "the still, sad music of humanity." But I have taken us now to the last dialectical movement of the poem, an alternation between metaphor and transumption, and I want to pause to brood on image-patterns before returning to the opposition between sight and sound.

The surprisingly beautiful passage from lines 134 through 146 juxtaposes nature as a benign *outside* force with Dorothy as a benign *inside* presence, but as always with the perspectivism of metaphor, Nature and Dorothy are taken further apart rather than being brought closer together by the juxtaposition. But the remarkable metaleptic reversals of lateness for earliness and earliness for lateness, which follow, give a much more powerful and convincing rhetorical illusion:

> nor, perchance—
> If I should be where I no more can hear
> Thy voice, nor catch from thy wild eyes these gleams
> Of past existence—wilt thou then forget
> That on the banks of this delightful stream
> We stood together

Those gleams are technically the metonymy of a metonymy—they trope upon an earlier trope in the poem, and so work as a trope-reversing trope. This allows Wordsworth a proleptic representation of his own death, and also of a kind of survival through the surrogate of Dorothy. I do not think this is literal death, despite Wordsworth's apparent intention, but the figural and much-feared death of the poetic imagination. The power of Miltonic transumption is worked again; defensively, Wordsworth introjects the past, projects the future except as a world for Dorothy, and utterly destroys the present moment, the living time in which he no longer stands. His gain in all this troping or defending is palpable; it is crucial to consider his loss, which will bring us back to memory, to writing opposing voicing, and at last to Milton again, and with Milton to the poem's full-scale staging of a Scene of Instruction.

Wordsworth's wishful prophecy for his sister would make her mind "a mansion for all lovely forms" and her memory "a dwelling-place / For all sweet sounds and harmonies." Because of the direct contrast the poet enforces between an earlier phase of "wild ecstasies" and a supposedly more "mature" one of "sober coloring" of the close of the *Intimations* Ode, there is something about that "mansion" and that "dwelling-place" that makes the reader a little uneasy. The mansion is a touch like a museum, and the dwelling-place a kind of tape- or record-library. But, setting this uneasiness aside, a curious preference seems to be shown here for "memory" over the "mind," since the preferred sensory impressions are harbored in "memory." Wordsworth of course, unlike Blake, made no sharp distinction between memory and poetry as modes of thought, but we must question still why *Tintern Abbey*, as a poem, ends with so emphatic an emphasis upon memory. Three times Wordsworth repeats his anxious exhortation to his sister, whom he loved and was always to love far more intensely than anyone else (with of course the single exception, always, of himself):

> oh! then,
> If solitude, or fear, or pain, or grief,
> Should be thy portion, with what healing thoughts
> Of tender joy wilt thou remember me,
> And these my exhortations! Nor, perchance—

If I should be where I no more can hear
Thy voice, nor catch from thy wild eyes these gleams
Of past existence—wilt thou then forget
That on the banks of this delightful stream
We stood together; and that I, so long
A worshipper of Nature, hither came
Unwearied in that service: rather say
With warmer love—oh! with far deeper zeal
Of holier love. Nor wilt thou then forget,
That after many wanderings, many years
Of absence, these steep woods and lofty cliffs,
And this green pastoral landscape, were to me
More dear, both for themselves and for thy sake!

I think we learn in time, however much we love this poem, that we must read the last line with four words added: "More dear, both for themselves and for thy sake, and for my sake!" I am not attacking this superb poem, but I wish to acknowledge two very different readings or misreadings of the poem, the powerfully revisionist or deconstructive one implied by Paul de Man, in which the whole poem is an *aporia*, an "uncertain notice" like the smoke sent up among the trees, or the powerfully canonical one, in which Keats pioneered and which culminates in Hartman's *The Unmediated Vision*. Is *Tintern Abbey* an *aporia*, or is it the prolepsis of a dark passage, a major internalization of Milton's *agon* with tradition? Or is it, as an antithetical reading or misreading would seem to tell us, a very great visionary lie, not as much a myth of memory as it is a utilization of memory as a lie against time? Actually or potentially, these are all strong misreadings, and they may not differ from one another as much as they would like to, though clearly they also cannot be reconciled. Which of the three readings/misreadings would cost us too much of the poem's strength? Or to say it in more Nietzschean terms, of these three errors, these three composite tropes, which is the most necessary error?

Why, mine of course, though of the three it is the one I like the least, because it increases the problematics-of-loss in the poem. Memory, in *Tintern Abbey*, attempts to become a trope and/or defense that overcomes time, which means that memory, going bad, would fall into the realm of paranoia, but working properly would project or spit-out Wordsworth's fears of the future. I think we must praise Wordsworth, almost always, as a poet so strong that he does make his defenses work, a strength in which we could contrast him, most favorably, to a poet like Eliot, whose *Gerontion* is a curious compound of *Tintern Abbey* gone bad, and one of *Tintern Abbey*'s stronger descendants, Tennyson's *Tithonus*. Eliot is a poet whose poems, with some exceptions, tend to become weaker rather than stronger, the more provocatively they trope, defensively, against the burden of anteriority. Wordsworth also deforms himself, or rather his poem-as-self, but in him the deformation has a power so immense that after one hundred and seventy-five years it has not stopped surprising us.

Why is Wordsworth so afraid of time in *Tintern Abbey*? Surely it *is* time that is the hidden reference in the enigmatic: "more like a man / Flying from something that he dreads than one / Who sought the thing he loved." Yet Wordsworth's dread of mortality impresses us because more than any poet's, at least since the Milton of *Lycidas*, it seems to turn upon the magnificent, primal poetic urge for *divination*, in the complex sense best defined by Vico, the poet's apotropaic concern for his own immortality. Milton and Wordsworth alike feared premature death, "premature" meaning before their great epics had been written.

On an antithetical reading, *Tintern Abbey* is a Scene of Instruction in which the poet brings a Sublime response to a place or state of heightened demand, but the genius of the state counts for more than the genius of place, which means that Milton counts for more than nature does, both here and in *The Prelude*. It is Milton whose hidden presence in the poem makes the heightened demand that forces Wordsworth into the profoundly ambivalent defensive trope of memory. Renovation, or "tranquil restoration" as the text terms it, is only a mystification, a mask for the real concern of the poem. The Hermit is the synecdoche for Milton's hiddenness, and so for Milton's triumphant blindness towards anteriority. To see the writing or marking of nature is to see prophetically one's own absence or imaginative death. To see the "uncertain notice" of the Hermit's presence is to be disturbed into sublimity by way of repressing the mighty force of remembering Milton's sublimity, particularly in the Creation of *Paradise Lost*, Book VII, which haunts every Wordsworthian account of the subject- and object-worlds approaching one another again.

Wordsworth, where he is most self-deceiving, remains so strong that the self-deception finally does not matter. For no other poet since Milton holds Milton off so triumphantly, without even always knowing that he is engaged in a wrestling-match. The greatness of *Tintern Abbey*, no matter what the necessity is or is not of any particular strong misreading of it, is assured by its paradoxical triumph over its own hidden subject of memory. *Our* memory of the poem, any of our memories, is finally not a memory of nature's marking nor of Milton's writing, but of *hearing again*, with Wordsworth, "These waters, rolling from their mountain-springs / With a soft inland murmur." Though he was far inland, too far really from the oceanic autonomy he craved, his literally incredible strength of misprision rescued him, nearly intact, from a Scene of Instruction that had destroyed Collins, and partly malformed Blake. It is the peculiar and extravagant greatness of Wordsworth that only he supplanted Milton as the tutelary genius of the Scene of Instruction, and it is the scandal of modern poetry that no one, not even Yeats or Stevens, in turn has supplanted Wordsworth. The Hermit of *Tintern Abbey* is Milton, but the Hermit in *Notes toward a Supreme Fiction* is William Wordsworth, even if Wallace Stevens repressed his memory of who it was:

> That sends us back to the first idea, the quick
> Of this invention; and yet so poisonous
>
> Are the ravishments of truth, so fatal to
> The truth itself, the first idea becomes
> The hermit in a poet's metaphors,
>
> Who comes and goes and comes and goes all day.

FRANCES FERGUSON

The "Immortality Ode"

The irregular ode had served as a vehicle for ecstasy in the Miltonic example of standing outside of a particular time, as in the late eighteenth-century example of contemplating the contents of the mind as projected birth and personifications (Collins's "Ode on the Passions," "Ode to Fear"). In Wordsworth's Ode, however, the ecstasy is that of the mind standing outside of itself—without any firm commitment to any inconceivable conception other than its consciousness or itself. For the birth of the god which Wordsworth celebrates is his, and anyman's, rather than the birth of Christ or the hypostasized figures of subjectivity taken as objects. If the Great Ode is traditionally a form which revels in an ecstatic ascent "from earth to heaven," Wordsworth's ecstasy of contemplation traces the descent to earth of the god who is man.

The first two stanzas, in fact, provide a miniature myth of history within the life of the individual. For, with characteristic Wordsworthian suppression of the explicitly iconic, their images move from the pagan to the Judeo-Christian. De Selincourt indicates in his notes that Wordsworth's first lines are "both verbally and metrically reminiscent" of Coleridge's "Mad Monk"—"There was a time when earth, and sea, and skies, / The bright green vale, and forest's dark recess, / With all things, lay before mine eyes / In steady loveliness." And a comparison of Wordsworth's lines with Coleridge's is instructive in locating the procedure of Wordsworth's first stanza. For while Coleridge immediately gestures toward as much of the universe as a man can see (and then proceeds to narrow his scope), Wordsworth begins with a reconstruction of the classi-

From *Wordsworth: Language as Counter-Spirit.* Copyright © 1977 by Yale University. Yale University Press, 1977.

cal *locus amoenus,* and thus encloses a space which then begins to fit all of the world to itself ("There was a time when meadow, grove, and stream, / The earth, and every common sight . . ."). As Curtius describes the *locus amoenus* (or pleasance), it is "a beautiful, shaded natural site," the "minimum ingredients" of which "comprise a tree (or several trees), a meadow, and a spring or brook." And the opening lines of the "Immortality Ode" present a *locus amoenus* which is no more than minimal, a shorthand sketch rather than a description. Although it incorporates more territory in the second line, the vestiges of the *locus amoenus* remain to bracket both space and time against the postlapsarian world of flux.

> There was a time when meadow, grove, and stream,
> The earth, and every common sight,
>> To me did seem
>> Apparelled in celestial light,
> The glory and the freshness of a dream.

Thus, instead of simply remembering an acceptance of the world which the poet can no longer maintain, the passage recalls a myth which is both personal and conventional, the image of garden-as-paradise which seems to merge man and nature so thoroughly that neither empiricism nor idealism is an appropriate description of relationship. The force of his plaint—"The things which I have seen I now can see no more"—rests upon temporal rather than spatial dislocation. Moreover, it is a dislocation which describes a personal predicament with gestures toward the predicament of the race. For the line, "It is not now as it hath been of yore" comes to rest on that archaistic "yore" both to emphasize the speaker's sense of remoteness from those past days of "celestial light" and to recall the romance storyteller's distancing formula, "In days of yore," which introduced the incredible to listeners by reminding them that the way men are now is radically different from the way men were long ago. And in seeing the history of the race in his own history, the poet's hymn to himself (and to other individual men) as a god bringing celestial light already moves precariously close to the fall of man in the fall of Adam.

The poem begins with a paradise which could be pagan as easily as Judeo-Christian, but the opening lines of the second stanza enumerate images which have such marked resonance in the Judeo-Christian tradition—or the primer tradition—that their apparently nonsymbolic quality here is suspicious:

> The Rainbow comes and goes,
> And lovely is the Rose,
> The moon doth with delight
> Look round her when the heavens are bare.

The catalogue is so perfunctory as to suggest querulousness or impatience and the refusal to assimilate the items of the catalogue appears as an almost willful suppression of significance. It is as though the poet were countering—and banishing—his recollections of the rainbow as God's covenant with man, of the rose as a symbol of the heavenly paradise, of the trackings of the moon in Isaiah and Job. And the heavy use of capitals in the first three lines of the stanza (when no other lines of the first two stanzas have words beginning with capitals except in the first position in the line) only heightens the awareness of the poet's suppressive diffidence towards these symbols which struggle for a voice. For if the "description" of nature in the first stanza yields a world garden which is set aside as purely mythic, the description of the second yields images which are not content to remain submerged in nature—to be taken as significant or insignificant as one chooses. These images lay claim to supranatural meaning, which is overridden by the nay-saying device of pure iteration. Yet they become forms which are letters rather than spirits, as the final lines of the stanza come as a judgment on them in which the poet can see them and still affirm "But yet I know, where'er I go, / That there hath past away a glory from the earth."

These first two stanzas occur in a time lapse—a temporal vacancy that registers the memory of a "time when" and that marks time in only the most cursory way. Yet, suddenly, the Ode focuses upon a point, "now," which extends itself within the confines of particularity.

> Now, while the birds thus sing a joyous song,
>   And while the young lambs bound
>   As to the tabor's sound,
> To me alone there came a thought of grief:
> A timely utterance gave that thought relief,
>   And I again am strong.

"Now" and "I alone" become expansive points—incorporating several turns in time and "their perception" as well as the poet's. If the birds sing and the lambs bound, the poet does not merely perceive them but also their perception of the world on this May morning. And the curious intrusion of the lambs bounding "As to the tabor's sound" turns the poet's earlier rejection of mythic explanations back on itself: the thought of the ancient instruments provoking the lambs' dance justifies a sympathetic recognition of the reasons why the myths were constructed, and the will to banish ancient error virtually disappears. In fact, that fierce clear-sightedness comes to seem a new evasion, and what had been a demystifying knowledge in the first two stanzas is immediately trivialized, summed up as "a thought of grief" for which the preceding stanzas were merely a purgative. Yet the enthusiasm of the poet's new tack is one of almost insistent excess—suggesting that, like a particularly severe thunderstorm, it will be over soon. For the poet is accepting a specious mediation here; while the objects of nature did not evidence enough celestial light to convince him of Celestial Light, his sense of the music that they hear now becomes a token of an unheard "celestial" music—like the music of the spheres. An imputed "something else" that they hear hovers beyond what the poet hears, and the assertions that he hears bear the traces of the optative: if he can conjure them into enough of their plain song, he may hear the song behind their song.

The difficulty of this movement is that sound, like sight in the first two stanzas, is only a medium of perception rather than a decisive testimony for the inevitable satisfactoriness of this world or any other. Thus, even when the two senses work in tandem in the fourth stanza, the poet begins to "hear" sights (like the babe leaping up on his mother's arm) which finally appear to open, to discover a world of sight and sound behind them. But this brave new world is the "wrong" one, full of sights which speak of vacancy.

> I hear, I hear, with joy I hear!
> —But there's a Tree, of many, one,
> A single Field which I have looked upon,
> Both of them speak of something that is gone:
> The Pansy at my feet
> Doth the same tale repeat:
> Whither is fled the visionary gleam?
> Where is it now, the glory and the dream?
> (50–57)

The tree, field, and pansy almost constitute a parodically attenuated counter image to the already attenuated *locus amoenus* of stanza one. But the escalation into mythicizing capitals which appeared fleetingly in the second stanza and settled into the poem with the third provides these simple natural objects with a residue of ideality which the initial *locus amoenus* lacked. It is as though these are Platonic ideal forms which had once been imbedded in the ground, only to spring out of sight and reach as the gravity of human attentiveness gradually ceased to bind them to the earth. And the pansy itself bears witness to the peculiarity of the process. Although the tree and the field exist as memories of the former fusion between mind and the objects of its contemplation, the pansy at the poet's feet in the present stands tied to earth as the physical incarnation of its etymological source—*pensée*. Yet the very fragility of the flower suggests the evanescence of this identification: if tree and field have not remained, how can the flower? And its questioning bespeaks the erosion of the frail union of pansy-*pensée* as it registers in the present the inevitability of its own passing.

Although there might seem to be some elevation for the pansy as a natural object when it is personified and given a speaking voice, the movement of the precarious identification between flower and thought ultimately redounds to disclose the alienation of the mind from itself, the inability of thought in the present to imagine fully the thoughts of the past. Thus, what began in the Ode as a problem of metaphysics—the relation of the poet to nature—has become a problem of memory, in the full Wordsworthian extension of that term. And the apparent literalness of the pansy hovers over and masks the abyss of *pensée* in the memory, as if to put an idiot question to the Cartesian "cogito, ergo sum." For at no point in the poem has Wordsworth questioned the ontology of nature, while the multiplicity of stances toward nature issue in the ultimate problem of the memory: if human ontology is grounded in thought, what is the ontology of thought?

The ascent of this human god in a May celebration of his nativity thus becomes an inquiry into the possibility of the very process upon which the Ode rests—the mind's attempt at relationship in standing outside of its own past thoughts. Perhaps the project of seeking a reflective vision of thought in its pastness is a self-dooming one, a process which erodes the objective status of remembered thought so thoroughly that the reflection itself seems to be suspended over pure nullity. Precisely this concern governs Wordsworth's meditation upon one of the "spots of time" in Book XII of *The Prelude:*

> The days gone by
> Return upon me almost from the dawn
> Of life: the hiding-places of man's power
> Open; I would approach them, but they close.
> I see by glimpses now; when age comes on,
> May scarcely see at all; and I would give,
> While yet we may, as far as words can give,
> Substance and life to what I feel, enshrining,
> Such is my hope, the spirit of the Past,
> For future restoration.
>
> (XII, 277–86)

And despite the philosophical authority which the Socratic tradition had lent to the investigation of the relationship between thought and recollection, the inevitable sense of alienation of the mind from itself in exploring that relationship could raise the specter of madness. After all, just this linkage between thought and memory was taken for a symptom of Ophelia's madness:

> OPHELIA: There's rosemary, that's for remembrance. Pray you, love, remember. And there is pansies, that's for thought.
> LAERTES: A document in madness, thoughts and remembrance fitted.
> (*Hamlet*, IV, v, 174–78)

We have been tracing a progression from the rejection of illusion to a willed participation in illusion to an impasse. And recognition of the impasse—in which thought and remembrance seem reciprocally to annihilate one another—may help us to see the two-year gap between the composition of the first four stanzas and the composition of the remaining stanzas as more than accidental. The gap does not necessarily indicate lack of poetic inspiration, a dejection over mislaid talent. And accounts which emphasize poetic or psychological distress reduce the problem to a question of Wordsworth's final disillusionment, when such final disillusionment frequently proves to be the last and strongest illusion of all. If we consider the increasingly prominent role of memory in the poem, however, the compositional hiatus itself comes to seem appropriate. The first four stanzas themselves become a memory of the past which the remaining stanzas attempt to assimilate. Thus self-reading (or the reading of the words of a now alien self) enters into the process of writing in a most explicit way.

The relationship between the 1802 stanzas and the 1804 stanzas, the readings and the writing, has suggestive resemblances to Wordsworth's fragmentary essay on "The Sublime and the Beautiful," in which he sketches the relationship between the mind and the forms of nature. Here Wordsworth rehearses the Burkean theme of power as a constituent of sublimity and he depicts terror as destroying sublimity in as much as it indicates a disequilibrium between the power contemplated and the contemplating mind. In a condition of terror, "self-consideration & all its accompanying littleness takes place of the sublime, & wholly excludes it." Yet the precise operation of such terror becomes murky as the discussion continues:

> For connect with such sensations [of pain and individual fear] the notion of infinity, or any other ideas of a sublime nature which different religious sects have connected with it: the feeling of self being still predominant, the condition of the mind would be mean & abject.— Accordingly Belial, the most sensual spirit of the fallen Angels, tho' speaking of himself & his companions as full of pain, yet adds:

> Who would lose those thoughts
> Which wander thro' Eternity?

The thoughts are not chained down by anguish, but they are free, and tolerate neither limit nor circumscription. Though by the opinions of many religious sects, not less than by many other examples, it is lamentably shewn how industrious Man is in perverting & degrading his mind, yet such is its inherent dignity that, like that of the fallen Spirit as exhibited by the Philosophic & religious Poet, he is perpetually thwarted & baffled & rescued in his own despite.

The logical connective "accordingly" locates Belial initially as an example of the meanness and abjectness of the mind set in opposition against a power that pain rightly leads it to fear—the wrath of God. Yet Wordsworth proceeds to quote Belial and to supplement the fallen angel's words with his own assertion of the self-vexing movements of mental abjection.

Wordsworth previously described the experience of sublimity as one in which the mind responds to objects in a spirit either of "participation" or "dread," in which a suspension of "the comparing power of the mind" and a sense of "intense unity" were achieved. Yet the multiplicity and nature of the qualities which he requires of sublime objects—individual form, duration, and power, all coexisting—tend to erode the internal unity of the objects with which the mind is to establish "intense unity." Thus, while we might see the mind's "union" with sublime natural objects as an effort to impute to itself (temporarily) a stability and continuity which it lacks, Wordsworth is repeatedly drawn to examples which are those of opposition and resistance (for example, the passive resistance of "the Rock in the middle of the fall of the Rhine at Chafhausen, as opposed for countless ages to that mighty mass of Waters"). The opposition between two natural forces, passive and active, the rock and the waterfall, represents an equilibrium of powers which can be rendered in an idealized schema, as being in "the state of opposition & yet reconcilement, analogous to parallel lines in mathematics, which, being infinitely prolonged, can never come nearer to each other." And Wordsworth's substitution of a geometric pattern for the quantitative one to be found in most sublime theories may lead us to recognize how difficult it is to imagine such a neutral analogy for Belial's opposition to God.

The example Wordsworth uses is one in which Belial's rhetoric is the only instrument of inducing any balance between the power of God and that of the fallen angels. As Wordsworth indicates by his characterization of Belial as "the most sensual spirit of the fallen Angels," bodily pain and the fear of bodily pain constitute a motive force for his speech—the most pusillanimous address in the congress in Pandemonium. Yet the passion (terror) which would seem to account for the "falsity" of Belial's words refuses to be suppressed or expunged by the speech which would assimilate it. Like all passions, Belial's terror is intrinsically uncontrollable, dictating a speech which recognizes neither the nature of God nor his own nature. The "error" of Belial's passion-dictated language cannot be attributed to any simple reversal of the dictates of the truth; for passion, in its errancy, can neither be directly expressed nor directly inverted. Rather, passion constitutes the most conspicuous moment of the noncoincidence of the subject with itself. And in the lines which Wordsworth hits upon, in which the sensual Belial speaks of cherishing "those thoughts which wander through eternity," the terror of physical pain has pursued such a wandering course that it has caused the fallen angel to speak as if he were unfallen. While Belial's defining characteristic is to think only of "present good," Wordsworth can see this brief passage as an index to his being "perpetually thwarted & baffled & rescued in his own despite" precisely because it abandons the present in insisting upon future presents.

Although the essay on "The Sublime and the Beautiful" tries to intimate the "mighty difference between seeing and perceiving," it concerns itself less with the relationship between subject and object than with the significance of the "unimaginable touch of Time" in determining that relationship. Similarly, the 1804 stanzas of the "Immortality Ode" reexamine the relationship between the subject and nature by investing the process of time with a new significance. In 1802, time entered primarily in the form of narrative conventionalism: "There was a time." But in the 1804 stanzas, Wordsworth's rereading of the earlier section of the poem yields a myth which attempts to trace the movement in which the mind masks the unimaginability of time by constructing such narrative devices.

Critics have justly called the fifth through the eighth stanzas a "negative answer" to the question of the lost visionary gleam. But perhaps the greatest difficulty which we face in these stanzas is that they introduce death into the midst of life with all the force of an Hegelian movement of negation.

> The life of mind is not one that shuns death, and keeps clear of destruction; it endures death and in death maintains its being. It only wins to its truth when it finds itself utterly torn asunder. It is this mighty power, not by being a positive which turns away from the negative, as when we say of anything it is nothing or it is false, and, being then done with it, pass off to something else: on the contrary, mind is this power only by looking the negative in the face, and dwelling with it.

If the earlier stanzas registered an unbridgeable gap between "then" and "now," these stanzas import continuity in the form of an implacable temporal lockstep. It is as though the famous fifth stanza ("Our birth is but a sleep and a forgetting . . .") recognized a wish for temporal continuity in the 1802 stanzas and proceeded to fulfill the wish as faithfully as possible—in accordance with the "facts" ("The things which I have seen I now can see no more"). "I could wish my days to be / Bound each to each in natural piety" is, in fact, a malicious epigraph in conjunction with these middle stanzas of the poem, in which "binding" is so clearly allied with oppression that continuity feels like confinement. According to this schema of "natural time," a time which bears no relationship to human subjectivity, the mind's memory of itself and its past experiences is precisely the element which is expunged. And the movement of declining vision finds an eerie completion in the sixth stanza, in which nature's wooings try to fit the mind to her inhuman time:

> Earth fills her lap with pleasures of her own;
> Yearnings she hath in her own natural kind,
> And, even with something of a Mother's mind,
>   And no unworthy aim,
>   The homely Nurse doth all she can
> To make her Foster-child, her Inmate Man,
>   Forget the glories he hath known,
> And that imperial palace whence he came.
>
>   (75–85)

After such molding of the mind to an unconsciousness like that of nature, human culture dissolves into nothing more than empty formalism, a collection of roles which are passed along not because they bespeak any significant collective consciousness but because they present themselves to the eye.

> But it will not be long
> Ere this be thrown aside,
> And with new joy and pride
> The little Actor cons another part;
> Filling from time to time his 'humorous stage'
> With all the Persons, down to palsied Age,
> That Life brings with her in her equipage;
>   As if his whole vocation
>   Were endless imitation.
>
>   (100–08)

Cleanth Brooks (while regretting the inclusion of the "weak Stanza VII") describes this stanza as the poet's act of "withdrawing to a more objective and neutral position. The poet's treatment of the child here is tender, but with a hint of amused patronage in the tenderness. There is even a rather timid attempt at humor." But it might be more appropriate to see the stanza as an "objective" demonstration of the fulfillment of the wish to see nature and man as perfectly analogous. And Wordsworth's account of this fulfillment reveals the limits of its possibilities: natural man here appears more than a little artificial because his naturalization converts him into a machine. When the poet translates *ecce homo* into "behold the Child among his new-born blisses, / A six years' Darling of a pigmy size!" the "attempt at humor" is strikingly unhumorous because it envisages a state in which the freakish and the mechanical are not lapses from consciousness but a permanent condition.

The heavily mimetic imagery of the seventh stanza in turn reveals the price which must be paid to secure a language in which words and the things they represent are perfectly unified—a price which is consciousness itself. And it is with the eighth stanza, deplored by Coleridge as an example of "mental bombast," that consciousness reasserts itself. Yet this counterimage to the little Actor rapidly exceeds the simple purpose of rejecting the reduction of human experience into pure form. For the assertion of the "soul's immensity" beyond the child's "exterior semblance" escalates into abstraction:

> Thou best philosopher, who yet dost keep
> Thy heritage, thou Eye among the blind,
> That, deaf and silent, read'st the eternal deep,
> Haunted for ever by the eternal mind,
>
> Thou, over whom thy Immortality
> Broods like the Day, a Master o'er a Slave,
> A Presence which is not to be put by.
>
> (111–21)

For all the magnificence of the passage, the difference between "thou" and "we" subtly exposes this rejection of nonhuman time (which is not, properly speaking, time in any meaningful sense) as yet another flight from the consciousness of time. The refutation of this bud is that it cannot become blossom and fruit. For the child as the "Eye among the blind" represents an hypostatized abstract spirit which sees the world in its own image rather than perceiving the surrounding blindness as alien.

> Why with such earnest pains dost thou provoke
> The years to bring the inevitable yoke,
> Thus blindly with thy blessedness at strife?
>
> (124–26)

As the culmination of the messianic strain in the poem, this stanza reflects the desire for a being which will create (or recreate) the world of conditions which would bind it. Although failed messianism manifested itself earlier in the form of guilt at "wronging" the season by bringing the world of nature too little light, this version of failure appears as an unnecessary self-martyrdom. The polarities which make this sacrifice "unnecessary"—a world of dead forms as opposed to a spirit which has all the trappings of an atemporal purity—do, however, also make it inevitable. Both are states which forestall the possibility of self-recognition by satisfying opposite myths of a desire for unity.

Yet both the intrusiveness of the poet's warning voice and the juxtaposition of these opposed pictures of the human erode the stasis of each. They are both projections which are presented as schemata based on memory. But memory forms no part of these projections unless they are both seen as negative moments which intimate by their oversimplification the difficulties of accepting memory as a truly temporal consciousness of the self's identity and difference from itself. For the achievement of memory involves dispensing with what Wittgenstein spoke of as "a false picture of the processes called 'recognizing'; as if recognizing consisted in comparing two impressions with one another. . . . Our memory seems to us to be the agent of such a comparison, by preserving a picture of what has been seen before, or by allowing us to look into the past (as if down a spy-glass)." Only the memory which recognizes that "the Child is father of the Man" precisely because the child does not remain a child enables self-consciousness to come into being.

The final three stanzas of the "Immortality Ode" attempt to frame positively this wisdom gained through negation. Yet the very tentativeness of their expression of joy renders them less consolatory and pious than many critics have taken them to be. The inability to "get back" to a state of childhood innocence and visionary unity with nature does not annihilate the meaningfulness of memory; but Wordsworth is careful not to overstate the "truth" which he has so painstakingly gleaned about the memory. "O joy! that in our embers / Is *something* that doth live" (my emphasis) delineates an unwillingness to see the problems of memory settled; for the "something" has not only been continually redefined in the course of the poem, but is also still to be redefined in the future. In fact, the "benediction" upon "the thought of our past years" specifically renounces the consolatory movement of a new creed which would imagine a lost unity:

not indeed
For that which is most worthy to be blest;
Delight and liberty, the simple creed

Of Childhood, whether busy or at rest,
With new-fledged hope still fluttering in his breast:—
    Not for these I raise
    The song of thanks and praise;
But for those obstinate questionings
Of sense and outward things,
Fallings from us, vanishings.

              (135–44)

But why, in a poem which began by crying out for more light, should the poet offer praise for these murkinesses and vanishings? The contrast between the opening stanzas and the three final stanzas underscores a radical difference in the word "thought" as it occurs throughout the poem. For the poem no longer strives to develop a synthetic definition of "thought" from the disparate connective matrices by which one characterizes thought. The first section of the poem seeks to make metaphysics prove itself, to make the natural and supernatural world change thought itself; the second section (in stanzas five through seven particularly) attempts to derive thought from various developmental myths of education which have no more to do with thought itself than Dr. Spock or Emily Post does. In the first stanzas, however, thought itself becomes the unseen absolute which was earlier rendered as "immortality." Instead of adding logic to memory to metaphysics in an effort to record the mysteries of the human mind, the poet now sees thought as a sum which is not to be arrived at but which is to be intuited and accepted.

    Although the word "thought" disappears from the poem after the early lines of stanza three, "To me alone there came a thought of grief: / A timely utterance gave that thought relief," it reemerges in the last three stanzas of the poem to become a quietly uttered refrain:

The *thought* of our past years in me doth breed
Perpetual benediction
              (IX, 134–35)

We in *thought* will join your throng
              (X, 172)

In the soothing *thoughts* that spring
Out of human suffering
              (X, 184–85)

And finally,

Thanks to the human heart by which we live,
Thanks to its tenderness, its joys, and fears,
To me the meanest flower that blows can give
Thoughts that do often lie too deep for tears.

                                        (XI, 201–04)

Like the earlier "thought of grief," these "thoughts" appear to spring unmotivated by anything except themselves. They are themselves "seeds," rather than being simply (and recognizably) the products of any other seeds. And the concluding return to a link between flowers and thoughts reiterates the association between "pansy" and *"pensée"* which we discerned in stanza four. Yet in its final form the association between flower and thought is no longer tied to any desire to see thought in an objectified form. "Pansy" and *"pensée,"* flower and thought, are curious—almost accidental—analogues, not mutual explanations of one another. And it is in this final abandonment of an insistence upon connections and explanations that the Ode commands attention to the education which is continually eluding its "possessor" rather than to the formal schemes of linkage which are taken for its substance. The almost universal invocation of the last three stanzas speaks of continuities and connections, but it affirms these connections in a rhetoric which suspends itself over a gap in demonstrable truths.

THOMAS McFARLAND

The Wordsworthian Rigidity

The attitude of defense—the armored attitude of the happy warrior—was one that Wordsworth maintained against the assaults of life for more than seventy years. So constant a posture of defense had as concomitant the rigidity that is so notable a feature of his later period. Almost everything Wordsworth espoused became rigid. For instance, his Christianity, which had developed in part under Coleridge's warnings against Spinozistic pantheism ("this inferred dependency of the human soul on accidents of Birth-place & Abode together with the vague misty, rather than mystic, Confusion of God with the World & the accompanying Nature-worship, of which the asserted dependence forms a part, is the Trait in Wordsworth's poetic Works that I most dislike, as unhealthful, & denounce as contagious. . . . It conjures up to my fancy a sort of *Janus*-head of Spinoza and Dr Watts"), became so rigid that Coleridge himself commented adversely on its orthodoxy.

Again, Wordsworth's pattern of first supporting, then repudiating, the revolutionary tendencies of the age was one he shared with many intellectuals; but with him the reaction was peculiarly rigid. "Most intensely did I rejoice at the Counter Revolution," admits Crabb Robinson: "I had also rejoiced when a boy at the Revolution, and I am ashamed of neither sentiment." Yet in the very entry in which this statement occurs, Robinson says of Wordsworth's hardening conservatism that "I am sorry that Wordsworth cannot change with the times. . . . Wise men and great men when carried away by strong feelings run with fools. Of the integrity of Wordsworth I have no doubt, as of his genius I have an unbounded admiration; but I doubt the discretion and wisdom of his latest political writings."

From *Romanticism and the Forms of Ruin: Wordsworth, Coleridge, and the Modalities of Fragmentation.* Copyright © 1981 by Princeton University Press.

It was as though Wordsworth's psychic muscles were constantly tensed. The initial life-giving radiance—the sense that "Heaven lies about us in our infancy"—was left further and further behind as the years went by. Though the growing boy beheld "the light, and whence it flows," the "Youth" daily traveled "farther from the east"; at length "the Man" perceived it "die away,/ And fade into the light of common day." The course of existence therefore offered the prospect not of an accession but a deprivation of being: "I see by glimpses now; when age comes on / May scarcely see at all"; "Life's autumn past, I stand on winter's verge; / And daily lose what I desire to keep." In this respect Wordsworth's life of eighty years, in itself an anomaly among ruptured Romantic existences, was a cruel irony, a long day's dying to augment his pain. What he always wanted was to experience unchangingly the joy he had felt as a child— "Stability without regret or fear; / That hath been, is, and shall be evermore." Thus the Solitary, commenting on the happiness of a "cottage boy," says "Far happiest . . . / If, such as now he is, he might remain."

But into the longing for eternal and blessèd childhood obtruded the iron claims of ravaging time:

> . . . a thought arose
> Of life continuous, Being unimpaired;
> That hath been, is, and where it was and is
> There shall endure,—existence unexposed
> To the blind walk of mortal accident;
> From diminution safe and weakening age;
> While man grows old, and dwindles, and decays;
> And countless generations of mankind
> Depart; and leave no vestige where they trod.

We recognize the lines as not merely the poetic precursor of Keats's "Ode to a Nightingale," but also as an index for the peculiarly tragic sense of Wordsworth's life. The cheerfulness of the egotistical sublime was an attempt to maintain the thought of "life continuous, Being unimpaired." The cost of such continual straining against the true situation of "mortal accident," "diminution," and "weakening age" was the Wordsworthian rigidity: the psychic muscles were always tensed. A trifling comment from the last decade of Wordsworth's life reveals, perhaps better than larger evidence, Wordsworth's own haunted sense of this fact:

> Nothing however said or done to me for some time has in relation to myself given me so much pleasure as a casual word of Anna's that the expression of my face was ever varying. I had begun to fear that it had lately been much otherwise.

Both Wordsworth's rigidity and his stoic defenses were raised to ideational formulation in his conception of "duty." The word, indeed, received an honorific charge in his vocabulary that only "love" and "joy" and "nature" can match. Even Kant's apotheosis of *Pflicht* at the expense of *Neigung* is no more insistent than was Wordsworth's rejection of "wayward inclination" for what he apostrophizes as the "Stern Daughter of the Voice of God."

The honorific charge seems to derive from two related defensive services that duty performed in Wordsworth's lifelong struggle against loss of being. First of all, duty was a principle by which an existence kept itself from being broken up and dissipated in protean change. It maintained the commitments of childhood in the circumstances of age, and thus bulwarked the aspiration to "life continuous, Being unimpaired." Without it, one would be, to use a phrase from the "Ode to Duty," the "sport of every random gust." For Wordsworth change meant loss, time was horror ("Mutability is Nature's bane"); he longed for "a repose that ever is the same." Underlying any possibility of a life of joy and love there accordingly was the necessity of keeping the past green; and duty helped to achieve this:

Serene will be our days and bright,
And happy will our nature be,
When love is an unerring light,
And joy its own security.
And they a blissful course may hold
Even now, who, not unwisely bold,
Live in the spirit of this creed;
Yet seek thy firm support, according to their need.

The "firm support" of duty thus was a major ally in the war against fears in solitude. As such, its call became in its largest description an obligation toward the significant group; as we see, to cite only one instance, in Wordsworth's dismay about Coleridge:

He *ought* to come to see after Hartley. . . . But because he ought to come, I fear he will not; and how is H. to be sent to College? These perplexities no doubt glance across his mind like dreams—but nothing ever will rouse the Father to his duty *as Duty.*

As we can infer from that passage and others like it, Coleridge's failure to recognize the sacredness of duty was, at least from Wordsworth's perspective, perhaps the single most important factor in the eventual estrangement of the two men.

The second function of duty was a complement to the first. If duty helped maintain the bonds of the significant group, it also rescued an individual from chaotic solitude—from the "being to myself a guide" that characterized the egotistical sublime. As Wordsworth says in the "Ode to Duty":

> I, loving freedom, and untried; . . .
> Yet being to myself a guide,
> Too blindly have reposed my trust: . . .
> But thee I now would serve more strictly, if I may.

The isolated self is free, but this freedom divorced from relationship and its responsibilities paradoxically becomes a burden: "Me this unchartered freedom tires; / I feel the weight of chance-desires."

Duty therefore both redeems one from the emptiness of self and asserts the bond with the significant group. In such functions we can understand the enormous importance Wordsworth attached to the idea, at the same time that we realize how rigid is the tendency of a life dominated by so demanding an allegiance. Both the importance and the rigid tendency can perhaps be illustrated by a single idiosyncratic example. Dorothy, in mourning the death of Thomas, ascribes as one of his finest qualities the attachment to "duty" as opposed to "wayward inclination." She is speaking of a child six years old! That Wordsworth's sister expressed such an almost grotesque sentiment about his son shows how magical, almost, was the conception of duty in the psychic economy of his own significant group. Dorothy writes:

> The ways of Providence are inscrutable. That child was taken from us who never disturbed our minds with one wayward inclination—Right forward did he tread the path of duty—and we looked at him with the fondest hopes, that in after years he would be our pride and comfort as he was then a source of tender delight.

Such a statement indicates very precisely the nature of duty in Wordsworth's vision. A child who treads "the path of duty" will, unlike Michael's Luke, be able to resist change and dissipation of being, will in "after years" support the significant group and be a "pride and comfort" to those of its members assaulted by diminution and weakening age.

If the Wordsworthian rigidity is apparent in the conception of duty, it also is a factor, as we have suggested above, in the almost feudal quality of his political conservatism. But the more *outré* aspects of that conservatism (he threatened to leave the country if the Reform Bill of 1832 were enacted!) were the result not solely of rigidity but of rigidity compounded with withdrawal of emotional affect. The affect withdrawn from the conception of society at large was bestowed on the significant group, whose features we now can clearly discern. For the significant group might most simply be defined as that society the loss of any member of which attacks the participant's sense of his own being. Furthermore, the significant group is composed exactly of those people, the loving of whom and then the loss of whom tested Wordsworth's stoic fortitude throughout his life. His mother, we remember, died in his early childhood; his father, in his early adolescence; his brother, in the poet's early manhood; his son and daughter together, in his early middle age. His best friend dropped off; his beloved sister became insane; his favorite remaining daughter died before him in his extreme old age. To all these hammer blows Wordsworth reacted with cheerful stoicism; but surely his was a being under assault, an existence exposed to "the blind walk of mortal accident." Central to the whole situation was the extreme depth of Wordsworth's capacity for emotional attachment. Only by loving so deeply could he lose so deeply. "We weep much to-day, and that relieves us," he said after his brother's death:

> As to fortitude, I hope I shall show that, and that all of us will show it,
> in a proper time, in keeping down many a silent pang hereafter.

It is in this regard that "We Are Seven"—a poem that shows marks of Coleridge's compositional symbiosis no less than does our other example of the yew-tree poem—can be seen as paradigmatic for the structure of the significant group. "We Are Seven" is a poem about disparaction denied: about the breaking of the significant group and the refusal to accept that breaking:

> "Sisters and brothers, little Maid,
> How many may you be?"
> "How many? Seven in all," she said,
> And wondering looked at me.
>
> "And where are they? I pray you tell."
> She answered, "Seven are we;
> And two of us at Conway dwell,
> And two are gone to sea.
>
> "Two in the church-yard lie,
> My sister and my brother;
> And, in the church-yard cottage, I
> Dwell near them with my mother."

The primary speaker in the poem, who ironically combines worldly wisdom with the denudation of being that for Wordsworth accompanied adulthood, repeatedly attempts to insist on the fragmentation of the significant group; but the child, combining in counter-irony inexperience of reality and more intense feeling for human relationship, has the last word:

"How many are you, then," said I,
"If they two are in heaven?"
Quick was the little Maid's reply,
"O Master! we are seven."

"But they are dead; those two are dead!
Their spirits are in heaven!"
'Twas throwing words away; for still
The little Maid would have her will,
And said, "Nay, we are seven!"

In the light of the foregoing discussion, it is evident that this poem, its deliberate simplicity notwithstanding, goes to the very heart of what Wordsworth valued and what he feared. Naive though its surface statement is, its deeper attitudes intertwine in a special complexity. The little girl is at once one who refuses to accept reality and one who serves a higher reality: she is that "best Philosopher" of the "Intimations Ode"; she is that "Eye among the blind"—and here as there the one who is blind is the informed adult who is the speaker. She is a specification of the way in which the child is "Mighty Prophet! Seer blest! / On whom those truths do rest, / Which we are toiling all our lives to find." She serves, still again, as parallel in figure and function to Dorothy in "Tintern Abbey":

> . . . thou my dearest Friend,
> My dear, dear Friend; . . . in thy voice I catch
> The language of my former heart, and read
> My former pleasures in the shooting lights
> Of thy wild eyes. Oh! yet a little while
> May I behold in thee what I was once,
> My dear, dear Sister!

The little girl of "We Are Seven" represents for Wordsworth the "language of my former heart"; he beholds in her "what I was once."

The child's denial of reality ironically echoes that tendency toward denial that guaranteed Wordsworth's own stoic cheerfulness, and that in a sense dictated his entire poetic effort—that thought of "life continuous, Being unimpaired," "existence unexposed / To the blind walk of mortal accident; / From diminution safe and weakening age." Still further, the "seven" who constitute the child's significant group contain among them both the living and the dead, and this, in Wordsworth's most mature conception, was indispensable to the idea of meaningful community:

> There is
> One great society alone on earth:
> The noble Living and the noble Dead.

He expounds more fully upon this fundamental of the significant group in his prose writing, where he refers to the great society as a "spiritual community":

> There is a spiritual community binding together the living and the dead; the good, the brave, and the wise, of all ages. We would not be rejected from this community; and therefore do we hope. We look forward with erect mind, thinking and feeling: it is an obligation of duty: take away the sense of it, and the moral being would die within us.

Here again we see "duty" functioning to bind together the significant group.

The child's significant group, lastly, is constituted by her family circle. Family relationships were for Wordsworth those most cherished, and those that, when torn apart by death, generated the most pain. "My loss is great, and irreparable," he writes of the death of his brother—and might well have written of any of the losses he sustained within his family group. On this occasion, indeed, he was so agonized as to pose the question whether "however inferior we may be to the great Cause and ruler of things, we have *more of love* in our Nature than he has?"—an attitude that, at least in this instance, is not far from Blake's gnostic essential that "the Creator of this World is a very Cruel Being." As De Quincey charged in 1816, with pique but not wholly without point, Wordsworth "is incapable of friendship out of his own family, and . . . is very secular in his feelings."

The family, in brief, was for Wordsworth both the archetype of the ideal society and the center of all he held holy: "the household of man" is his revealing phrase from the revised preface to *Lyrical Ballads*. In his remarkable letter to Fox, which constitutes an enchiridion for his social beliefs, he draws an implied distinction between human life that has meaning and human life that does not (the great society is not simply the living and the dead, but the *noble* living and the *noble* dead). Life that does have meaning is possible only through "domestic affections":

> The domestic affections will always be strong amongst men who live in a country not crowded with population, if these men are placed above poverty. But if they are proprietors of small estates, which have descended to them from their ancestors, the power which these affections will acquire amongst these men is inconceivable by those who have only had an opportunity of observing hired labourers, farmers, and the manufacturing Poor. Their little tract of land serves as a kind of permanent rallying point for their domestic feelings, as a tablet upon which they are written which makes them objects of memory in a thousand instances

when they would otherwise be forgotten. It is a fountain fitted to the nature of social man from which supplies of affection, as pure as his heart was intended for, are daily drawn.

If the human life that is most meaningful requires placement in a natural setting—proprietorship of "small estates" that have descended from "ancestors"—the insistence not only accords with values that others have emphasized but reflects the structure of Wordsworth's psychic investment as well. For if his preoccupation with nature be ultimately a projection of human situation, so it seems fitting that nature then be reintegrated into human needs and concerns. And if the "small estates" are a sheltering of exposed existence by the protective cloak of nature, so does their descent from their owners' ancestors sanctify the child's wisdom of denial in "We Are Seven." The inheritance of the "small estate" is precisely a major agency in "binding together the living and the dead." One may remark parenthetically that Wordsworth's stress on his kind of property ownership stands at the antipodes from that most corrupt practice of modern capitalism: New York speculators buying unseen land to subdivide in the Rocky Mountains. Against such desecration he might have sided with Proudhon and declared property to be theft; for the implication of Wordsworth's attitude is that property not *lived into* by its owner is immoral. The property should be both an extension of and bulwark for the unique personality that inhabits it (Wordsworth, had he known them, would almost surely have found himself in agreement with the social theories of his contemporary, Adam Müller, whereby possessions are justified by being regarded as extensions of the limbs of the body). Finally, the lived-into property, by its descent from ancestors, is above all the locus of family relationships.

This complex of Wordsworthian emphases is perhaps nowhere better illustrated than in what Coleridge termed "the divine Poem called Michael." The work contains some of the most limpid verse Wordsworth ever composed, and constitutes possibly the finest realization of his prosodic theories of simplicity and naturalness of diction. Furthermore, its charge of emotion is so strong that the pathos achieved is almost sublime— matched only, one thinks, if at all, by the pathos of "The Ruined Cottage."

"Michael" is, in short, a great and quintessentially Wordsworthian achievement, and thereby added significance is lent to the fact that in it the three aspects of the complex just elucidated are classically presented: the family as archetypal society; the small estate as extension of its owner's personality; and *lived-into* land as the arena of communal interaction.

Michael's land is the projection of his own heart, and his heart is in turn the land:

> Those fields, those hills—what could they less? had laid
> Strong hold on his affections, were to him
> A pleasurable feeling of blind love,
> The pleasure which there is in life itself.

This land is not inhabited in selfish isolation, however; it is the natural setting for the small but complete society of Michael's love:

> His days had not been passed in singleness.
> His Helpmate was a comely matron, old—
> Though younger than himself full twenty years.
> She was a woman of a stirring life,
> Whose heart was in her house:

The conception of the land as binding together the "great society" of living and dead, and simultaneously the sense of this society as personally connected—as familial in its history—is unequivocally set forth:

> I have been toiling more than seventy years,
> And in the open sunshine of God's love
> Have we all lived; yet if these fields of ours
> Should pass into a stranger's hand, I think
> That I could not lie quiet in my grave.

The significant group is completed by the son, Luke, who by his status as child symbolizes the blessedness of the situation and the hope of its continuation:

> The Shepherd, if he loved himself, must needs
> Have loved his Helpmate; but to Michael's heart
> This son of his old age was yet more dear—
> Less from instinctive tenderness, the same
> Fond spirit that blindly works in the blood of all—
> Than that a child, more than all other gifts
> That earth can offer to declining man,
> Brings hope with it, and forward-looking thoughts

But then the group is broken; Michael's heart and life are broken; the relationship to the land itself is broken. The monument to this massive onset of diasparaction is the sheepfold, eternally fragmentary and incomplete: "The length of full seven years, from time to time, / He at the building of this Sheepfold wrought, / And left the work unfinished when he died." And this monument focuses the pathos of the poem:

> Among the rocks
> He went, and still looked up to sun and cloud,
> And listened to the wind; and, as before,
> Performed all kinds of labour for his sheep,
> And for the land, his small inheritance.
> And to that hollow dell from time to time
> Did he repair, to build the Fold of which
> His flock had need. 'Tis not forgotten yet
> The pity which was then in every heart
> For the old Man—and 'tis believed by all
> That many and many a day he thither went,
> And never lifted up a single stone.

Luke's defection not only breaks the significant group but also indicates the kind of human assembly that to Wordsworth was the enemy of significance: the society of the city:

> . . . Luke began
> To slacken in his duty; and, at length,
> He in the dissolute city gave himself
> To evil courses: ignominy and shame
> Fell on him, so that he was driven at last
> To seek a hiding-place beyond the seas.

To Wordsworth, the transitory, anonymous, and chaotic life of the city stood in horrible antithesis to all he held dear in society. The significant group that redeemed man from the abyss of egotism was maintained by fewness in number, spatial placement in live-into property, and continuity in time. London, on the contrary, was a "monstrous ant-hill on the plain / Of a too busy world!" The variety of types and multiplication of numbers that to many have been fascinations in city life were to Wordsworth a deprivation of all meaning:

> How oft, amid those overflowing streets,
> Have I gone forward with the crowd, and said
> Unto myself, "The face of every one
> That passes by me is a mystery!"

This effect, whereby multiplication of people breaks down human meaning, is symbolized by the blind beggar—a derelict figure whose blankness as a city-dweller presents a strong contrast to the Old Leech-Gatherer's humanity in the country:

> Amid the moving pageant, I was smitten
> Abruptly, with the view (a sight not rare)
> Of a blind Beggar, who, with upright face,

Stood, propped against a wall, upon his chest
Wearing a written paper, to explain
His story, whence he came, and who he was.
Caught by the spectacle my mind turned round
As with the might of waters; an apt type
This label seemed of the utmost we can know,
Both of ourselves and of the universe

The groupings of the city thus diminished rather than enhanced the sense of the unique personality, and thereby paradoxically suppressed the very variety of relationship that for Wordsworth was necessary to redeem the egotistical sublime. Bartholomew Fair, which in Ben Jonson's art had been a place for affectionate if therapeutic sporting with human weakness and folly, became in Wordsworth's vision little less than pandemonium itself:

What a shock
For eyes and ears! what anarchy and din,
Barbarian and infernal,—a phantasma,
Monstrous in colour, motion, shape, sight, sound!

It was a collection of "All out-o'-the-way, far-fetched, perverted things, / All freaks of nature." But most of all, it negated, rather than preserved, the very spatiality and uniqueness of the individual necessary to a significant group:

Oh, blank confusion! true epitome
Of what the mighty City is herself,
To thousands upon thousands of her sons,
Living amid the same perpetual whirl
Of trivial objects, melted and reduced
To one identity

Wordsworth thus recoiled from what we have termed the liberal mythology of the meaningfulness of life in and of itself. If egotistical isolation was to be feared, so too was the immersion—the drowning rather—of the individual in the experience of the multitude. Only concrete and continuing relationships, constantly defined and renewed by love, gave value to existence.

Thus in his largest commitments—to begin to proceed to more modern instances—Wordsworth stood at the opposite extreme from Dickens's Mrs. Jellyby, who worried about Africa while her household and children were neglected. Mrs. Jellyby's eyes "had a curious habit of seeming to look a long way off," as if "they could see nothing nearer than Africa!"; and she held a discussion "of which the subject seemed to be—if

I understood it—the Brotherhood of Humanity; and gave utterance to some beautiful sentiments." But her daughter bursts out:

> "I wish Africa was dead!" she said, on a sudden. I was going to remonstrate.
> "I do!" she said. "Don't talk to me, Miss Summerson. I hate and detest it. It's a beast!"

The point of Dickens's satire is not restricted to Mrs. Jellyby. If Wordsworth's conservatism was to some extent dictated by a withdrawal of emotion from mankind at large and a redirection toward the significant group, the "radical chic" of our own day often simply reverses that process. I am mindful of a paradigmatic cocktail party conversation a few years ago, in which, after expressions of agonized concern for Biafra, my interlocutress briskly dismissed the suicide of a man we both knew with an attitude equivalent to sweeping him into the trash bin. What was true in this instance has been, in my rather dishearteningly extensive experience, almost a norm for the relationship of humanitarian protestation to actual practice. One recalls Burke's trenchant attack on Rousseau, who exhausted "the stores of his powerful rhetoric in the expression of universal benevolence, whilst his heart was incapable of harboring one spark of common parental affection." In Burke's observation, "Benevolence to the whole species, and want of feeling for every individual with whom the professors come in contact," were the hallmarks of Rousseau's philosophy. The spiritual descendants of Rousseau are with us yet and evermore.

As with Burke, Wordsworth's reaction against the French Revolution came about not as a rejection of humane ideals, but as a judgment that those ideals had been betrayed; and ultimately as the conclusion that they could not practically be realized. In a sense he always remained a republican; the structure of the significant group incorporated an honoring of liberty, equality, and fraternity. It was not in any way dependent upon a privilege of birth or wealth, and its feudal nature is qualified by that idiosyncrasy:

> It was my fortune scarcely to have seen,
> Through the whole tenor of my school-day time,
> The face of one, who, whether boy or man,
> Was vested with attention or respect
> Through claims of wealth or blood

Membership in a significant group was on the contrary open to all, for such a group was maintained by a valuing of human life that radiated out from primary relationships:

> . . . my affections first were led
> From kindred, friends, and playmates, to partake
> Love for the human creature's absolute self

His "heart" was through such relationships, and through nature,

> early introduced
> To an unconscious love and reverence
> Of human nature.

With such idealism, he, like ardent spirits throughout Europe, greeted the Revolution as a great step forward for humanity:

> Bliss was it in that dawn to be alive,
> But to be young was very Heaven!
> . . . the whole Earth
> The beauty wore of promise

From the wreck of the overthrown Bastille

> A golden palace rose, or seemed to rise
> . . . The potent shock
> I felt: the transformation I perceived,
> As marvellously seized as in that moment
> When, from the blind mist issuing, I beheld
> Glory—beyond all glory ever seen

He soon became "a patriot, and my heart was all / Given to the people, and my love was theirs"; "in the People was my trust." The ideals of the Revolution seemed such a logical extension of "love and reverence / Of human nature" that to stand against its tide seemed to argue a personal malignancy of spirit. All the weight of humanity seemed on the side of the great stirring—the "Domestic severings, female fortitude / At dearest separation, patriot love / And self-devotion, and terrestrial hope" that accompanied the early days of the Revolution were like

> arguments from Heaven, that 'twas a cause
> Good, and which no one could stand up against,
> Who was not lost, abandon'd, selfish, proud,
> Mean, miserable, wilfully deprav'd,
> Hater perverse of equity and truth

Such a hater Wordsworth neither was nor ever wanted to be.

His mind, as did that of other noble-spirited young men of the time, could move quickly from obvious wrong to exalted visions of apocalyptic amelioration:

> And when we chanced
> One day to meet a hunger-bitten Girl,
> Who crept along fitting her languid self
> Unto a Heifer's motion
> . . . at the sight my Friend
> In agitation said, ' 'Tis against *that*
> Which we are fighting,' I with him believed
> Devoutly that a spirit was abroad
> Which could not be withstood, that poverty
> At least like this, would in a little time
> Be found no more . . .
> All institutes for ever blotted out
> That legalized exclusion, empty pomp
> Abolish'd, sensual state and cruel power,
> Whether by edict of the one or few,
> And finally, as sum and crown of all,
> Should see the People having a strong hand
> In making their own Laws, whence better days
> To all mankind.

In this view of futurity, all society would participate in the structure of a significant group:

> . . . prophetic harps
> In every grove were ringing, 'War shall cease;
> Did ye not hear that conquest is abjured?
> Bring garlands, bring forth choicest flowers, to deck
> The tree of Liberty. . . .
> Henceforth, whate'er is wanting to yourselves
> In others ye shall promptly find;—and all,
> Enriched by mutual and reflected wealth,
> Shall with one heart honour their common kind.'

Disillusionment, when it came, was harsh. The very residence in France that so exhilarated Wordsworth made him more vividly aware of the rapid degeneration of Revolutionary ideals than was, for instance, "English Blake." His first realizations that "Lamentable crimes / . . . the work / Of massacre" had been committed were hopefully dismissed. Such occurrences were "Ephemeral monsters, to be seen but once!"; and "inflamed with hope, / To Paris I returned." But as terror continued, and the Moloch-figure of Robespierre rose over the scene, the exhilaration vanished:

> O Friend!
> It was a lamentable time for man. . . .
> A woeful time for them whose hopes did still
> Outlast the shock; most woeful for those few,

> They had the deepest feeling of the grief
> Who still were flattered, and had trust in man. . . .
> Most melancholy at that time, O Friend!
> Were my day-thoughts, my dreams were miserable; . . .
> I scarcely had one night of quiet sleep
> Such ghastly visions had I of despair
> And tyranny, and implements of death,
> And long orations which in dreams I pleaded
> Before unjust Tribunals,—

Robespierre—"a Caligula with the cap of Liberty on his head," in Cole-ridge's image—was followed by Napoleon and the Revolutionary mockery of the empire: "to close / And rivet up the gains of France, a Pope / Is summon'd in, to crown an Emperor— / This last opprobrium, when we see the dog / Returning to his vomit." From being the nourisher of human hopes France became a defiler of those hopes:

> And now, become Oppressors in their turn
> Frenchmen had changed a war of self-defense
> For one of conquest, losing sight of all
> Which they had struggled for

The cumulative effect of these progressive disillusionments led Wordsworth to what he memorably terms a "loss of confidence in social man." He had glimpsed and been repelled by what Taine retrospectively described as the social bestiality of the French Revolution: "from the peasant, the laborer, the bourgeois, pacified and tamed by an old civiliza-tion, we see suddenly spring forth the barbarian, and still worse, the primitive animal, the grinning, bloody, wanton baboon, who chuckles while he plays, and gambols over the ruin (*dégâts*) he has accomplished." Wordsworth had initially approached, "like other Youth, the Shield / Of human nature from the golden side"; but the Terror forced him to conclude that "the weak functions of one busy day" could not reclaim, extirpate, and perform "What all the slowly-moving years of time, / With their united forces, have left undone." His vision of building "social upon personal Liberty" gave way to ever more unrewarding examination of doctrine:

> Thus I fared,
> Dragging all passions, notions, shapes of faith,
> Like culprits to the bar, suspiciously
> Calling the mind to establish in plain day
> Her titles and her honours, now believing,
> Now disbelieving, endlessly perplex'd
> With impulse, motive, right and wrong, the ground

Of moral obligation, what the rule
And what the sanction, till, demanding *proof*,
And seeking it in everything, I lost
All feelings of conviction, and, in fine,
Sick, wearied out with contrarieties
Yielded up moral questions in despair

From this retreat into confusion and disillusionment, he was saved by the significant group—by his sister, "Companion never lost through many a league," who "Maintained for me a saving intercourse / With my true self"; and by Coleridge, "Thou, most precious Friend!" who "didst lend a living help / To regulate my Soul."

It was those two, Coleridge and Dorothy, who vitalized for Wordsworth the conception of the significant group. The entity as a whole contained also his brother John, his wife Mary, and his sister-in-law Sara; Coleridge and Dorothy, however, were the defining members. "But Thou art with us," writes Wordsworth of Coleridge,

with us in the past,
The present, with us in the times to come.
There is no grief, no sorrow, no despair,
No languor, no dejection, no dismay,
No absence scarcely can be there, for those
Who love as we do.

The emotional triplicity—that is, the changing of simple adhesion into the special structure of group—was completed by Dorothy. Wordsworth felt himself, and Coleridge as well, to be "blest" with a joy

Above all joys, that seem'd another morn
Risen on mid noon, the presence, Friend, I mean
Of that sole Sister, she who hath been long
Thy Treasure also, thy true friend and mine,
Now, after separation desolate
Restor'd to me—

Wordsworth withdrew into the significant group after having been both pulled away and pushed away from the vision of social panacea initially offered by the French Revolution. The pushing away was effected by the Terror and its bloodshed; the pulling away, by his personal and idiosyncratic involvement in the egotistical sublime—the need to restore "intercourse / With my true self." It was henceforth no longer the case that "in the People was my trust"; rather, his idealism was displaced into the conviction that only the few can raise themselves to meaningful life: "Endeavour thus to live . . . / . . . and a stedfast seat / Shall then be yours among the happy few / Who dwell on earth, yet breathe empyreal air, / Sons of the morning." The displacement in effect aligned him morally and politically with Plato, who, to the continuing dismay of Karl Popper and his followers, equated the many with a "great beast," and was convinced that "Philosophy, then, the love of wisdom, is impossible for the multitude."

In this altered vision, Wordsworth's love of humanity (even as early as "An Evening Walk" he had expressed "Entire affection for all human kind") became increasingly qualified by recognitions of disabling defects in social man:

> Neither vice nor guilt,
> Debasement undergone by body or mind,
> Nor all the misery forced upon my sight,
> Misery not lightly passed, but sometimes scanned
> Most feelingly, could overthrow my trust
> In what we *may* become.

Thus he came in effect to share the sentiment of Keats: "I admire Human Nature but I do not like *Men*."

As years went by, both Wordsworth's tendency to rigidification and his withdrawal of emotional affect from the idea of society at large left their marks. The husks of these later attitudes are well described by Mrs. Moorman:

> His extreme horror of Lord Grey's Reform Bill has to be understood in the light of his own depressive temperament which always tended to expect the worst consequences from all measures which he could not approve. He had given way entirely to his uncontrollable dread of 'the mob' which had been increasing in him ever since the days of Robespierre.

His fear of and contempt for the undifferentiated mass—"the mob" (an abhorrence he shared with Shakespeare no less than with Plato) —were complemented, however, by the more positive aspect of his ever-deepening commitment to the significant group. For the "mob" was merely people too crowded and deracinated to participate in meaningful relationship. In this context, we are justified in saying that Wordsworth's ideals never changed; only his cognizance of their possibilities changed. As a commentator sees:

> Wordsworth's sympathy with the French Revolution was . . . never an independent or a primary matter. It was the corollary of a prior loyalty, his faith in the sort of persons whom he later made his chosen heroes. . . . At this point Legouis, and all who have followed his lead, have misread the poet. William Wordsworth was from first to last a stubborn north-country Englishman, anxious above all else, in political

matters, to perpetuate the society in which he had grown up as a boy and youth.

His one desire was to insure to the world men like Michael. He was a revolutionist as long as the Revolution promised to yield him such men. When the Revolution failed him here, degenerating into a new tyranny, he lost all interest in it. He turned to Toryism because political thinking of that type seemed to him at the time more likely than any other to guarantee him his freeman.

There is a third factor that demands consideration. Pushed into commitment to the significant group by disillusionment with universal social solutions, and pulled into it by his tendency to the egotistical sublime, Wordsworth held ever-tighter to it in response to the dwindling of those who constituted its being. The loss of each uniquely valuable relationship hammered him, as it were, further into himself, and caused him to question the whole purpose and meaning of mankind. "Alas! what is human life!" he exclaimed after his brother's death; and such a shaking of assumption and value could hardly help restore his loss of confidence in social man.

Rigid and reactionary though Wordsworth's political attitudes eventually became, however, they should not be dismissed as nothing more than idiosyncrasy. The name of Burke alone should remind us that Wordsworth's cherishing of the significant group was not solely the expression of his special cognizance of meaning in human life, but also participated in broader historical currents. It would, indeed, be an interesting and illuminating task to explore in detail the historical analogies to Wordsworth's conservatism. Although, as we have been at pains to elucidate, his attitudes arose primarily from tensions in his own psychological development and needs, they none the less conformed in important respects to those of contemporary conservative thinkers.

Romanticism, in fact, though in a sense inaugurated by the French Revolution (which was, in Shelley's words to Byron, "the master theme of the epoch in which we live"), distributed the energy thus stirred up in a polar form. Although figures such as Blake, and Shelley himself, espoused what may loosely be termed the Jacobin tradition ("The system of society as it exists at present," said Shelley, "must be overthrown from the foundations with all its superstructure of maxims & of forms"), figures such as Wordsworth and Coleridge opposed it. "No man," claimed Coleridge in retrospect,

> was more enthusiastic than I was for France and the Revolution: it had all my wishes, none of my expectations. Before 1793, I clearly saw and often enough stated in public, the horrid delusion, the vile mockery of

the whole affair. When some one said in my brother James's presence that I was a Jacobin, he very well observed—"No! Samuel is no Jacobin; he is a hot-headed Moravian!" Indeed, I was in the extreme opposite pole.

In this polar opposition, Burke, as Cobban and others have shown, was the intellectual leader. But Burke was not the only philosopher of conservatism, and Wordsworth's opinions exhibit affinities to the thought of such continental writers as Justus Möser—"der herrliche Justus Möser," in Goethe's words—and Adam Müller (the latter's *Die Elemente der Staatskunst* [1809] is of special relevance to Romantic conservatism in general). Later contributions, such as Taine's massive *Les Origines de la France contemporaine* and the writings of Maurice Barrès, extend the historical perspective of anti-revolutionary conservatism. In fact, Barrès, both by his insistence on the continuity between the living and the dead, and by his stress on human relationship to the soil, seems in certain ways an unintentional epigone of Wordsworth. In Wordsworth's own era, moreover, other conservative thinkers such as Bonald, Joseph de Maistre, and Friedrich Schlegel were active and are pertinent to his position.

Among these and other theorists, however, and without discounting the special importance of Wordsworth's similarity to both Müller and Möser, one might say that the conservative analogies for the great poet's stance are most satisfyingly embodied by Burke. Hazlitt identifies the "clue" to all Burke's "reasoning on politics" in these words:

> He saw in the construction of society other principles at work, and other capacities of fulfilling the desires, and perfecting the nature of man, besides those of securing the equal enjoyment of the means of animal life. . . . He thought that the wants and happiness of men were not to be provided for, as we provide for those of a herd of cattle, merely by attending to their physical necessities. He thought more nobly of his fellows. He knew that man had affections and passions and powers of imagination, as well as hunger and thirst and the sense of heat and cold. He took his idea of political society from the pattern of private life, wishing, as he himself expresses it, to incorporate the domestic charities with the orders of the state, and to blend them together. He strove to establish an analogy between the compact that binds together the community at large and that which binds together the several families that compose it. He knew that the rules that form the basis of private morality are not founded in reason . . . but in the nature of man, and his capacity of being affected by certain things from habit, from imagination, and sentiment, as well as from reason.

The congruence of these essentials of Burke's political philosophy with Wordsworth's object-oriented, family-vitalized social vision is apparent. Equally so is that between Wordsworth's commitment to the significant group and Burke's ordering of the priorities of human concern. To Burke, in Hazlitt's words,

> the reason why a man ought to be attached to his wife and children is not, surely, that they are better than others, (for in this case every one else ought to be of the same opinion) but because he must be chiefly interested in those things which are nearest to him, and with which he is best acquainted, since his understanding cannot reach equally to every thing; because he must be most attached to those objects which he has known the longest, and which by their situation have actually affected him the most . . . ; that is, because he is by his nature the creature of habit and feeling, and because it is reasonable that he should act in conformity to his nature.

Such, in Hazlitt's description, were Burke's basic tenets. Strikingly apposite to those of Wordsworth, they assume special importance as the considered conclusions of a political mind of the first magnitude. As Hazlitt says (his tribute is the more remarkable in that he regarded Burke as "an ememy" of his own radically democratic principles), Burke's "stock of ideas did not consist of a few meagre facts, meagrely stated, of half a dozen common-places tortured in a thousand different ways; but his mine of wealth was a profound understanding, inexhaustible as the human heart, and various as the sources of nature. He therefore enriched every subject to which he applied himself, and new subjects were only the occasions of calling forth fresh powers of mind which had not been before exerted. It would therefore be in vain to look for the proof of his powers in any one of his speeches or writings: they all contain some additional proof of power."

In addition to the correspondences obtaining between the basic priorities of Burke and Wordsworth, Wordsworth's turning from support to repudiation of the French Revolution duplicated in his private experience the pattern that Burke, on the larger stage of national political life, exhibited in turning from espousal of the American Revolution to rejection of the French; and perhaps the best political commentary to the metamorphosis of Wordsworth's attitude to French Republican dogma is supplied by the *Reflections on the Revolution in France*.

In such contexts of similar conviction and fellow-feeling, it was entirely fitting that the 1850 version of "The Prelude" should incorporate a direct salutation to Burke:

> Genius of Burke! forgive the pen seduced
> By specious wonders. . . .
> I see him,—old, but vigorous in age,—

Stand like an oak. . . .
While he forewarns, denounces, launches forth,
Against all systems built on abstract rights,
Keen ridicule; the majesty proclaims
Of Institutes and Laws, hallowed by time;
Declares the vital power of social ties
Endeared by Custom; and with high disdain,
Exploding upstart Theory, insists
Upon the allegiance to which men are born—

To be sure, there are differences between Burke and Wordsworth; Wordsworth was a relative novice in politics, whereas Burke was one of the great governmental practitioners and theorists ("He knew more of the political machine than a recluse philosopher," said Hazlitt, "and he speculated more profoundly on its principles and general results than a mere politician"). But the differences are less urgent than the deep-lying similarities. Indeed, two similarities not previously adduced are that, for both men, the reaction to the French Revolution was the result of proximity in both space and time to its specific features; and, secondly that neither endorsed those more aggressive strains of conservative thought that, departing from Maistre's glorification of warfare and Stirner's celebration of pure egotism, led through Nietzsche and Sorel to fascism and the Nazi cataclysm.

KENNETH R. JOHNSTON

"Home at Grasmere" in 1800

The identification of William Words-
worth with the English Lake District is so elemental a fact of literary
history that one easily forgets there was a time when the fact had to be
created in competition with other available options. Despite the fine
biographical and poetical inevitability of the Wordsworths' move to Grasmere, the principals in the case were by no means sure of destiny's
direction. In their correspondence of 1798–99, the question of where to
settle (closely linked to questions of what to do) is indeed preeminent; but
by far the most important variable was how to remain close to Coleridge.
Grasmere and the Lakes entered into the decision belatedly, as an enter-
taining diversion. Once their dissatisfaction with Germany had set in
(December 1798), Dorothy wrote to Coleridge that they should all explore together "every nook of that romantic country" the following summer, "wherever we finally settle." Coleridge, during the whole year, held
out for the south as being better for Wordsworth because it was nearer the
intellectual company he felt Wordsworth needed more than books. In July
he reported with disappointment that Wordsworth "renounces Alfoxden
altogether," but William and Dorothy's letters indicate no clear alternative
except for "William's wish to be near a good library, and if possible in a
pleasant country."

These domestic decisions are important poetically as well as bio-
graphically because they help to explain the peculiarly aggressive vehemence of Wordsworth's joy in the portions of "Home at Grasmere" written

From *Wordsworth and "The Recluse."* Copyright © 1984 by Yale University. Yale University
Press, 1984.

in the spring of 1800 as a fresh start on *The Recluse*. There is undoubtedly creative psychological significance in the curious fact that almost all major segments of *The Recluse* were undertaken when the Wordsworths had just completed, or were just beginning to contemplate, a move to a new home—and, moreover, that this occurred with each of the residences they occupied from Alfoxden on. That this is more than mere coincidence is strongly suggested by one of the poet's few post-1815 efforts to work on his masterpiece, "Composed When a Probability Existed of Our Being Obliged to Quit Rydal Mount as a Residence," 1826, a meditation of over two hundred lines in which *The Recluse*'s frequent discrepancy between grand themes and small occasions is especially marked. In 1800, the Wordsworths were not returning home to Grasmere but going to Grasmere *as if* it were home, a situation "conducive to a self-conscious awareness of himself as an observer," not to the recapture of an "indigenous" childhood. Their seven-month stay with the Hutchinson family at Sockburn had shown them brothers and sisters reunited as a happy, independent family of adults, a potent image because of their own painful childhood memories of being scattered abroad after the death of their father in 1783. They had also been living for four years in what seemed to their elder relations a state of semivagabondage and were very eager to stop it. The question of Wordsworth's career—indeed, of his profession—was crucial in deciding where to go from the temporary hospitality of the Hutchinson farm. Careers were not to be made in Grasmere; not the least of Wordsworth's imaginative achievements was his establishment of a national literary reputation from so remote a provincial spot. Cowper and Collins and others may have suggested models, but they were gentlemanly recluses on church, university, or family sinecures, and in any case they did not plan to save the world with their poetry. The November walking tour was not the summer vacation jaunt Dorothy had proposed but an effort to interest Coleridge in the North; yet it also had the effect of allowing Wordsworth to see the Lakes with newly approving eyes—Coleridge's. His letter back to Dorothy at Sockburn concentrates on Coleridge's responses— "Coleridge enchanted with Grasmere and Rydal"—and Coleridge's enthusiasm catalyzes his own: "Coleridge was much struck with Grasmere and its neighbourhood and I have much to say to you, you will think my plan a mad one, but I have thought of building a house by the Lake side . . . ." Barely a month before the great move "home" to Grasmere, the idea struck its proposer as "mad," as it surely must have seemed to his relatives and to received ideas of how and where a not-so-young man of uncertain promise would establish his independence in the world. Nor was the author of "The Mad Mother," "Incipient Madness," and other lyrics of

the psychopathology of everyday life likely to use the word with sophisticated frivolity.

William and Dorothy's return in December of 1799 was full of
wonder and loving observation. They were returning, brother and sister,
aged twenty-nine and twenty-seven, to the general neighborhood of their
childhood, reentering after long absence a childhood dream. The reestablishment of their feelings for this landscape was inextricably tied up with
the re-formation of their family. Their brother John's behavior upon
arriving for a visit to the new household in January is expressive of the
powerful emotions underlying these changes. From the inn, he twice
walked up to the door of William and Dorothy's cottage, put his hand
on the latch, and twice walked away. Finally, he sent word from the
inn to warn them. He was struggling with a terrific ambivalence of
joy and sorrow as he anticipated entering the first household they had
had, as a Wordsworth family, since their father's death nearly twenty years
earlier. The return to childhood memories entailed a wrenching of adjust-
ments to adult life that had been made with great precocious sacrifice;
they were trying to return to simpler, more usual, or normal relationships
that had been interrupted or postponed. The reunion with John was soon
followed by the reestablishment of other old ties broken by the German
misadventure, culminating with Coleridge's return in April for a visit,
which by June had become a new residence. The James Loshes, once
invited to join the "little colony" in Germany, came to greet the new
couple during the extended housewarming of 1800; Losh was another
ex-radical who had tempered revolutionary enthusiasm with domestic
bliss, and (like Wordsworth and Coleridge themselves) was one of the
disillusioned intellectuals whose fading idealism Coleridge proposed *The
Recluse* to revive. The re-formation of their family led naturally to thoughts
of family growth by marriage and children, for which the Loshes and other
friends offered plenty of models. For a period of a year or two it was not
clear who would marry whom, but the two Hutchinson sisters, Mary and
Sara, were eligible, and the two Wordsworth brothers, William and John,
were interested. The entire milieu was one of young people entering
optimistically into adulthood. Mrs. Coleridge bore a son soon after her
arrival, and her husband promptly named him Derwent, after the river
that Wordsworth had involved at the beginning of "the poem to Coleridge." Other identifications of themselves with the place would soon
follow, in "Poems on the Naming of Places"; although their controlling
fiction suggests that they build on childhood associations, their operative
model is the sophisticated pastoral one of literary young adults concocting
emblems for themselves in the wild.

Moorman's claim that William had established "familiar and affec-tionate" relations with Grasmere by the end of the summer of 1800 is certainly true but also suggests that it was a project involving conscious effort. Coleridge's picture of them all dancing around a bonfire on Gras-mere island that summer is a fit image of the childlike joy indulged in by these young adults, and of the sense of recovered innocence that imbues Wordsworth's return to *The Recluse* in "Home at Grasmere": "I lay and saw the woods, and the mountains, and lake all trembling, and as it were *idealized* through the subtle smoke . . . and the Image of the Bonfire, and of us that danced round it—ruddy laughing faces in the twilight—the Image of this in a Lake smooth as that Sea to whose waves the Son of God had said, '*Peace*'." His friend's resumption of their idealized master-poem would continue to manifest the same predilection for picturing the life-works of this "happy band" in divine images and analogies.

Both Wordsworth and Coleridge later associated the start of *The Recluse* with the year 1800 rather than with the 1,300 lines Wordsworth had announced in 1798. As a return to *The Recluse*, "Home at Grasmere" is indeed more like a new beginning than a continuation; such radical freshness was to become characteristic of each resumption of the project. Each new start has much more in common with other work Wordsworth was doing at the moment than with the most recent prior state of *The Recluse*. This is not surprising to common sense, but it illumines the unstable, ad hoc nature of the philosophy on which the poem was to have been founded. "Home at Grasmere" thus resembles the 1798–99 *Prelude* far more than it does *The Recluse* of 1797–98. Its extremity of joy is from a different world than the extreme suffering of Margaret, the old Cumber-land beggar, and the discharged veteran. In his determined efforts to finish "Home at Grasmere" in 1806, Wordsworth inserted specimens of decrepitly enduring mankind to reassert his epic's socially responsive intentions, but the 1800 portions of "Home at Grasmere" are a direct continuation of the moods and scenes of the 1799 *Prelude*, from whose composition they are separated only by the very similar "Poems on the Naming of Places," in which the Wordsworth entourage claimed Grasmere valley by naming its striking features after themselves, like latter-day Adams and Eves. "Home at Grasmere" brings the 1799 *Prelude* into the present tense, installing Wordsworth in propria persona, age twenty-nine, amid the scenes the first *Prelude* had described up to his age seventeen.

However, "Home at Grasmere" is even less straightforward autobi-ography than *The Prelude*. Lionel Stevenson acutely views it as a transi-tion from autobiography to something else, once Wordsworth's autobio-graphical record had reached the present and no longer offered a convenient formula for composition; perhaps the "topographical unity of an isolated region" would offer a spatial coordinate to extend the temporal one, pressing landscape into the service of biography. It opens with a "spot of time" which shows him gazing on the valley during a boyhood ramble, experiencing in a visionary moment some distinctly unboyish thoughts:

> "What happy fortune were it here to live!
> And if I thought of dying, if a thought
> Of mortal separation could come in
> With paradise before me, here to die."
>
> (9–12)

The recently composed "spots of time" in the 1799 *Prelude* had shown "the imaginative power" acting upon ordinary sight; this compositional moment of March 1800 shows imagination sharing its power with a more extraordinary place. In moving from *The Prelude* in 1799 to "Home at Grasmere" in 1800, Wordsworth skipped, as it were, his intervening awful decade, from Cambridge to Sockburn. At this point, a biographical record was not his intention. But he would not be able to complete "Home at Grasmere" until he gave that decade its full due in his greatest poem, *The Prelude* of 1805. Only then could the promise of *The Recluse* be once more assayed.

His sense of returning to Grasmere as if in response to a *vocation* is adumbrated in some lines he incorporated from the poem he wrote on Hart-Leap Well, a notable local sight he and Dorothy had passed in their December march on Grasmere. These lines identify a millennial moment of newly established right relations between Man and Nature with the Wordsworths' advent in Grasmere:

> Among the records of that doleful place
> . . . we found
> A promise and an earnest that we twain,
> A pair seceding from the common world,
> Might in that hallowed spot to which our steps
> Were tending, in that individual nook,
> Might even thus early for ourselves secure,
> And in the midst of these unhappy times,
> A portion of the blessedness which love
> And knowledge will, we trust, hereafter give
> To all the Vales of earth and all mankind.

Attuned to the inarticulate lore of "grey-headed Shepherds," they can appreciate the almost supernatural powers that attend upon conscious homecomers and interpret the meaning of the wounded hart's bleeding out its life at the wellsprings of its birthplace. In "awful trance," Wordsworth sees "the Vision of humanity and of God / The Mourner, God the Sufferer, when the heart / Of his poor Creatures suffers wrongfully" (243–46). But "Home at Grasmere" falters when this vision tries to shift the referent of "poor creatures" from animals to men.

Although "Home at Grasmere" deserves to be read as a complete poem, that has been done elsewhere, and the present context requires that it be separated out into its two main compositional eras, 1800 and 1806, in order to appreciate how the break between them manifests Wordsworth's difficulty in turning *The Recluse* toward human life—and how much of the structure of the great *Prelude* of 1805 is determined by the necessity to heal the breach human suffering causes here. If we consider the five hundred-odd lines of "Home at Grasmere" written in 1800 as a unit, we discover a Romantic Ode to Joy written in one of the highest keys ever attempted. No small part of Wordsworth's achievement in these lines, incomplete and unbalanced as they are, is his avoidance of the outright hysteria to which such odes were prey, like some of the youthful effusions of Shelley and Keats. This Ode to Joy launches itself, moreover, by its own design, over the brink into the depths of its counterpoint, the Ode to Dejection, as in such dialectically mature works as Keats's "Ode to Melancholy." Wordsworth "breaks Joy's grape against his palate fine," and then hangs his poem up, defeated, among the "shadowy trophies" of the goddess Melancholy. Unlike the conventional pastoral poet who writes himself into his landscape as a refuge from worldly pain and corruption, Wordsworth writes himself out of it, as he gradually, reluctantly, recognizes the social responsibility he is shirking. Beyond its repeated "braving" of Milton—"paradise before me" tops *Paradise Lost*'s "the earth was all before them"—it courts resemblance to Milton's biblical sources, especially the thanksgiving Psalms and the *Song of Songs*, with the striking variation that the body of the beloved is not the expectant community but the receptive landscape: "Embrace me then, ye Hills, and close me in" (129).

These lines effuse the eager anticipation of a man rubbing his hands together before a satisfying piece of work. There is not a risk Wordsworth fears to take, literary or psychological. This is the place, and he is in it.

> What Being . . . since the birth of Man
> Had ever more abundant cause to speak
> Thanks . . . ?

> The boon is absolute
> . . . among the bowers
> Of blissful Eden this was neither given
> Nor could be given. . . .
>
>   (117–25)

Better than Eden, Grasmere provokes expressions of paradise consciously regained, suited to Coleridge's vision of *The Recluse* as a philosophic displacement of *Paradise Lost.* Both self and world seem born again, and Wordsworth feels his experience to be archetypal:

> The unappropriated bliss hath found
> An owner, and that owner I am he.
> The Lord of this enjoyment is on Earth
> And in my breast.
>
>   (85–88)

All his past life has led to this place and these moments. The sign of true miracle is how easy it turned out to be:

> And did it cost so much, and did it ask
> Such length of discipline, and could it seem
> An act of courage, and the thing itself
> A conquest? Shame that this was ever so. . . .
>
>   (64–67)

This open rhetorical question is like a rebuttal to the hanging question of the 1799 *Prelude,* "Was it for this . . . ?" The discipline, courage, and conquest lay not in his disappointed efforts to break successfully into print in London, but in his rejection of London's terms in favor of his own. Everything becomes easy if seen in the right light—seen, that is, not as a regressive retreat to "that romantic country" of childhood memory, but as a mature choice which supersedes the false values of the world with a higher calling.

   The 1800 segments of "Home at Grasmere" advance by a series of rhetorical leaps and bounds, excited verse-paragraphs each ending in exclamations more sweeping than the last. These rhetorical periods are more oratorical than narrative or descriptive in form, like the "prolusions" which both Milton and Wordsworth knew at Cambridge as compositional models in Latin. After the opening "spot of time" (1–43) there is a thematic introduction (44–170), followed by a general biographical perspective (171–215), the specific biographical context of the December walk to Grasmere (216–77), and the immediate confirmation of their expectations in the coming of spring, celebrated in the winter birds' riotous pleasure in the new warm weather (277–321). To this point, the

poem works toward identification with the very moment of its composition—
toward saying, here am I, writing this poem. If all its linguistic peculiari-
ties were generalized into a single compressed sentence, they would collapse
all tenses into one: "Once upon a time I am living happily ever after." It
bursts into, and eventually through, its moment of inspiration. Every
aspect of its structure and language strives toward self-identification.
Everything about it is circular: its arguments tautological, its syntax
redundant and repetitious, its imagery full of rounded reflections which
reinforce the circling tensions of its structure. Proofs are presented osten-
sively, not argued: "For Proof behold this Valley and behold / Yon Cottage,
where with me my Emma dwells" (97–98). It is nothing if not internally
coherent, since it virtually implodes itself. All these traits taken together
make it an absurdist or fabulist text, in the technical sense; this, of course,
was not Wordsworth's intention but the dramatic result of his radical
literalism. Its absurdism is a function of its modes of presentation, not its
contents, which are familiarly Wordsworthian but juxtaposed in extreme
patterns, half caricature, half sublime allegory: baroquely plain, simply
rococo. Its favorite images are themselves images: things seen in reflection. Wordsworth's description of the joyous birds wheeling "in wanton
repetition" is apt for the style of the whole poem and a fit culmination of
the poem's upbeat movement, as Grasmere mirrors their heavenly motion:

> Behold them, how they shape,
> Orb after orb, their course, still round and round,
> Above the area of the Lake, their own
> Adopted region, girding it about
> In wanton repetition, yet therewith—
> With that large circle evermore renewed—
> Hundreds of curves and circlets, high and low,
> Backwards and forwards, progress intricate,
> As if one spirit was in all and swayed
> Their indefatigable flight.
>
> (292–301)

"As if" is a suspect simile, and "adopted region" may point to troubling
questions of true origin, but the vigor of Wordsworth's style does not allow
such problems to emerge into conscious discourse to challenge the wide
claims he makes for Grasmere:

> A Centre, come from wheresoe'er you will,
> A Whole without dependence or defect,
> Made for itself and happy in itself,
> Perfect Contentment, Unity entire.
>
> (167–70)

Rather, these effusive prolusions run into trouble at the level of
literal description. It comes as no surprise to any level-headed reader that
this dizzying, surreal absurdism cannot be long sustained, that the denomi-
nation of the first wild day of March 1800 as an imaginative entity—new
century, new career, new revolutionary agenda—should falter in the face
of real time. But it came as an untoward shock to Wordsworth, and we can
see it in the poem. At the very height of his "O altitudo!" Wordsworth
looks down, sees death, poverty, and evil, and plunges to ground, not to
resume the poem for over five years. Just when he seems to be parsing his
poem off the page of the landscape, he reads something he doesn't like:

> But two are missing—two, a lonely pair
> Of milk-white Swans. Ah, why are they not here?
> These above all, ah, why are they not here
> To share in this day's pleasure?
>
> (322–25)

The repetitions, the reiterated gasp, the insistent questioning, all show
the poem's intrinsic characteristics imploding in upon it. And the reason is
as honestly presented as the ecstasy: he and Dorothy have identified
themselves with these two swans to an extraordinary extent:

> From afar
> They came, like Emma and myself, to live
> Together here in peace and solitude,
> Choosing this Valley, they who had the choice
> Of the whole world.
>
> . . . to us
> They were more dear than may be well believed,
>
> . . . their state so much resembled ours;
> They also having chosen this abode;
> They strangers, and we strangers; they a pair,
> And we a solitary pair like them.
> They should not have departed . . .
>
> Shall we behold them yet another year
> Surviving, they for us and we for them,
> And neither pair be broken?
>
> (325–29, 333–34, 338–42, 348–50)

The poem's extreme symbolism rebounds upon the narrating observer.
Finch notes interesting parallels between Wordsworth's description of the
missing swans and Milton's account of Satan's rebellion, but rebelliousness

in this instance attaches not to the objects described but the describing subject (Wordsworth), a characteristic example of the poem's tendency to deconstruct its own structural principles. If the swans are gone, just like that, with no explanation or meaning, what does it signify for the fate of another "solitary pair" coming into this valley?

Wordsworth has pitched his claims for the special qualities of Grasmere so high that this ridiculous literalism threatens to spoil it. In the sequence of *The Recluse*'s development, he has sailed off the top of the axis of vision, just as in the 1,300 lines written by March 1798 he came close to bottoming out on the axis of things, where mental power dwindles to a mere feature of physical existence, subject to "animal decay." He goes immediately on the defensive, and the bulk of the remaining lines composed in 1800 show him back-pedaling furiously to restore the damage he has done. But it is no good; he ultimately backs himself into a corner, out of the poem, and breaks it off.

The extremes to which he goes to explain the swans' absence are the best guarantee of the sincerity of the joy which preceded his discovery of it. Given the situation, it is not surprising that "Home at Grasmere"'s subversion of normal language becomes most radical in the hundred-odd lines in which the poet tries to rectify the damage a gap in reality has wreaked upon the fabric of his literalistic art. His first conjecture is that the swans may have been shot by Grasmere "dalesmen," but this leads to an even worse crisis, lack of moral confidence in Grasmere's residents. He apologizes both to the place and to his own poem for "harbouring this thought": "Recall, my song, the ungenerous thought; forgive, / Thrice favoured Region, the conjecture harsh." His determination to make amends leads beyond this reflexive hypostasis of his own text to a surreal identification of language with place, in which moral predication of any sort becomes redundant.

> Ah! if I wished to follow where the sight
> Of all that is before my eyes, the voice
> Which is as a presiding Spirit here
> Would lead me, I should say unto myself,
> They who are dwellers in this holy place
> Must needs themselves be hallowed. They require
> No benediction from the Stranger's lips,
> For they are blessed already. None would give
> The greeting "peace be with you" unto them,
> For peace they have; it cannot but be theirs.
>
> (362–71)

This curious apology implies that all apologies are unnecessary because morally irrelevant. The unsubtle repetition of cognate forms as predicates ("holy / hallowed," "benediction / blessed," "peace / peace") risks the charge of illogic only to flaunt the irrelevance of logic to the tautological self-sufficiency of the situation. Grasmere is placed once more beyond the realm of ordinary discourse. Partly, of course, he is simply seeking to avoid the presumption of bestowing upon the dalesmen virtues they already have in surplus. But a deeper impulse is at work (after all, they may indeed have killed the swans): to deny that anything need be predicated of Grasmere because it is literally self-validating. To say that people who dwell in a holy place are themselves holy is a form of predication. But to deny they need benediction, which presumably all people can benefit from, is to move toward asserting that anyone who does not fully share their special condition cannot possibly predicate anything of them. The rest of the passage moves further in the same direction, claiming Grasmerians need nothing because they have "charity beyond the bounds of charity" (375). In denying the efficacy of strangers' benedictions of the dalesmen, Wordsworth is denying the power of "performative verbs" to perform "speech acts" upon them. In a speech-act, to say is to do (for example the "I do" of marriage); it is thus one of the most powerfully self-sufficient uses of language, and its redundant uselessness in Wordsworth's Grasmere further highlights the radical uniqueness he attributes to the place.

The effort of each succeeding verse-paragraph to correct the over-stated extremes of its predecessor leads further and further away from the missing swans and the real fact they imply, that Grasmere is not *necessarily* congenial to solitary pairs who choose it. Wordsworth stoutly avers that he and Dorothy did not come hither "betrayed by tenderness of mind" (398); they were well aware that accusations of romantic sentimentalism would be leveled at them. As evidence that they know men are not angels, he cites the profane language he has heard the shepherds utter. This bit of social realism is important for the poet who will in a few months write the most famous manifesto in English defending ordinary language for art (Preface to *Lyrical Ballads*), and is introduced by a belated attempt to unravel his own tautologies. They did not expect to find "in midst of *so much loveliness / Love, perfect love, of so much majesty / A like majestic* frame of mind in those / Who here abide, the *persons* like the *place*" (401–04; italics added). But even in denial, the tautological redundancies suggest residual longings for affirmation. He who has heard the human voice in harmony with nature's power has, he insists, heard "that voice, the same, the very same":

> Debased and under prophanation, made
> An organ for the sounds articulate
> Of ribaldry and blasphemy and wrath

> The common creature of the brotherhood,
> But little differing from man elsewhere
> For *selfishness* and *envy* and *revenge*,
>
> *Flattery* and *double-dealing*, *strife* and *wrong*.
>   (424–26, 434–38; italics added)

The bearing of this evidence is clearer in the context of *The Recluse*'s development. From the 1799 *Prelude*, as well as the 1798 *Lyrical Ballads*, we recognize Wordsworth's peculiarly intense yet narrow characterizations of human evil ("greetings where no kindness is, nor all / The dreary intercourse of daily life"). He is not saved from being "betrayed by tenderness of mind" because he can stand to hear profanity; he is not so dainty. Rather, to have heard profane language and recognized the human weakness it implies is for Wordsworth to have heard language as it is used in cities, especially under conditions of competitive work. His not being "betrayed by tenderness of mind" here closely parallels his faith in "Tintern Abbey" that "Nature never did betray the heart that loved her," with the immediate proof provided there against "evil tongues, rash judgment [and] the sneers of selfish men." Wordsworth generalizes these narrowly particular abuses of language under conditions of ambitious competition into a morally corrupt condition for so-called normal, "worldly" language, against which he defines his vocation-cum-location as a restoration to real normal health. There is a quality of courageous naiveté in these assertions that resembles the admission of another famous self-biographer, Henry Adams, that his education did not attain to comprehending Wordsworth until he was thirty; neither, in a sense, did Wordsworth's.

But this evidence has introduced a complication into the argument which proves insuperable and soon breaks off his composition of "Home at Grasmere" in 1800. Other human beings have been recognized, and *The Recluse*'s theme of "Human Life" once again disrupts the Man-Nature bonding Wordsworth celebrates, because of his extremely unguarded defense of Grasmere's moral significance. He tries desperately to assert that Grasmere's dalesmen could not be swearing, wrathful, selfish, envious beings (or shoot swans) for the usual external reasons—that is, because they are poor, hungry, or ill-clothed—since "Labour here preserves / His rosy face . . . extreme penury is here unknown . . . they who want are not too great a weight / For those who can relieve" (440–48). But the strain of this special pleading is too much, for reasons closer to the springs of Wordsworth's genius than his "rentier's" view of Grasmere, and the poem breaks off, at the interesting words, "so here there is . . ." (457). The conjunction is meant to complete a moral or human simile drawn from the geographic form of the valley: "*as* these lofty barriers break the force / Of winds—this deep vale *as* it doth in part / Conceal us from the storm—*so* here there is. . . ." But nothing follows; there is no moral counterforce equivalent to Nature's forms. Instead, there is only a brief coda, which will in fact become the predicating guarantee, in a variety of forms, of all subsequent *Recluse* fragments. It is the image of the one spiritually creative community Wordsworth can vouch for and actually could complete the interrupted simile:

> And if this
> Were not, we have enough within ourselves,
> Enough to fill the present day with joy
> And overspread the future years with hope—
> Our beautiful and quiet home, enriched
> Already with a Stranger whom we love
> Deeply, a Stranger of our Father's house,
> A never-resting Pilgrim of the Sea,
> Who finds at last an hour to his content
> Beneath our roof; and others whom we love
> Will seek us also, Sisters of our hearts,
> And one, like them, a Brother of our hearts,
> Philosopher and Poet, in whose sight
> These mountains will rejoice with open joy.
> Such is our wealth: O Vale of Peace, we are
> And must be, with God's will, a happy band!
>   (859–74)

The necessary social dimension which has been raised in "Home at Grasmere" by Wordsworth's fantastically literal effort to save his own unifying symbols, the two swans, is finally put in terms of an extended family. This is as far as Wordsworth's social vision could extend with confidence in 1800. Resuming the poem in 1806, he will try specifically to generalize Grasmere's joy through a series of tales of men and animals intended to prove "that solitude is not where these things are," to show that this happy band in this valley is not as naive as Rasselas and his friends in their Happy Valley in Abyssinia, and that "Home at Grasmere" is more than a domesticated Oriental tale of self-indulgent escapism. In the interim, in the introduction to the 1805 *Prelude*, he will insert, between the "glad Preamble" of late 1799 (so close in spirit to "Home at Grasmere") and the abrupt, "Was-it-for-this?" beginning of the two-part *Prelude*, a series of possible epic subjects, all of which deal with historical or mythic versions of his own "happy band," followers of an unjustly expelled leader who flee, usually to the north, only to return in body or in spirit after years of creative exile to wreak their just revenge on the corrupt, tasteless civilizations to the south which cast them out (chapter 5).

But in the 1800 portions of "Home at Grasmere," the identification of the master-poem with the master's life was too quick and insufficiently mediated. Wordsworth still conceived writing about himself and about Man, Nature, and Human Life as separate tasks, and he thought he had just finished with himself in the two-part *Prelude* of 1799. The first sequence of *Recluse* compositions, with its depressed vision of human conditions, had pushed him into investigations of his own mental condition (the two-part *Prelude*) in order to raise his sights back to the work at hand. Now, after this second sequence, he is again forced to return to his own mind because his new start has soared too high. Having cast himself and Dorothy as Adam and Eve in a new Eden, the strain of saving the whole world *from this place* has quickly proved to be too much. Wordsworth's return to his "*Prelude*-movement" within *The Recluse* is, therefore, not simply a second rebound back to investigations of his own mind, but to investigations of the growth of mind in terms of the *places* in which it found—or did not find—itself at home as it did at Grasmere. Thus the 1805 *Prelude*, which he began haltingly in late 1803, begins as a "residential" elaboration of both the social faith evident in Part Two of the 1799 *Prelude*, and of the social impasse which "Home at Grasmere" reached in 1800.

THE GREAT PROSPECTUS

Between abandoning "Home at Grasmere" in about March 1800 and resuming *The Prelude* in full swing by March 1804, Wordsworth worked on two other texts important to *The Recluse*'s history: a revision of "The Ruined Cottage" into "The Pedlar," and the famous "Prospectus" of *The Recluse*, eventually published in the preface to *The Excursion* (1814). The result of his efforts on the first of these may be summarized by one of Dorothy's pained journal entries: "Disaster Pedlar." This was the most intense of several efforts over the years to separate the character of the Pedlar from the tale of Margaret, efforts which we can see, in the *Recluse*-context, as attempts to adjudicate between the claims of the narrative character and the authorial character, and as enactments of Wordsworth's dilemma in relating his story, *The Recluse*, to its teller, *The Prelude*: were they to be joined or separated? Butler's summary of these changes indicates their congruence with Wordsworth's other work during the three years between the interruption of "Home at Grasmere" and the resumption of *The Prelude:* [they] "change *The Pedlar* from a philosophic exposition to a character sketch which resembles some of the *Lyrical Ballads* and the poems of 1802 in which Wordsworth returned to portrayals of character. Besides adding many personal details to give the Pedlar's folk-wisdom biographical (rather than philosophical) plausibility, Wordsworth's most interesting change was the temporary insertion of a little girl precisely into the lines which establish a special relationship between the poem's aesthetic young narrator and the Pedlar, thereby distancing two characters who were both essentially versions of himself and preventing the Pedlar's interest in the young man (as a boy) from collapsing into a virtual identity that would destroy the usefulness of their conversation as a framework of conversion ("And for myself / He loved me, out of many rosy Boys / Singled out me, as he in sport would say / For my grave looks, too thoughtful for my years"). The little girl, by contrast, cannot believe the wise old Pedlar could ever have been the ragged litle poor boy he says he was, cannot believe the child could be father to the man—an appropriately challenging audience for a Wordsworthian conversion poem. But this little girl did not stay in the poem long, for the Pedlar's finding "a kindred heart to his" in the young narrator guarantees that his history will be heard aright, in much the same way Wordsworth could rely on Coleridge's correct audition of *The Prelude.*

But in the stirring lines of the "Prospectus," all doubts and displacements between tale and teller are overridden by the most sustained grandeur Wordsworth ever achieved. Despite their prospective function, they speak so wonderfully of the relationships imagined between *The Recluse*'s universal themes—"On Man, on Nature, and on Human Life" —that we hardly require anything to follow from them. As a prayer for inspiration, the "Prospectus" constitutes an act of faith that ennobles itself. Much of its splendor drives from Wordsworth's successful appropriation of Milton's idiom to his own concerns, a humanistic "counter-cry" to Coleridge's "Religious Musings." Beyond this, the structure, theme, and movement of the "Prospectus" bear rhetorical comparison with two other texts that are similarly prospective yet self-sufficing, the Lord's Prayer and the Apostles' Creed, which the boy Wordsworth would have read every Sunday on facing pages of the *Book of Common Prayer.* Like the former, it moves from a redefined heaven ("the mind of Man") through the fullness of earthly beauty to the social world of trespasses, temptations, and evil: "the tribes / And fellowships of men" (1017–18). Yet the structure of the "Prospectus" lines is exactly homologous to a text even closer to hand: the portions of "Home at Grasmere" itself that Wordsworth had just com-

pleted, which also move, as we have seen, from an initial state of radically
Edenic self-consciousness ("This solitude is mine; the distant thought / Is
fetched out of the heaven *in which it was*," 83–84; italics added), to an
extremely unguarded celebration of full interchange between human consciousness and earthly beauty, which fetches up abruptly on the simplest
contradiction in its metaphoric terms (the two missing swans), and then
descends helplessly into successively inadequate efforts to come to terms
with human evil. The structure of the "Prospectus" recapitulates that of
"Home at Grasmere," but succeeds in making a coherent poetic statement
where "Home at Grasmere" fails, by praying for inspiration rather than
essaying its realization, and by transmuting the simple places and persons
of Westmorland into the highest possible levels of mythological significance. Ultimately, Wordsworth will complete "Home at Grasmere" by
attaching these prospective lines to it as a conclusion.

Whether considered as a conclusion or a prospectus, the "Prospectus" is, like "Home at Grasmere" itself, preeminently a definition of poetic
inspiration in terms of the *places* which nurture it and which it must in
turn minister to. Indeed, it simply elaborates, as poetical regions, the
three basic terms of *The Recluse* announced in its opening line: "On Man,
on Nature, and on Human Life." The "mind of Man" displaces the
Christian "Heaven of heavens" and "darkest Pit of the profoundest Hell"
with the heaven and hell of human consciousness (976–90). Second, the
"living home" of Nature's beauty is a constant invitation to a daily
promised land: "An hourly Neighbour" (991–1001). After these two
passages Wordsworth inserted, in 1805 or 1806, the lines (1002–14)
celebrating the "great consummation" of the wedding of "the individual
Mind" and "the external world," a connection that has come to seem so
quintessentially Wordsworthian that it deflects us from his original determined turn to the third region of his song, Human Life, which follows
immediately after the first two in the earlier versions of the "Prospectus":

> Such [pleasant haunts] foregoing, if I oft
> Must turn elsewhere, and travel near the tribes
> And fellowships of men, and see ill sights
> Of passions ravenous from each other's rage,
> Must hear humanity in fields and groves
> Pipe solitary anguish, or must hang
> Brooding above the fierce confederate storm
> Of Sorrow, barricaded evermore
> Within the walls of cities—may these sounds
> Have their authentic comment, that even these
> Hearing, I be not heartless or forlorn!
> (1015–25)

If the lines about passing Jehovah "unalarmed" into "the mind of Man" are brave (though even Blake found them crazily blasphemous) and those on Nature's Beauty greatly promising, Wordsworth in his Human Life triad achieves an acuity of insight that is as shockingly compressed as the other two are grandly expansive. All forms of human suffering are swiftly included—mutual, solitary, and social-historical. The perverse way in which human emotions feed upon the frustration, not the satisfaction, of others' emotions is breath-takingly stated in a half-dozen words ("passions ravenous from each other's rage"), then generalized into a vision of human life as a self-contained siege *against itself* ("confederate storm") that recalls, for sheer paradoxical power, Blake's "mind-forg'd manacles." In between these two images, the anguish of the individual mind is put in terms of a sad pastoral (ll. 1019–20), whose "fields and groves" are ill-matched with the "paradise and groves Elysian" that Wordsworth has, just ten lines earlier, promised will be "the growth of common day." So much does the human factor complicate Wordsworth's vision, that all of the biblical, Exodus imagery in the "Prospectus" comes together in it. Instead of following "Beauty . . . pitch[ing] her tents before me," he is side tracked from the Promised Land, traveling "near the tribes and fellowships of men," those Moabites or Philistines of alienation, a veritable Confederation of the Cities of the Plain of Sorrow.

Wordsworth's reluctance to make this detour is matched only by his determination to complete it: "if I oft / Must turn elsewhere . . . may these sounds / Have their authentic comment, that even these / Hearing, I be not heartless or forlorn!" Yet for all the acute analytic power of the "Human Life" lines, we must ask if they are not too unremittingly negative, just as the "Mind of Man" section is too expansively grandiose, and the natural beauty section too confidently tempting? The question, whether addressed to the "Prospectus," to "Home at Grasmere," or to most of Wordsworth's poetry, reveals that *The Recluse*'s presumptive relations between Man, Nature, and Human Life were skewed in a way that predetermined Wordsworth's failure to keep them balanced. He could not see Human Life wedded to Man and Nature as he could imagine them wedded to each other. Jonathan Wordsworth and Stephen Gill assert that the objective poetry implied by "Human Life" was simply impossible for Wordsworth; this has been the criticism of Wordsworth's egotism from the beginning. Yet at each stage of *The Recluse*'s development we see that Wordsworth's failure was not simply in turning his eyes "from half of human fate," as Arnold gibed, but turning *toward* "the tribes and fellowships of men" with a determination to make an "authentic comment" that was immediately undercut by his representation of general human experience in the terms of his own painful individual experiences. His determination not to neglect Human Life spelled the doom of his *Recluse,* but also gave it its fitful glory.

Wordsworth's own experience also provided the way out of the dilemma that the "Prospectus" lines reached. Invoking a "prophetic Spirit" like the Holy Spirit that concludes the Apostles' and Nicene creeds, and that was associated by Milton and tradition with poetic inspiration and the final redemption of mankind in a New Jerusalem, he gets himself back on track for the Promised Land via his own poetry:

> Come, thou prophetic Spirit, Soul of Man,
> Thou human Soul of the wide earth that hast
> A metropolitan Temple in the hearts
> Of mighty Poets . . .

>   (1026–29)

He comes in from the Wilderness to a Holy See of Imagination that both rescues and completes the Exodus imagery of the "Prospectus" lines. But whereas Milton's spirit prefers "Before all Temples th'upright heart and pure" (*P.L.* I.18), Wordsworth's is not only humanized but localized in hearts of genius rather than virtue. When these lines were published in 1814, the "metropolitan Temple" resonated with the "gothic church" to which Wordsworth then compared his entire oeuvre. In MS D, the "metropolitan Temple" of poetry contrasts directly with the "vacant commerce" of the man "by the vast Metropolis immured . . . where numbers overwhelm humanity" (595–99). Considering Grasmere as a "strategic retreat" from the public world, Finch compares Wordsworth's replacement of politics by imagination to the biblical prophets' denunciations of the sinful cities from the spiritual purity of the desert. This redemption of the sinful city is also . . . the fundamental pattern of *The Prelude*'s search for satisfactory "residences" for Imagination. The city of Human Life will finally be redeemed as a city of poetry. And when Wordsworth prays that his "verse may live and be / Even as a Light hung up in heaven to chear / Mankind in times to come!" (1032–34), we may be sure, both from the imagistic development of the "Prospectus" and from the entire *Recluse*'s pattern of spiritual-edifices-humanistically-redeemed, that it is not just any Star in the sky, but one of very distinct house and lineage, hanging above a region which, though provincial, is confident of out-shining the nominal capital (Jerusalem or London) as a center for the world's admiration. Tracing the star's lineage will in fact be the next order of business: "with this / I blend more lowly matter . . . describe the mind and man / Contemplating, and who and what he was . . . when and where and how he lived" (1034–39).

Thus the "Prospectus" lines end, in context, not as a prospectus to *The Recluse* but to *The Prelude*, turning back from their universal scope to their person of origin. Their redemptive hope ("chear Mankind in times to come") is identical with that expressed at the end of the 1805 *Prelude*, but its realization first requires the full examination of "the mind and man contemplating." Wordsworth tried to keep the *Prelude—Recluse* relationship sequential, or one of cause and effect; but in tracing closely the history of their mutual development, we see how often and how easily this relationship collapsed into an identity. The crisis of the first *Recluse* poems was: how could this poetically immature narrator deal with those terrifying sufferers? Wordsworth's first response, in 1798, was to revise "The Ruined Cottage" to give the Pedlar plausible explanatory insights from his own biography; his second (in 1799), to begin the poem to Coleridge on the growth of his own mind. That, in substance, is exactly what happens again in the next stage of *The Recluse*'s development. Determined to give the storms of human sorrow their "authentic comment," "Home at Grasmere" breaks off in a crisis of confidence, which in the "Prospectus" lines is elided by promissory mythopoeic notes. In 1802, Wordsworth again returned to "The Ruined Cottage," tried to recast it as an independent poem, "The Pedlar," abandoned the effort after great pain, and then, slowly in 1803 and massively by 1804, dropped his pedlar guise and again returned to the poem to Coleridge, *The Prelude*.

Chronology

1770	Born April 7 at Cockermouth in Cumberland.
1778	Death of mother, Ann Wordsworth.
1779	Enters school near Esthwaite Lake in the Lake Country.
1783	Death of father, John Wordsworth.
1787–91	Attends St. John's College, Cambridge University.
1790	Walking tour of France, Germany and Switzerland.
1791	Walking tour of North Wales, where he ascends Mount Snowdon.
1791–92	Residence in France, where he associates with moderate faction of the Revolution. Love affair with Annette Vallon. Birth of their daughter, Anne-Caroline.
1793	Publication of *An Evening Walk* and *Descriptive Sketches*.
1795	Death of college friend, Raisley Calvert, whoe legacy enables Wordsworth to devote himself to his poetry.
1795–98	Settles with his sister Dorothy first at Racedown, and then at Alfoxden. In 1797–98, he is constantly in the company of Samuel Taylor Coleridge.
1798	In September, *Lyrical Ballads* is published, with Coleridge.
1798–99	Winters with Dorothy at Goslar in Germany.
1799	Moves with Dorothy to Dove Cottage, Grasmere, where he writes *The Prelude* in its first version, in two parts.
1800	Second edition of *Lyrical Ballads*, with "Preface" added.
1802	Marries Mary Hutchinson.
1805	Death of his brother, John Wordsworth, who goes down with his ship in February. *The Prelude*, in thirteen books, is finished, but the poet chooses not to publish it.
1807	Publishes *Poems in Two Volumes*.
1810–12	Rift with Coleridge; subsequent friendship is never the same.
1813–42	Becomes government tax collector for Westmoreland. Lives at Rydal Mount, near Ambleside.
1814	Publishes *The Excursion*.
1835	Dorothy's madness begins.
1843	Becomes Poet Laureate.
1850	Dies April 23 at Rydal Mount. *The Prelude*, in fourteen books, is published posthumously.

Contributors

HAROLD BLOOM, Sterling Professor of the Humanities at Yale University, is the author of *The Anxiety of Influence, Poetry and Repression* and many other volumes of literary criticism. His forthcoming study, *Freud: Transference and Authority*, attempts a full-scale reading of all of Freud's major writings. A MacArthur Prize Fellow, he is general editor of five series of literary criticism published by Chelsea House.

FREDERICK A. POTTLE is Sterling Professor Emeritus of English at Yale. He is best known as the editor and biographer of James Boswell.

The late PAUL DE MAN was Sterling Professor of Comparative Literature at Yale. His influential work in critical theory includes *Blindness and Insight* and *Allegories of Reading*.

GEOFFREY HARTMAN is Karl Young Professor of English and Comparative Literature at Yale. Besides his writings on Wordsworth, his books include *Beyond Formalism* and *Saving the Text*.

JOHN HOLLANDER is equally renowned as a poet and as a scholarly critic. He is Professor of English at Yale, where he also serves as Director of Graduate Studies in English. His criticism includes *Vision and Resonance* and *The Figure of Echo*. Much of his most accomplished poetry is gathered in *Spectral Emanations: New and Selected Poems*.

M. H. ABRAMS, the most distinguished living scholar of romanticism, is Class of 1916 Professor of English at Cornell University. His masterwork is *The Mirror and the Lamp*, the definitive study of Romantic critical theory, which ought to be read in conjunction with his other major books, *Natural Supernaturalism* and *The Correspondent Breeze*.

THOMAS WEISKEL, who died in a tragic accident at the age of twenty-nine, taught English at Yale. His *The Romantic Sublime* was published posthumously.

FRANCES FERGUSON is Professor of English at the University of California, Berkeley. Her writings on Romanticism and the Sublime include her book, *Wordsworth: Language as Counter-Spirit*.

THOMAS MCFARLAND is Professor of English at Princeton University. He is widely known for his books on Coleridge and on Shakespeare, as well as for his *Romanticism and the Forms of Ruin.*

KENNETH R. JOHNSTON is Professor of English at Indiana University, and the author of *Wordsworth and "The Recluse."*

Bibliography

Abrams, Meyer Howard, ed. *Wordsworth: A Collection of Critical Essays*. Englewood Cliffs, N.J.: Prentice-Hall, 1972.

Averill, James H. *Wordsworth and the Poetry of Human Suffering*. Ithaca: Cornell University Press, 1980.

Baker, Jeffrey. *Time and Mind in Wordsworth's Poetry*. Detroit, Mi.: Wayne State University Press, 1980.

Beer, John Bernard. *Wordsworth and the Human Heart*. New York: Columbia University Press, 1978.

Bialostosky, Don H. *Making Tales: The Poetics of Wordsworth's Narrative Experiments*. Chicago: The University of Chicago Press, 1984.

Brett, R.L., and Jones, A.R., eds. *Lyrical Ballads, 1798 and 1800*. London: Methuen, 1978.

Butler, James, ed. *The Ruined Cottage and The Pedlar*. Ithaca: Cornell University Press, 1979.

Byatt, Antonia Susan. *Wordsworth and Coleridge in Their Time*. London: Nelson, 1970.

Davies, Hunter. *William Wordsworth, A Biography*. London: Weidenfield and Nicolson, 1980.

Devlin, David Douglas. *Wordsworth and the Poetry of Epitaphs*. London: Macmillan Press, 1980.

————. *Wordsworth and the Art of Prose*. London: Macmillan Press, 1983.

Ferguson, Frances. *Wordsworth: Language as Counter-Spirit*. New Haven: Yale University Press, 1977.

Gérard, Albert S. *English Romantic Poetry: Ethos, Structure and Symbol in Coleridge, Wordsworth, Shelley and Keats*. Berkeley: University of California Press, 1968.

Gill, Stephen, ed. *The Salisbury Plain Poems of William Wordsworth*. Ithaca: Cornell University Press, 1975.

————, ed. *William Wordsworth*. New York: Oxford University Press, 1984.

Grob, Alan. *The Philosophic Mind: A Study of Wordsworth's Poetry and Thought. 1797–1805*. Columbus: Ohio University Press, 1973.

Halliday, F.E. *Wordsworth and His World*. London: Thames and Hudson, 1970.

Hartman, Geoffrey. *Wordsworth's Poetry*. New Haven: Yale University Press, 1971.

————, ed. *New Perspectives on Coleridge and Wordsworth*. New York: Columbia University Press, 1972.

Havens, Raymond Dexter. *The Mind of a Poet*. Baltimore: Johns Hopkins University Press, 1941.

Hayden, John O. ed. *The Poems of William Wordsworth*. New Haven: Yale University Press, 1981.

Heath, William. *Wordsworth and Coleridge: A Study of Their Literary Relations in 1801–1802*. New York: Oxford University Press, 1970.

Heffernan, James A. W. *William Wordsworth's Theory of Poetry: The Transforming Imagination*. Ithaca: Cornell University Press, 1969.

Hodgson, John A. *Wordsworth's Philosophical Poetry, 1797–1814*. Lincoln: University of Nebraska Press, 1980.

Jackson, Wallace. *The Probable and The Marvelous: Blake, Wordsworth and the 18th Century Critical Tradition*. Athens: University of Georgia Press, 1978.

Jacobus, Mary. *Tradition and Experiment in Wordsworth's Lyrical Ballads (1798)*. Oxford: Clarendon Press, 1976.

Johnson, Lee M. *Wordsworth's Metaphysical Verse: Geometry, Nature and Form*. Toronto: University of Toronto Press, 1982.

Johnston, Kenneth R. *Wordsworth and "The Recluse."* New Haven: Yale University Press, 1984.

Jones, Henry John Franklin. *The Egotistical Sublime: A History of Wordsworth's Imagination*. London: Chatto and Windus, 1954.

King, Alexander. *Wordsworth and the Artist's Vision*. London: Athlone Publishers, 1966.

McConnel, Frank D. *The Confessional Imagination: A Reading of Wordsworth's Prelude*. Baltimore: Johns Hopkins University Press, 1974.

McFarland, Thomas. *Romanticism and the Forms of Ruin: Wordsworth, Coleridge and the Modalities of Fragmentation*. Princeton: Princeton University Press, 1981.

Murray, Roger N. *Wordsworth's Style, Figures and Themes in the Lyrical Ballads of 1800*. Lincoln: University of Nebraska Press, 1967.

Onorato, Richard. *The Character of the Poet: Wordsworth in The Prelude*. Princeton: Princeton University Press, 1971.

Owen, W. J. B., ed. *Wordsworth's Literary Criticism*. London: Routledge and Kegan Paul, 1974.

Owen, W. J. B., and Smyser, Jayne Worthington, eds. *The Prose Works of William Wordsworth*. Oxford: Clarendon Press, 1974.

Parrish, Stephen Maxfield. *The Art of the Lyrical Ballads*. Cambridge: Harvard University Press, 1973.

———, ed. *The Prelude, 1798–1799*. Ithaca: Cornell University Press, 1977.

Perkins, David. *The Quest for Permanence: The Symbolism of Wordsworth, Shelley and Keats*. Cambridge: Harvard University Press, 1959.

———. *Wordsworth and the Poetry of Sincerity*. Cambridge: Belknap Press, 1964.

Pirie, David. *William Wordsworth: The Poetry of Grandeur and of Tenderness*. London: Methuen, 1982.

Reed, Mark L. *Wordsworth: The Chronology of the Middle Years, 1800–1815*. Cambridge: Harvard University Press, 1975.

Reguerio, Helen. *The Limits of Imagination: Wordsworth, Yeats and Stevens*. Ithaca: Cornell University Press, 1976.

Rehder, Robert. *Wordsworth and the Beginnings of Modern Poetry*. Totowa, New Jersey: Barnes and Noble, 1981.

Roper, Derek, ed. *Lyrical Ballads, 1805*. London: Collins, 1968.

Sheats, Paul D., ed. *The Poetical Works of Wordsworth*. Boston: Houghton Mifflin Co., 1982.

Sherry, Charles. *Wordsworth's Poetry of the Imagination*. Oxford: Clarendon Press, 1980.

Simpson, David. *Wordsworth and the Figurings of the Real*. London: Macmillan Press, 1982.

Watson, J. R. *Wordsworth's Vital Soul: The Sacred and the Profane in Wordsworth's Poetry*. London: Macmillan, 1982.

Acknowledgments

"Introduction" by Harold Bloom from *The Visionary Company* by Harold Bloom, copyright © 1961 by Harold Bloom and © 1971 by Cornell University. Reprinted by permission of the publisher.

"The Eye and the Object in the Poetry of Wordsworth" by Frederick A. Pottle from *The Yale Review*, vol. 40 (Autumn 1950), copyright © 1950 by Yale University. Reprinted by permission of The Yale Review.

"Intentional Structure of the Romantic Image" by Paul de Man from *The Rhetoric of Romanticism* by Paul de Man, copyright © 1984 by Columbia University Press. Reprinted by permission.

"The Romance of Nature and the Negative Way" by Geoffrey H. Hartman from *The Unmediated Vision* and from *Wordsworth's Poetry 1787–1814* by Geoffrey H. Hartman, copyright © 1954 and © 1964 by Yale University. Reprinted by permission of Yale University Press.

"Wordsworth and the Music of Sound" by John Hollander from *New Perspectives on Coleridge and Wordsworth*, edited by Geoffrey H. Hartman, copyright © 1972 by Columbia University Press. Reprinted by permission.

"Two Roads to Wordsworth" by M. H. Abrams from *Wordsworth: A Collection of Critical Essays* edited by M. H. Abrams, copyright © 1972 by Prentice-Hall. Reprinted by permission.

"Wordsworth and the Defile of the Word" by Thomas Weiskel from *The Romantic Sublilme: Studies in the Structure and the Psychology of Transcendence*, copyright © 1976 by The Johns Hopkins University Press. Reprinted by permission.

"The Scene of Instruction: *Tintern Abbey*" by Harold Bloom from *Poetry and Repression* by Harold Bloom, copyright © 1976 by Yale University. Reprinted by permission of Yale University Press.

"The 'Immortality Ode' " by Frances Ferguson from *Wordsworth: Language as Counter Spirit* by Frances Ferguson, copyright © 1977 by Yale University. Reprinted by permission of Yale University Press.

Index

Rilke, Rainer Maria, 55–56, 80
Rimbaud, Arthur, 28
River Duddon Sonnets, 70, 71
Robespierre, Maximilien, 165–67
Robinson, Crabb, 50, 151
romanticism, 23, 29–30, 56, 122, 168
Rousseau, Jean Jacques, 30, 31, 34–35, 120, 122, 123, 162
Ruined Cottage, The, 85, 89, 158, 186, 191
"Ruines of Time, The," 57
Ruskin, John, 20, 121

S
Sappho (Grillparzer), 69
Schlegel, Friedrich, 169
Schelling, Friedrich, 117
Schöne Müllerin, Die, 69
Scott, Sir Walter, 45
self-discovery, 47
Selincourt, Ernest De, 108, 137
Shakespeare, William, 13, 43, 167
Shelley, Mary, 46
Shelley, Percy Bysshe, 7, 18, 45, 46, 50, 53, 68, 70, 168, 178
Simple Wordsworth, The (Danby), 85
Smart, Christopher, 73–76, 78
Solitary Reaper, The, 20
solipsism, 120–22
solitude, 14, 20, 40, 84
"Song for St. Cecilia's Day, A" (Dryden), 73
Song of Songs, 178
sound, 55–80
Spenser, Edmund, 46, 53, 57, 63
Sperry, Willard, 51
Spinoza, Baruch, 151
spots of time, 101–11, 141, 177, 179
Stevens, Wallace, 1, 3, 7, 90, 118, 121, 135
Stevenson, Lionel, 176
structuralism, 86
Swift, Jonathan, 62

T
Taine, Hippolyte-Adolphé, 165, 169

Tate, Allen, 73
Tennyson, Alfred, Lord, 16, 72, 133
Theocritus, 65
Thompson, James, 69
Thoreau, Henry David, 69
Thorn, The, 85
Tintern Abbey, 5, 37, 51, 52, 57, 62, 90, 113–35, 156, 184
"Tithonus" (Tennyson), 133
Tolstoy, Leo, 8
Trilling, Lionel, 89

U
Unmediated Vision, The (Hartman), 124, 133

V
"Vale of Esthwaite, The," 70, 109
Van den Berg, J. H., 120–24
Vico, G. B., 134
Virgil, 45, 53, 65, 69

W
Walden (Thoreau), 69
Waller, Edmund, 74, 75, 76
Warton, Thomas, 57, 61
"We Are Seven," 155–56, 158
Weiskel, Thomas, 93–111
White Doe, The, 46, 49, 70
Whitman, Walt, 57, 121
"Witch of Atlas, The (Shelley)," 46
Wittgenstein, Ludwig, 147
Wordsworth, Christopher (brother), 46
Wordsworth, Dorothy (sister), 11–14, 19, 47–48, 50, 131–32, 154, 156, 166, 173–75, 177, 181, 183, 186
Wordsworth, John (brother), 58, 85, 89, 166, 175
Wordsworth, Mary (wife), 46, 47, 166, 175
Wordsworth, Thomas (son), 154

Y
Yeats, William Butler, 118, 135
Young, Edward, 77